Welfare Economics

Although it was an important specialization in economics in the mid-twentieth century, welfare economics has received less attention in the twenty-first century. This book explores the history of welfare economics, with a view to explaining its rise and subsequent decline.

Drawing on both philosophy and economics, the book offers a new and original perspective on the history of welfare economics, starting with Pigou and charting the trajectory of applied and theoretical welfare economics throughout the twentieth century.

This book will be of interest to students and researchers of philosophy, economics and history of economic thought.

Roger A. McCain is Professor of Economics at Drexel University, USA.

T0384099

Routledge Advances in Social Economics

Series Editor: *John B. Davis, Marquette University*

This series presents new advances and developments in social economics thinking on a variety of subjects that concern the link between social values and economics. Need, justice and equity, gender, cooperation, work poverty, the environment, class, institutions, public policy and methodology are some of the most important themes. Among the orientations of the authors are social economist, institutionalist, humanist, solidarist, cooperatist, radical and Marxist, feminist, post-Keynesian, behaviouralist, and environmentalist. The series offers new contributions from today's most foremost thinkers on the social character of the economy.

Publishes in conjunction with the Association of Social Economics.

For more information about this series, please visit: www.routledge.com/ Routledge-Advances-in-Social-Economics/book-series/SE0071

Welfare Economics
An Interpretive History

Roger A. McCain

Routledge
Taylor & Francis Group

LONDON AND NEW YORK

First published 2019 by Routledge

2 Park Square, Milton Park, Abingdon, Oxon, OX14 4RN

605 Third Avenue, New York, NY 10017

Routledge is an imprint of the Taylor & Francis Group, an informa business

First issued in paperback 2020

British Library Cataloguing-in-Publication Data
A catalogue record for this book is available from the British Library

Library of Congress Cataloging-in-Publication Data
Names: McCain, Roger A., author.
Title: Welfare economics : an interpretive history / Roger A. McCain.
Description: Abingdon, Oxon ; New York, NY : Routledge, 2019. |
Series: Routledge advances in social economics ; 26 | Includes
bibliographical references and index.
Subjects: LCSH: Welfare economics--History.
Classification: LCC HB99.3 .M39 2019 | DDC 330.15/5609--dc23
LC record available at https://lccn.loc.gov/2019007130

ISBN: 978-1-138-68564-2 (hbk)
ISBN: 978-0-367-72959-2 (pbk)

Typeset in Times New Roman
by Taylor & Francis Books

Contents

1 Objective and scope of the work

Welfare economics is a systematic study of normative policy recommendations in economics. Applied welfare economics is an attempt to say "what ought to be" with respect to government policy, and theoretical welfare economics is the attempt to learn how to create a reliable applied welfare economics. The history of welfare economics is a strand of the history of the twentieth century. During the twentieth century, welfare economics emerged from neoclassical economic theory as a specialized field of study, only to strangely disappear from the mainstream of economics by the end of the century, as Sir Anthony Atkinson observed in 2001. Following mid-century, welfare economics was widely taught. (I was hired in my first faculty position in part because I was considered qualified to teach welfare economics.) Today it is far less commonly taught, and while some research continues, it is largely ignored. In Atkinson's words (p. 193), "The 'strangeness' is that, despite the prevalence of welfare statements in modern economics, we are no longer subjecting them to critical analysis." This book will attempt to trace and, perhaps, explain that rise and dissolution.

Now, economists in earlier centuries, like those of the twenty-first century, did not hesitate to make policy recommendations. Adam Smith could advocate for free trade and laissez-faire on the ground that it would increase the revenue of the nation; Ricardo could oppose the corn laws because they would raise the price of corn and shift income to the landlords. However, the emergence of neoclassical economics, particularly in the work of Marshall, made possible a narrower focus and more precise answers. Any excise tax will discourage production, no doubt, but there is no civilized society without some taxation. *How much* will a particular tax discourage production, and could it be that some taxes are less burdensome in this way than others? The apparatus of elasticity of supply and demand, consumer and producer surpluses showed the way to answer questions at that level of detail, questions that classical economics could not have answered. This is the opportunity that arose, for economists, with the maturation of neoclassical economics in the work of Marshall and Pigou. In *Wealth and Welfare* (1912) and *Economics of Welfare* (1920), A. C. Pigou presented a highly coherent account of the relation of economic activity to welfare as he conceived it, an account that was to influence both the construction of economic statistics that remains standard, and generations of research by economists.

There was, of course, some hesitation to adopt the Marshallian kit of tools. Many economists had followed Smith and Ricardo in arguing for free markets, for laissez-faire; others had argued the contrary. These large issues seemed to be the ones that mattered. To ask *which* taxes are *less* burdensome must have seemed a distraction from the more important question whether markets, on the whole, could better promote the prosperity of the many than could direct action by the state. There was probably less doubt about the value judgments that underlay the neoclassical tools. Advocates of free markets and advocates of state action could alike claim that the policies they advocated would encourage the prosperity of the many. The two sides in this great controversy shared the same, rather vague, value judgments. Their differences had to do with the nature of the economic system.

A further source of hesitation was the very precision of the Marshallian approach itself. To say that we can determine which taxes are less burdensome, and how much less burdensome, is to imply that the government ought to consider the taxes case by case, and choose those that are least burdensome. More generally, the government would be able to consider the merits of market processes as against regulation case by case. But, to the believers in laissez-faire, this would require the state to be the very meddlesome busybody they opposed. The precision of Marshallian analysis, if it could really be applied, was itself a defeat for their program. And the opponents of the free-market position were no more comfortable with the case-by-case approach. They were convinced that market systems were just chaotic and unreasonable, so that a simple set of bureaucratic rules could easily bring about a vast improvement of prosperity. Neoclassical economics, with a predictable logic of market equilibria and a focus on marginal improvements, must simply be wholly false, a fraud rather than a theory.

Further, the neoclassical apparatus was complex and tricky. This was a third major reason to hesitate: may we really be sure that these arcane graphs and computations could be a guide to the policies that would bring about greater prosperity of the many? What does consumer surplus really mean, and how should we really measure it? These questions would occupy many of the pages of the newly founded research journals in economics in the early years of the twentieth century, and several of Pigou's early papers were important contributions.

The questions that remained largely unasked, even by those who hesitated to adopt the Marshallian approach, were those of value: just what constitutes the prosperity of the many, and why should it be a goal of public policy or of right action? Why should we favor policies that increase the revenue of the nation? Why should we not favor policies that shift income from the working class to the landlords? What, to use Pigou's phrase, is the national dividend and why should we favor public policies that increase it? But these questions had to be addressed. The very precision of the neoclassical theoretical apparatus demanded that the value questions be addressed with similar precision. Pigou addressed them, and in the process reinforced a dilemma for many economists. Pigou's welfare economics was firmly based in utilitarian ethical theory as Pigou understood it. This theory provided the most transparent support for the argument that free markets could result in increased prosperity in a morally significant sense. On the other hand, it had been known since the work of John Stuart Mill that utilitarianism could imply an argument for redistribution of income toward equality. Mill had also called for a separate consideration of efficiency and distribution. This was the dilemma economists had inherited from Mill, and to accept Pigou's analysis of the efficiency of competition seemed to make a distinction between efficiency and distributive norms impossible.

Pigou also developed Marshall's discussion of externalities, creating the modern concept of externalities. In the retrospect of a century, this may seem more important than the utilitarian case for (a limited amount of) redistribution. However, it was the Millian dichotomy of efficiency and distribution that motivated the attempt by the New Welfare Economics to reconstruct welfare economics on a different, though closely related, value theory. It will be argued that the creativity and success, and ultimate failure, of the New Welfare Economics led both to the rise and the disappearance of welfare economics in the twentieth century.

Pigou's welfare economics is described as "highly coherent" in somewhat the sense of C. I. Lewis (1946), or Laurence BonJour (1985): a body of discourse is coherent only if it is logically consistent; and is relatively more coherent to the extent that it comprises propositions that entail or enhance the conditional probability of one another; and is less coherent to the extent that it can be divided into unconnected subsets of propositions and to the extent that it contains unexplained anomalies. This is not to assert a coherence theory of truth or justification, to assert, that is, that coherence is either necessary or sufficient to evaluate truth or to justify belief in all or part of the discourse. However, coherence is useful. In particular, it is useful to have coherence between the concept of economic welfare and the theory of the motivations, decisions and actions of people in the marketplace. If we were to adopt a concept of welfare and a theory of economic action that contradict one another or are without logical or probabilistic connections, we would raise the questions why (on the one hand) people are unmotivated by what we suppose to be their welfare or (on the other hand) whether a concept of welfare can be meaningful if it is unrelated to, or indeed contradicts, the motives that people reveal by their actions. Pigou's welfare economics was highly coherent in that sense. A large part of the story to follow is of the attempt to retain that coherence without the specific utilitarian basis that Pigou gives it, and the failure of that attempt.

Pigou's work did not of course take place in a vacuum, but quite the contrary, could reasonably be considered the maturity of the neoclassical tradition that had been growing in the last third of the nineteenth century. Much of this prehistory is well known and will not require a resume here. Some other parts – the utilitarian argument for redistribution, consumer and producer surpluses and the "measuring rod of money," and externality – are best discussed along with the development of those ideas in Pigou's writing and after. The ideas of utilitarians, and the incorporation of their ideas into economics after Mill and Jevons, deserve separate attention. It will be the topic of Chapter 2. Pigou's welfare economics will then be discussed in Chapter 3. The fourth chapter will review the rise of the New Welfare Economics, its critique of Pigou and its attempt to refound welfare economics. Such further developments as the social welfare function, community indifference curves and the renewed interest in externalities will be considered in the chapters that follow. The challenges to welfare economics from the Arrow impossibility theorem, the second-best principle, and "the impossibility of a Paretian liberal" will be the topic of Chapter 7. Subsequent chapters will consider more recent developments, largely parallel but to a considerable extent independent, such as justice as fairness and fairness as the absence of "envy," self-assessed happiness, behavioral anomalies and transaction costs. The last chapter is a brief summary and prospect.

Several ideas from twentieth-century philosophy will be called on. The work of Douglas Walton (1989, 2007, 2011) on informal logic and defeasible reason will play a double role. On the one hand, the book as a whole and its successive parts are organized around the judgment that the development of welfare economics at its best is an instance of what Walton calls a reasonable dialog.[1] On the other hand, some scholars – Pigou, Little and Sen may be mentioned – have taken the view that discussions of public policy both among economists and in the population in general cannot avoid reliance on arguments that, while reasonable, are inconclusive. Here, again, Walton's ideas and the concept of reasonable dialog are applicable. From the philosophy of perception and subjective experience, we will find the concepts of qualia and the associated ideas useful. These will be defined in Chapter 2 and used from time to time in subsequent chapters. For welfare economics, clearly, the relation of factual and valuative assertions is a key issue. Here, relatively recent philosophic discussions of "thick" concepts provide a standpoint for reconsidering economists' debates about these matters. A thick concept is one that links an evaluative expression with one that is descriptive or non-evaluative, in such a way that the evaluation is merited *because* the object described is as it is in non-evaluative terms. Can we do welfare economics without relying on thick concepts? If not, what are the implications of this, and what may we learn about the economists' controversies on this point in the twentieth century? Further discussion about thick concepts will be deferred to Chapter 5.

Note

1 Compare the retrospective view of Hicks (1975, p. 326), which concludes, "What I am saying, at the conclusion of this essay, is that Welfare Economics, in the broad as well as in the narrow sense, is itself a Critique."

References

Atkinson, Anthony B. (2001) The Strange Disappearance of Welfare Economics, *Kyklos* v. 54, no. 23 (May–Aug) pp. 193–206.

BonJour, L. (1985) *The Structure of Empirical Knowledge* (Cambridge, Mass.: Harvard University Press).

Hicks, J. R. (1975) The Scope and Status of Welfare Economics, *Oxford Economic Papers* v. 27, no. 3 (Nov) pp. 307–326.

Lewis, C. I. (1946) *An Analysis of Knowledge and Valuation* (LaSalle: Open Court).

Pigou, A. C. (1912) *Wealth and Welfare* (London: Macmillan).

Pigou, A. C. (1920) *Economics of Welfare* (London: Macmillan).

Walton, Douglas (1989) *Informal Logic: A Handbook for Critical Argumentation* (Cambridge: Cambridge University Press).

Walton, Douglas (2007) Evaluating Practical Reasoning, *Synthese* v. 157, no. 2 (July) pp. 197–240.

Walton, Douglas (2011) Defeasible Reasoning and Informal Fallacies, *Synthese* v. 179, no. 3 (April) pp. 377–407.

2 Utilitarianism for Pigou's welfare economics

The prehistory of the marginal utility theory of demand is well known and will be briefly sketched here for context. The classical political economists, from Smith through Mill and Cairnes, saw market prices as unrelated to utility. This was expressed in Smith's paradox of diamonds and water. Accordingly, the classical political economists focused on a long-run, cost theory of price with labor as the measure of cost. There were, of course, some passages in the classical writings that pointed toward the marginalist theory. Malthus hinted, in a little-known essay (1800), that demand price would be the marginal willingness to pay, and his proposition of diminishing productivity of land would be generalized in neoclassical economics. John Stuart Mill had a modern conception of demand, applied in exceptional cases such as international trade and monopoly, though he did not derive it from utilitarian premises. Utilitarianism and price theory cohabited in Mill's thought but he did not marry them, nor did they have issue.

Jevons, however, did marry utility and price theory, writing (1866, p. 282) "A true theory of economy can only be attained by going back to the great springs of human action – the feelings of pleasure and pain." It is hard to imagine a more emphatic assertion of Benthamite utilitarianism, at least as a theory of individual economic choices. Yet one could – and many economists would – adopt Jevons' theory of market equilibrium without adopting a Benthamite ethical theory or Benthamite norms of public policy. In itself, Jevons' market equilibrium theory per se is not utilitarian. It is an explanatory theory. Jevons tells us that exchange will produce a surplus for at least one of those entering into exchange, but he adds by way of qualification that "There are motives nearly always present with us, arising from conscience, compassion, or from some moral or religious source." However, as soon as Jevons' successors and co-discoverers began to argue that the mutual gains from exchange justify a market economy and public policies that encourage a market economy, they were making a utilitarian judgment.

The ideas of Henry Sidgwick deserve some comment here, if only because it has been suggested that he anticipated Pigou's foundation of welfare economics (Schultz 2017, p. 312). Sidgwick can be ranked along with Bentham and Mill among the great English nineteenth-century utilitarian philosophers (e.g. Schultz 2017, ch. 4). His book *Methods of Ethics* (1874) is probably the most important basis for this assessment. Sidgwick's *Principles of Political Economy* (1883) is a restatement of the classical political economy incorporating, among other modifications, Jevons' model of demand (pp. 72, 180). In Book III, "The Art of Political Economy," Sidgwick addresses political economy as a public-policy discipline and relies mainly on utilitarian judgments as the decisive criteria. To this extent we may say that he raised the questions that Pigou would address. There is some difficulty of interpretation here. "As in the case of the *Methods*, the structure of these works has often made it difficult to see precisely where Sidgwick comes down on many issues" (Schulz 2017, p. 312). Sidgwick does say (1883, p. 518), like Pigou and perhaps less equivocally than Mill, that redistribution toward equality will *ceteris paribus* increase aggregate utility. In practice, though, Sidgwick never sees *ceteris* as *paribus*, systematically rejecting actual proposals for redistribution on account of his view that they would reduce productivity excessively. In one case (1883, p. 521) he abandons the *homo oeconomicus* theory to argue that an increase of leisure on the part of recipients of redistributed income would not increase utility. All in all, Sidgwick's "Art of Political Economy" does not approach the coherence either of Pigou's welfare economics or Cairnes' latter-day classical political economy (McCain 2012).[1]

2.1 Utilitarianism as a value theory

Executive summary of the section: Utilitarianism is a kind of consequentialist ethical theory, though its application might be limited to public policy. But there are several varieties of consequentialism and utilitarianism. Pigou's is an instance of satisfaction utilitarianism.

In the first instance, utilitarianism is a moral philosophy. That is to say, utilitarian thinking is first and foremost concerned with the actions we ought to undertake, with the way decisions ought to be made, how we ought to decide how to act. (Utilitarian thinking can be applied also to the psychology of decision making, as Jevons did, with more or less success.) Utilitarianism per se is subject to a number of criticisms as a moral philosophy, as are other moral philosophies. Some of those criticisms will be taken up below.

   In particular, utilitarian thinking can be applied to the decision among alternative public policies. This has been central to utilitarianism from its beginning in Bentham's writing. Some of the criticisms of utilitarianism as a general moral philosophy will not apply to the particular case of public policy decisions, so that a reasonable person might adopt a utilitarian standard for public policy decisions while rejecting it as a general moral theory. Some of these distinctions will be taken up below.

   Second, utilitarianism is a form of *consequentialism*. That is, a utilitarian holds that the rightness of actions and decisions depends only on their consequences, and not in anything intrinsic to the act itself nor any revelation or other source of knowledge independent of the consequences. One may believe that God will be pleased with the action, even if it does nobody any good; but God's attitude is not considered a consequence. (One may argue that God is pleased when we act according to utilitarian norms – both Mill and Pigou sometimes seem to make that argument – but that is to say that God's evaluations, like those of a fully informed utilitarian human being, are utilitarian, not that God's pleasure is among the consequences of the act.) However, consequentialists can and do differ among themselves as to which consequences should count and how they should be counted. Some might hold, for example, that a decision is right to the extent that it increases the ability of people throughout the world to meet basic needs, such as the needs for food, shelter and health care.[2] While consequentialist, this position would not be utilitarian. In part, this follows from a distinction of needs from wants and desires: needs are objective (McCain 2017, p. 152). It is an important position for economics, and in what follows, it will be referred to as basic-needs consequentialism.

It would not be utilitarian because, third, for a utilitarian the consequences that must be considered are subjective states of mind or of consciousness. Other, material consequences are excluded – or, to be more precise, all the material consequences of any act or decision are themselves to be evaluated on the basis of the subjective states of mind that arise from them. Thus, it may be important that a decision increases the ability of poor people to meet their basic needs, and it is quite important to some welfare economists, but this importance follows from a judgment that the subjective states of mind that accompany the reduction of hunger are more intense, urgent or important than the subjective states of mind that correspond to the enjoyment of an operatic performance.

Any utilitarian will hold that the objectives of public policy and ethical norms or actions should be to increase some kinds of subjective states of mind and decrease others. Bentham has a point. Pains and pleasures are pure subjective experiences that a reasonable person might want or prefer to other experiences, or want to avoid, and prefer other experiences to. Nevertheless, if with Bentham we consider pleasures and pains as consequences that matter, this will sacrifice some of the power of utilitarian thinking as a tool. Consider the experience of a successful mountain climb. (As I write, El Capitan has just been climbed for the first time by free climbers.) This experience is likely to include considerable dimensions of pain, fatigue and discomfort. It may also include dimensions of pleasure, exhilaration, exaltation and relief of anxiety. As a mountaineer friend said to me, he likes to get high on a mountain. Can the exhilaration, exaltation and relief really be credibly reduced to "pleasure?" Contrast this experience to the experience of settling into a familiar armchair with a good book, a glass of a mildly intoxicating beverage and a warm fire. This experience combines a good deal of comfort with a familiar intellectual challenge, probably some pleasure, but probably little exhilaration and exaltation and at the same time little or no pain or fatigue. A reasonable person might *want* both of these experiences at different times and might *prefer* one or the other at a particular time. For a utilitarian, subjective experiences of this sort – subjective experiences that often are the predictable consequences of particular actions or decisions and the material consequences that follow from them – are the ultimate consequences on the basis of which decisions (especially of public policy) ought to be decided.

But this poses questions of comparability and measurement. How are these multidimensional experiences to be compared? This is not only a matter of *interpersonal* comparability. Suppose I have to choose between climbing a mountain and settling back to reread Pigou's *Wealth and Welfare*. How can I compare these multidimensional alternatives in order to decide which one to choose? It seems that this question cannot be answered without some reference to *desires* or *preference*.

Thus utilitarians may, and do, disagree among themselves as to the subjective states of consciousness that are to be considered and how they are to be considered and compared or aggregated. For the purposes of this book, three distinct utilitarian philosophies will be important (Sinnott-Armstrong, 2012).

The first, chronologically, is hedonism, which is the utilitarianism of the first founder of utilitarianism, Jeremy Bentham. For hedonism, the subjective states of mind to be considered are pleasures and pains. On the Benthamite view, these sensations can be compared in terms of intensity and duration in such a way that the pains can be subtracted from the pleasures and the net, pleasure minus pain, aggregated over the whole population (or indeed over the whole universe of sentient creatures) is the moral value of the action.

The second of the utilitarian frameworks is satisfaction consequentialism. A satisfaction consequentialist would hold that an action is right when it is more effective in *satisfying* desires, wants, or needs than alternative actions would be. This is not necessarily a utilitarian position, as the example of basic-needs consequentialism shows. But a satisfaction utilitarian could hold that it is *the subjective states of mind associated with the satisfaction of desires* that are to be considered. Bentham would not have seen this as a different position than his, on the ground that what a person desires is to increase pleasure and avoid pain. Even if we reject this argument, and some good reasons to do so will be considered below, satisfaction-utilitarianism might encompass hedonism within a broader framework.

The third framework is preference utilitarianism. The preference utilitarian holds that an action is better than another if the first satisfies a more highly ranked preference than the second. This in turn can have two variants. First, preferences might simply replace desires in a satisfaction utilitarianism that would hold that it is the subjective experience (pleasure or pain or whatever) associated with the satisfaction of the preference that is the basis of evaluation of the first situation as better than the second. But, second, it might be held that it is simply the brute fact that the first situation satisfies a higher preference than the second that leads to the evaluation of the first as better, independent of the subjective experience, pleasures or pains, that the person associates with the satisfaction. This is the "ordinal preference theory" at the basis of modern economic theory. Since a preference is a subjective state of mind, this is a form of utilitarianism, though different from the other kinds. Note that the first sort of preference utilitarianism presents no new difficulties for aggregating utilities. Indeed, we could think of a very Benthamite sort of preference hedonism, in which we somehow measure the intensity and duration of the pleasures and pains associated with the satisfaction of particular levels of preference. (In courses of the principles of economics, we often reverse that, deriving the preferences from the previously postulated utilities, to help the slower students understand preferences.) For the second sort, however, the neoclassical preference utility, aggregation faces some familiar limitations.

Clearly these concepts can overlap, but the overlap may not be as great as it seems. It may seem that a preference utilitarian of the second sort, accepting Bentham's claim that what people prefer is more pleasure and less pain, would agree with a simple hedonist in his assessments. But the difference is in the states of mind that are made the basis of evaluation of actions, decisions and public policies. A neoclassical preference utilitarian might agree that the preference ranking is derived from a linear sum of pleasures and pains, and nevertheless hold that the pleasures and pains of one person cannot meaningfully be compared with those of another person, so that only the preference rankings themselves should be considered in the evaluation of public policy. This seems to have been Pareto's position and is consistent with the ideas of Paul Samuelson. But further, the neoclassical preference theorist might concede that the pleasures and pains of different people can meaningfully be compared, but hold that an evaluation of public policy based on the offsetting of one person's gains against another person's losses is invalid normative reasoning.

Another important distinction among kinds of utilitarianism is the distinction of act utilitarianism from rule utilitarianism. The rule utilitarian would hold that people ought to act according to a rule, but should choose the rule that yields the greatest aggregate utility in the average or in some normal case. An act utilitarian by contrast demands that every action and decision be based on the assessment of the total utility of that individual action, regardless of rules. The rule utilitarian could call for action according to a rule either because we often do not know the consequences of our particular acts except as a normally expected average or instead because only action according to rules is properly considered ethical, or both. This is important for utilitarian ethics, but not for public policy, since public policy is unavoidably a kind of rule, that is, a rule for the deployment of government power. Thus a utilitarian evaluation of public policy can only be rule utilitarian.

Some approaches to the economic evaluation of public policy are not utilitarian in any of these senses. As we have seen, this would include a basic-needs consequentialism, and Sen (e.g. 1983) proposes a consequentialist approach to the evaluation of public policy that takes into account "capabilities," which, like satisfactions of basic needs, seem to be objective circumstances. In so doing, Sen tells us that he is rejecting "welfarism." This identifies "welfare economics" with utilitarianism in some form.

2.2 Economics and the integrability problem

Executive summary of the section: Because of the complication of integrating a system of demand functions (considered as partial differential equations) it might not be possible to derive a utility function from market data, unless it is assumed that the utility function is separable.

As noted above, Jevons' (1866, 1871) understanding of the psychological basis of economics was emphatically utilitarian. While Edgeworth (1881) provided the tool that modern economics uses to express preference utilitarianism – indifference curves and the indifference map – Edgeworth did not hesitate to postulate a numerical utility that might be measureable and interpersonally comparable, suggesting (pp. 60–62) that the minimum perceptible difference, which had been investigated by the psychologists Fechner and Wundt, could be the basis of reliable interpersonal comparisons of utility. However, other economists preferred to avoid association with psychology and philosophy, and particularly utilitarian philosophy, and to place economics on what they deemed a more scientific, objective basis. Pareto, particularly, is associated with this view, and with the attempt to avoid even the word utility by substituting "ophelimity." However, it was Irving Fisher (1892) who pointed out that observable data might simply be inconsistent with any measure or indeed comparison of utility, if the data did not possess mathematical properties derived from integral calculus. This is the integrability problem. Pareto's rejection of interpersonal comparison seems to have been influenced by Fisher.

Suppose, as we often do in economics, that the utility an individual enjoys from consumption is a function of the quantities of various goods and services she consumes, $U=f(q_1, q_2, ..., q_n)$; and suppose the individual treats prices as given and maximizes utility given a limit on total spending. What we can observe *at best* are the quantities and prices that define her demands for the various goods at the various prices charged. Since these constitute a set of partial differential equations, the problem of constructing a utility function from those observations is a problem of integration of the system of partial differential equations. Now, consider two vectors of consumption, $q_1^1, q_2^1, ..., q_n^1$ and $q_1^2, q_2^2, ..., q_n^2$ and the respective utilities U^1 and U^2. The difference $U^1 - U^2$ is the definite integral of the system of partial differential equations constituting the demand functions. Treating U^2 arbitrarily as 0, then U^1 is the quantity of utility at $q_1^1, q_2^1, ..., q_n^1$. From a mathematical and hypothetical point of view, there are an uncountable infinity of paths from $q_1^2, q_2^2, ..., q_n^2$ to $q_1^1, q_2^1, ..., q_n^1$, and the integral could be computed along any of them "by adding up the infinitesimal changes" (to use an illegitimate but expressive phrase.) Since the difference U^1-U^2 is *assumed* to be well defined, these path integrals must all give rise to the same total. Suppose, however, that the observed demand data are such that integration along different paths gives rise to different quantities. Then the difference U^1-U^2 and consequently the quantity U^1 itself are not defined. Conversely, we may not suppose that, merely because price and quantity observations corresponding to demand curves can be observed, there is a well-defined utility function.

In the first part of his dissertation, Fisher considers a special case in which the problem of integrability does not arise: a case in which the utility function is additively separable, that is, considering just two categories of goods, $U=f_1(q_1)+f_2(q_2)$. For his example he identifies q_1 as bread. He then observes that the ratio of the marginal utilities of e.g. the 150th and 100th loaves of bread (per year) can be measured by the relative quantities of another good that he would substitute for bread, given that the quantity of the other good that he consumes at the same time is a constant. Given separability, the utility of the other good will not depend on whether the individual has 100 or 150 loaves of bread, so a quantity of the other good corresponds to the same utility at 150 loaves as it does at 100 (1892, pp. 6–8). He designates the other goods that would be substituted for 100 loaves as the unit of utility. He notes (p. 8) that if the utility of the other good depends on the quantity consumed of bread, this would fail – the correspondence of units of the other good to quantities of utility would be different at 100 than at 150 loaves.

Thus, for his special case, Fisher claims he has defined a *unit* of utility (given an arbitrary independent commodity and a quantity of that commodity) and denotes it as "a util" (p. 10). He defines consumer surplus or "gain" at p. 11. To get total utility it is necessary to integrate under the demand curve (p. 10) but this presents no difficulty since the demand curve for bread in this case is an ordinary differential equation. That is, the marginal utility of bread is a function only of one variable, the quantity of bread consumed, so the only "path" from 0 to 150 loaves of bread is the straight line along the axis of the quantity of bread and the integral is determined up to a constant of integration.

Fisher then discusses the implications of maximizing utility subject to a spending constraint with extensive use of an analogy to the common level of water in a connected series of cisterns, and with many diagrams of water tanks. In Part II, he eliminates the special case assumption of separability. At pp. 56–58 he introduces "competing" (strongly substitutable) and "completing" (complementary) goods. He notes that the unit of utility now cannot be defined as it was in the first part and promises an alternative at the end. But, since the demand curves for various goods will now be a system of partial, not ordinary differential equations, and *unless we assume the existence of a well-defined utility function*, the integrability problem does arise in this case. Thus, what we find at the conclusion is not an alternative approach to define and measure utility, but an argument that price theory does not need utility functions, but can proceed instead with something like indifference curves. In fact, Fisher was not committed to that view (Fisher 1918; Fellner 1967), and considered the separability assumption as a workable assumption. For example, the utility of food as an aggregate commodity might be treated as separable from the utility of other goods. Fisher considered a project to estimate a utility function for a representative consumer using that approximation (Fellner 1967).

Pareto (1971 [1906]) attempted to follow the program Fisher had suggested in his conclusion, developing price theory on a basis of an indifference curve analysis. However, the mathematician Vito Volterra (1906) pointed out that, with three or more goods, it might be impossible to define indifference curves, again because of an integrability problem. This was not to be resolved for a generation. (This discussion follows Samuelson 1950.)

Fisher rejects Jevons' utilitarianism as "psychology" or "metaphysics," and claims a more scientific status for economics. In that sense, his dissertation might seem to be something of a failure – unless one *assumes* the existence of a utility function, there is no prospect of extracting a utility function (or indeed indifference curves) from empirical observations. Most economists for the next generation simply set the integrability problem aside as a mathematical curiosum and proceeded to use utility functions or indifference curves according to their preference. That was Marshall's position. The first edition of his *Principles* had appeared in 1890, and Marshall had no hesitation either in assuming a utility function or in comparing utilities as between people, and drawing conclusions for public policy. The influence of Marshall largely eclipsed the issues Fisher raised, and in any case Marshall's ideas were the principal influence on Pigou.

Now, it might seem that a utilitarian would not see the integration problem as a difficulty, but that is not quite self-evident. The utilitarian would have no difficulty justifying the idea that decisions are based on comparison of subjective states, such as pleasures and pains, but that does not in itself imply that there is a well-defined function relating utility to quantities of goods consumed. The relation of consumption of goods and services to utility might be too complex to be expressed as a function, and even if it could be so expressed, might not have the properties of continuity and continuous first and second derivatives that the utility-maximization model presupposes. Even so, the utilitarian probably would not hesitate very long: if utility does not increase with the quantity of a good consumed, then why would we think of it as a good? And the tendency of marginal utility to decrease is not only an observable tendency, but essentially a condition for the existence of markets; and markets are known to exist. Thus, for the utilitarian, the *assumption that there is a utility function* is a relatively modest step. In a laudatory review of Fisher's monograph, Edgeworth (1893, p. 112) says, "At the same time he throws out some hints which will be valuable to the utilitarian." And he quotes from p. 87 of the monograph as follows:

> The statistician might begin with those utilities in which men are most alike – food utilities – and those disutilities in which they are most alike as the disutilities of definite sorts of manual labour. By these standards he

could measure and correct the money-standard, and if the utility curves for various classes of articles were constructed, he could make rough statistics of total utility, total disutility, gain, and utility-value which would have considerable meaning. Men are much alike in their digestion and fatigue. If a food or a labour standard is established, it can be easily applied to the utilities in regard to which men are unlike, as of clothes, houses, furniture, books, works of art, &c.

As we will see in a later section, this is still a reasonable program.

2.3 Pigou's satisfaction utility

Executive summary of the section: For Pigou, utility is the "psychic return of satisfaction." His remarks on the telescopic faculty make it clear that he thought of such an increment as a discrete occurrence, however subjective and whenever experienced.

In *Wealth and Welfare* and *The Economics of Welfare*,[3] Pigou reduced questions of public policy to questions of economic theory, and he did this by adopting a utilitarian standard for public policy. Pigou's welfare economics rests on two propositions for which he argues consistently in works written over half a century: "first, any additions to the real income of an individual makes satisfaction larger; secondly, transfers of money income from better-to-do people to worse-to-do people make satisfaction larger" (Pigou 1951, p. 293).

As this passage suggests, Pigou's utilitarianism was satisfaction utilitarianism, but satisfaction utilitarianism of a particular sort. He says it is "the psychic return of satisfaction" (Pigou 1912, p. 4) which seems to mean a subjective state of mind that arises from the satisfaction of a want or desire; not, for example, the acquisition per se of the desired object. Pigou observes that the "measuring rod of money ... can only be brought into relation with satisfactions and dissatisfactions through the medium of desires and aversions" (1912, p. 8). Further, "But what does satisfaction mean? Not simply happiness or pleasure; for a man's desires may be directed to other things than these and may be satisfied" (1951, p. 288). For Pigou,

- utility is a subjective state of mind, a "psychic return," associated with a satisfaction;
- satisfaction presupposes that something is satisfied;
- that something is a desire;
- the magnitude of the utility is (imperfectly) correlated with the degree of desire.

This can hardly be dismissed as a "thin" account of human motivation. But what seems to be missing here is that a desire is a desire for something. If the desire is for the "psychic return," the subjective state of mind, then the circle is closed: what people desire is good states of mind, and sometimes they do experience them. What does the language of satisfaction add? If I want a fine automobile, not for the good feelings it will bring me but simply for itself; but nevertheless I take pleasure in driving it, then, on the one hand, the pleasure of driving has little to do with my demand for it, and consequently cannot be measured by "the measuring rod of money" and, on the other hand, seems incidental to the satisfaction of my desire.

Both want and satisfaction are subjective states of mind. If I say, "I want my breakfast," I am describing a subjective state of mind, the way things seem to me. In that sense, my report is incorrigible. To say that I am mistaken is to say that things do not seem to me as they seem to me, a bit of nonsense. Expressions of satisfaction are similar in this. Further, a want and its satisfaction are not different things. Rather, a want is a potentiality and the satisfaction is its realization. If owning a fine automobile both affords me pride of ownership and the pleasure of driving it, this is to say that pride of ownership and pleasure of driving are potentialities for me and the car is the material means necessary for their realization. But while I can hardly be mistaken about my wants and satisfactions, I might lie about them. It is here that *incentive compatibility* becomes a problem. Further, what we observe in the marketplace are decisions, and decisions are based on expected future satisfactions. These expectations might be mistaken. As we will see in a later chapter, learning from economic psychology tells us that we must take such errors into account. Pigou would agree.

Pigou's utilitarianism is illustrated by his comment on the "telescopic faculty." He writes

> Generally speaking, everybody prefers present pleasures or satisfactions of given magnitude to future pleasures or satisfactions of equal magnitude, even when the latter are perfectly certain to occur. But this preference for present pleasures does not – the idea is self-contradictory – imply that a present pleasure of given magnitude is any greater than a future pleasure of the same magnitude. It implies only that our telescopic faculty is defective, and that we, therefore, see future pleasures, as it were, on a diminished scale … It follows that the aggregate amount of economic satisfaction which people in fact enjoy is much less than it would be if their telescopic faculty were not perverted, but equal (certain) satisfactions were desired with equal intensity whatever the period at which they are destined to emerge.
>
> (EW, p. 21)

Pigou is saying that it is irrational to value the same state of mind differently because that state of mind occurs at a later rather than an earlier time. For a preference utilitarian, by contrast – and this would include most modern neoclassical economists – a rational act or valuation is one that is in accordance with individual preferences, and if, as a given fact, people prefer present to future gratifications, then it is rational and indeed necessary to value them differently.

If the future pleasure is *the same experience* as the present pleasure, then to prefer the present to the future experience seems questionable. But can they be the same experience? One might argue that, since the future experience entails also the experience of waiting, the two cannot be the same. Moreover, there is an ambiguity here. Pigou thinks of *economic* welfare as "satisfactions," that is, satisfactions of desires. And desires for a particular experience at different times could be thought of as different desires; and pari passu, their satisfaction different satisfactions. On the other hand, "welfare includes states of consciousness only, and not material things or conditions" (WW, p. 3) and elapsed time is a material condition. Then again, "the elements of welfare are states of consciousness and, perhaps, their relations" (EW, p. 13). Perhaps the elapse of time could be admitted as a relation between the satisfactions of wants at the two different times. In any case, Pigou excludes elapsed time, presumably as a material thing rather than a state of consciousness.

Still, Pigou may have been troubled by an intuition of a real problem for the discounting of utility. A generation after Pigou, this problem was introduced and analyzed by Strotz (1956; for an example see McCain 2015, pp. 155–8). If the individual discounts future benefits to present value at different rates depending on the time elapsed, the decision maker may adopt a plan of future consumption at time τ and then find at $t > \tau$ that the plan is not optimal but that another, quite different plan leads to a greater discounted utility than would be gained by completing the earlier plan. This is *time inconsistency* (Strotz 1956, p. 170). Strotz treats this as a predictive behavioral hypothesis, but most economists since have instead assumed that the rate of discount is a constant, in order to avoid the problem for the sake of "mathematical tractability." Pigou's assumption that discounting utility to present value is irrational is another way of avoiding the problem.

Pigou to the contrary notwithstanding, we might treat states of consciousness at different times as different states of consciousness, and thus assign different magnitudes to them. But this would mean that "the same pleasure" must be evaluated on the basis of two dimensions: one of the magnitude or intensity of the pleasure itself, and one on the time of realization. This raises an issue that any utilitarianism must face: how are pleasures and pains to be aggregated? Should pains simply be subtracted from pleasures, as Bentham had it, or should they be differently weighted, with some reduction of pains taking priority over the increase of pleasures? What about qualitative differences? Certainly pleasures and pains are of different quality. Mill had made quite a point of that. We may again call on the contrast of the states of mind accompanying a mountain climb and those accompanying a rereading of WW. How are the two qualitatively different experiences to be compared?

Pigou says "Every conscious state is a complex of many elements, and includes not only satisfactions but also cognitions, emotions and desires"

(WW, p. 5). For Pigou, this is the basis for a distinction of economic from other components of welfare with economic welfare depending only on satisfactions. We may find, however, that more than one want is satisfied by a single experience, and specifically that "the same pleasure" at an earlier date would satisfy both wants for that specific pleasure and wants for early gratification. These differences of dimension would have to be reduced to a common measure. Pigou demands no more. He asserts as a second necessary condition for welfare economics "that welfare can be brought under the category of greater and less" (WW, p. 3).

Preference is a relation among states of mind, and so we might bring multidimensional states of consciousness "under the category of greater and less" by treating as greater the states of consciousness that are more highly preferred and as lesser those that are less highly preferred, whether because of date of realization or for any other reason. This would provide a sort of hybrid of preference utilitarianism and satisfaction utilitarianism or hedonism. While it might present some problems for interpersonal comparisons, the components of utility in this sense would still be "states of consciousness" with magnitude in terms of intensity and duration, and intercomparable in themselves. This could resolve the problem of interpersonal comparison in some cases, on the plausible argument that, for example, the reduction of the pains of hunger could take precedence over other satisfactions and pleasures, so that poor people who expend a large proportion of their income on the reduction of hunger could be said to have a greater marginal utility of income than do rich people who would spend their marginal dollar for less urgent purposes.[4] Indeed, the problem of interpersonal comparisons would seem to present no more difficulties than the intertemporal comparison of utilities.

We then may summarize Pigou's position as follows: it is the subjective experiences, the pleasures and pains and other affective states, the psychic returns of satisfaction of desires that are the values on the basis of which we can say that a decision is wrong or right. With the exception of satisfactions that occur at different times, the different intensities of desire enable us to evaluate the complex and multidimensional psychic returns on a scale of more or less: while the psychic returns of satisfaction are multidimensional or even beyond description in quantitative terms, the intensity of desire provides the single dimension on which they can be scored. This solves the problem of intrapersonal comparison of utilities. Further, desires of relative intensity are highly correlated with observable material circumstances, the desires for food, water and warmth being instances. Knowing by our own subjective experience something of the relative intensities of desires in given circumstances, we plausibly suppose that others experience wants of similar magnitude in similar circumstances, and make that supposition the basis of interpersonal comparison of utilities. The supposition is not, of course, conclusive – but, as Descartes' example of the demon warns us, we have no *conclusive* grounds for supposing that other minds exist at all. To attribute to other minds desires of similar intensity in similar material circumstances, and consequently satisfactions of similar magnitude, is no less plausible than the supposition that other minds exist at all. This is what Pigou means when he says that it is the intensity of desire that enables us to bring satisfactions into correspondence with the measuring rod of money: "For the most general purposes of economic analysis, therefore, not much harm is likely to be done by the current practice of regarding money demand price indifferently as the measure of a desire and as the measure of the satisfaction felt when the desired thing is obtained" (EW, p. 24).

2.4 Utilities as qualia

Executive summary of the section: In a philosophic language from the later twentieth century, utilities as conceived by Pigou are qualia of a particular kind. This could solve some problems that would arise later.

In the philosophy of the past century, qualia have been a topic of deep controversy. Qualia are the subjective seemings of things, as illustrated by Nagel's (1974) essay "What is it like to be a bat?" Economists seem largely unaware of this discussion.[5] The terminology of *qualia* was not available to utilitarians and economists of the nineteenth and early twentieth centuries. This section introduces qualia and will explore the relation of utility, as economists of that period conceived it, to qualia as they have been discussed in the late twentieth and twenty-first centuries.

The definition of qualia from the *Internet Encyclopedia of Philosophy* (Kind 2015) is clear and will be sufficient.

> Qualia are the subjective or qualitative properties of experiences ... The term "qualia" (singular: quale and pronounced "kwol-ay") was introduced into the philosophical literature in its contemporary sense in 1929 by C. I. Lewis in a discussion of sense-data theory ... In contemporary usage, the term has been broadened to refer more generally to properties of experience. Paradigm examples of experiences with qualia are perceptual experiences ... and bodily sensations (such as pain, hunger, and itching).

The reference to pain and hunger suggests that utilities might be a kind or category of qualia. On this score Sen (2009, p. 285) paraphrases Wittgenstein: "If you feel pain, then you have a pain, and if you don't feel pain, then no external observer can sensibly reject the view that you do not have pain."

Of course, qualia are controversial among philosophers. The existence of qualia is denied by some, and among philosophers who concede that qualia exist, their interpretation is also controversial. A key difficulty is to reconcile the existence and character of qualia with physicalism, or in terms more familiar to non-philosophers, with materialism. On the one hand, it is argued that qualia are irreducibly subjective. Nagel's provocative paper, "What is it like to be a bat?" made that point strongly. Chalmers (1996) makes it the basis of a challenge to materialism. On the other hand, if one holds with materialists that every material event is determined by material causes, then qualia must be epiphenomena, that is, they can have no material consequences. "Intuitively, we believe that the qualitative character of pain – the fact that it hurts – causes us to react the way that we do when we feel pain. But if qualia are epiphenomenal, then the painfulness of pain is causally inert" (Kind 2015). This seems a crucial point for utilitarianism and welfare economics, which would consider the avoidance of pain both as a common "reason" for individual action and as an objective of ethical actions and of public policy. The relation of qualia to utilities does not seem to have been much explored by philosophers. Stalnaker (2004) seems a partial exception.

This difficulty can be illustrated by one of the common mind experiments in the literature on qualia: zombies (e.g. Speaks 2014, p. 76) In this literature, a zombie is a hypothetical creature without any subjective consciousness, but the responses of which to any observable stimuli duplicate those of a conscious being, such as oneself. "Zombies are creatures who behave exactly like us, they run around, they laugh, they cry, they dance to music, and yet there is nothing it is like to be one of them. For them, there are no experiences" (Dietrich and Gillies 2001, p. 365). The logical possibility of zombies challenges materialism because it seems that consciousness must be logically independent of material causes, in that we can conceive of a world identical to our actual material world in which there is no consciousness. Of course, this view remains extremely controversial among philosophers.

It may be that consciousness has evolutionary consequences. The obvious instance is that the qualia of hunger may lead an organism to seek food, and thus enhance her chances of survival and reproduction. For example, Morsella et al. (2016) argue that consciousness is fundamentally a means of coordination of the skeletal musculature and is involved in the choice of one course of action rather than another. (Qualia of decision making will be important in what follows.) This does not remove the zombie problem. It remains apparently a logical possibility that this coordination and decision might be accomplished by some neurological process that does not involve subjective experience.

There are several ways to avoid the problems of interpretation of qualia. One is simply to reject materialism and adopt in its place something like substance (Cartesian) dualism. This will be attractive, of course, to philosophers and others, including economists, who are committed to that view for other reasons. However, philosophers who are skeptical about substance dualism do not seem to be persuaded simply by consideration of qualia.

Second, one may attempt to explain qualia in some physicalist terms. One such approach treats qualia as (mental) representations of physical phenomena, as, for example, the experience of something that seems to be red is a representation of a certain frequency of light. The point seems to be that a representation is dependent on the material state that is represented, rather than independent of it. This has been central to a large number of mind experiments and seems to work best with qualia that accompany sensations, such as visual sensations. Since the discussion began with feelings of this kind, this view has been influential; however, it may not work well in some other cases of interest to an economist. "Objections to representational views of qualia often take the form of putative counter-examples ... But there are more mundane cases. Consider the exogenous feeling of depression. That, it may seem, has no representational content. Likewise, the exogenous feeling of elation. Yet these experiences certainly differ phenomenally" (Tye 2011). Pleasures and pains are not clearly equivalent to elation and depression in this argument. Pains may be said to represent injuries (though the representation may be false, as with a pain felt in a limb long ago amputated). The pleasure that accompanies an ample meal might be said to represent the well-nourished physical state that results. While pleasures may shade into elation, and pains into depression, the "representational content" of many pleasures and pains may be sufficient to identify Benthamite utility as a representation of physical states.

A third possibility, and probably the most controversial, is to adopt a naturalist position that is not physicalist, that is, one that allows for subjective phenomena that follow natural laws but are not physical. "Chalmers' [1996] dualism is a version of property dualism. This view does not posit the existence of any nonphysical or immaterial substances, but instead posits the existence of properties – qualia – that are ontologically independent of any physical properties" (Kind 2015). This faces two kinds of shortcomings. First, if qualia are natural, they are likely to be widespread. This is more important for public policy than might be supposed at first: arguments for animal welfare, whether utilitarian or not, often seem to presuppose that animals can experience qualia, particularly including pain. But it might also correspond to "panpsychism," and "Panpsychism is almost universally regarded with skepticism, if not outright scorn" (Kind 2015). Some presence rather like God might come in by the side door, though probably not a God that any orthodox religion would recognize. However, it is one thing to say that many physical objects other than human beings (dogs and bats, for example) experience qualia, and another to say that all natural objects somehow experience qualia. Thus a person can reasonably adopt the property-dualist position while rejecting panpsychism. Here again, philosophers and others committed to panpsychism for other reasons will not be troubled by this, nor, presumably, by the scorn of most philosophers.

Second, this approach does not clearly avoid the problem that qualia seem to be epiphenomena. But perhaps it is not a problem that qualia are epiphenomena (Jackson 1982). Consider the following example. (What follows is an economist's example, not that of a person learned in philosophy.) Suppose I feel an itch and a corresponding impulse to scratch it. However I hesitate and decide not to scratch the itch, but instead to go and find some salve for it. Grant that these events – the feeling of an itch and the decision not to scratch it – are all neurophysical events and determined by material causes. The itch may react to some irritation, and when I decide not to scratch it, a sequence of neurophysical events follows one creod (Waddington 1977, p. 82) rather than another. The qualia of an itchy feeling and the sense of deciding not to scratch are simply the way that I experience those neurophysiological events. If I satisfy my hunger with a delicious meal, and this causes pleasure, the qualia of pleasure are simply part of the way I experience a sequence of bio-logical and neurophysical events. This does not, of course, tell us why we feel anything at all, but that will have to be left to the philosophers. For the pur-poses of economics, it will be sufficient that the qualia that we want to enjoy or to avoid are correlated with determinate[6] physical events.

Indeed the idea that qualia are epiphenomena correlated with particular neurophysical events is helpful with two problems of welfare economics and utilitarian ethics. One is the problem of interpersonal comparability. Since qualia are subjective, they cannot be compared from one person to another. Indeed, even intrapersonal comparisons – over time, for example, or for qualia experienced under different circumstances – might well be impossible. This latter difficulty means that qualia would not be very helpful for decision theory, which in turn would eliminate most economic theory. However, even if we cannot compare the qualia we may be able to compare the neurophysical states with which they are correlated. For example, if I know from my own experience and from the widespread reports of others that the pain of hunger is greater than the fatigue of working at a particular job for a certain period, then it will be reasonable for me to accept the job, and if I observe that cer-tain people experience hunger because they have no opportunity to work at comparable jobs, I may make a reasonable judgment that (at least in some ways) their qualia could be improved more than in proportion by an improvement in their economic opportunities. We may see a parallel between this argument and both Fisher's comments quoted by Edgeworth and the interpretation of Pigou given in the last section. These parallels suggest that, for these economists, utility may indeed implicitly be a category of qualia.

More generally, what basis have we to suppose that other creatures experi-ence qualia? There is no conclusive argument for this belief. We simply cannot be certain that our qualia, and the apparent reports of others about their qualia, are not implanted in our mind by a Cartesian demon or an "experi-ence machine." But there are plausible grounds. If we observe that our own qualia are correlated with observable states of our neurophysiological system, and further find that the reports of other human beings as to their qualia are similarly correlated with the states of their neurophysiological systems in many cases, then a reasonable prima facie inference is that their reports are true. In the absence of any direct counterargument we may reasonably con-tinue to entertain our prima facie inference. Further, as we have already noted, while we may not imagine the experience of dogs and bats, we may know something about their neurophysical states. Observation may suggest that a particular creature is experiencing pain and hunger, and further biological inquiry may reveal malnutrition or injury that supply further evidence. Now, these creatures may or may not be able to form complex concepts that we human beings experience as desires and preferences, but nevertheless a rational person might draw the conclusion that ethical action and public policy should try to prevent avoidable pains to these creatures.

For our purposes, then, it will be assumed that utilities, disutilities, pleasures, pains, and any other dimensions of utilities are qualia or are like qualia in the sense that they are irreducibly subjective and epiphenomenal but reliably correlated with physical processes that in some cases, such as injury and hunger, have implications for the survival and material well-being of humans and some other creatures. Strictly, it does not matter whether the utility qualia are representations or epiphenomena or (as a Cartesian dualist would have it) causally efficacious. The qualia are what we experience and it is reasonable to act to improve the quality of our experiences and the experiences that we infer that others have. Whether this improvement comes through the causal efficacy of our freely willed decisions or through the causal efficacy of the neurophysiological processes that we experience as freely willed decisions seems to make very little difference.

Thinking in terms of utility as qualia suggests solutions to some long-standing problems of welfare economics. For this, we must depart from the chronology of the history, as these were problems that emerged only later in the twentieth century.

For a first example, recall that Sen (1970) proved "the impossibility of a Paretian Liberal." A key to his proof was the possibility of what we might call "busybody preferences." In Sen's example, a prude prefers that his neighbor not read *Lady Chatterley's Lover* (p. 155). Another possible example would be an advocate of temperance who prefers that his neighbor does not drink alcoholic beverages. Sen here is working within neoclassical preference utilitarianism and follows Arrow's interpretation of preferences as being defined over "states of the world," which would include the activities of others as well as one's own activities. Certainly if preference or desire is the criterion of social choice, the problem seems unavoidable, since people may well prefer or desire that others abstain from, or engage in, certain activities.

How would this appear to a utilitarian who understands utilities as some dimensions of qualia? Suppose that A has a preference for B to abstain from liquor, and the state of the world is transformed in such a way that B takes a vow of abstinence. If A's utility, preference ranking or desire satisfaction is determined by the state of the world, then the temperance advocate is better off. But how does A *experience* being better off? A does not *experience* B's abstinence. If A is *informed* that B will henceforth abstain, and A believes this, A may experience pleasure or the relief of something unpleasant like a pain or anxiety. But this is a consequence of the change of A's belief system, not of B's abstinence. Indeed, so long as she believes it, it does not matter – for the subjective experience of the temperance advocate – whether the information that B has become an abstainer is true or not.

Beliefs and changes of belief, like pleasures and pains, are subjective states of mind, are qualia or dimensions of qualia. But they are dimensions that need to be kept distinct. Probably changes in the state of belief can produce pleasures and relieve pains, or induce other subjective mind states that we would reasonably wish to experience. However, if we wish to evaluate the state of the world, or of the specific part of the state of the world that is denoted as public policy, we will wish to focus on states of mind that arise from changes in the state of the world, independently of our states of belief.

Are there such utilities? Certainly there are some. The pleasure I derive from eating a crème caramel does not derive from my belief that I am eating a crème caramel but from the experience of eating it. If I sip a glass of wine, I may derive pleasure both from the experience of drinking the wine and from my mistaken belief that it is a famous and costly vintage. Only the first of these pleasures is the utility of the wine. Now, this may create some difficulty for demand theory. My marginal willingness to pay for the wine will most probably reflect both pleasures – I may be willing to pay a higher price because I mistakenly believe it to be a famous vintage. But this is a flaw of demand theory, not a flaw of the utilitarian standard for evaluating public policy.

We will find this helpful in another context: the "warm glow" interpretation of self-sacrificing decisions. Suppose, for example, that I have an opportunity to choose between two packages of coffee: one labeled as "fair trade," and at a higher price than the other. Suppose the two packages are otherwise identical. Out of a value that I put on fairness, I may buy the "fair trade" coffee. Some economists (e.g. Andreoni 1990) may say that I am motivated by a "warm glow" from doing what I believe to be right; and that taking into account my utility from the "warm glow," I am maximizing my utility. But if I feel a "warm glow" it is because I *believe* that the coffee growers gain a higher income and thus more utility from the fair-trade coffee. If the utility of my "warm glow" and the coffee growers' increased utility are both counted in valuing the resulting social state, that would seem to be double-counting.

But I have no subjective experience of the coffee grower's increased income, and so can derive no utility from it. That is, the utility from my purchase of the "fair-trade" coffee is the grower's quale, not mine. And if I am wrong, and the coffee grower does not get more income from the fair-trade coffee, then I have simply been defrauded. Here, again, my willingness to pay for the fair-trade coffee reflects both my utility and the state of my beliefs – but is that not always true of anyone who is defrauded?

This seems to be a key test. If a person's subjective experience could be produced by a false report that X, then utility is not attributable to X. Otherwise, we are forced to the conclusion that utility would be systematically increased if people in general were defrauded to believe that the state of the world is as they wish it to be. And common as such frauds are – often indeed as we defraud ourselves along these lines – it is hardly plausible that such a fraud makes the world a better place. And since any belief about the state of the external world could be mistaken, or the result of a fraud by a being like Descartes' demon, utility can never be a consequence of states of belief about the external world or a consequence of a change in those beliefs. The qualia that are consequences of states of belief, pleasurable or painful as they may be, and regardless of the desires that they satisfy, are not utilities; at least not for the purpose of a utilitarian evaluation of public policy.

One might argue that they are not utilities either for a *rational* decision maker. Consider a person with some (limited) knowledge of wine who takes great satisfaction in drinking a wine he mistakenly believes is a rare vintage. A skeptic will say that his pleasure is irrational, and that it would be equally irrational even if he were right that the vintage is rare – that for a rational person, only the taste of the wine and not its vintage are rational bases by which to judge it. Should we conclude that qualia consequent on states of belief should play no part in the decisions of a rational person? No, that would go too far. The (self-designated) connoisseur's pleasure at drinking what he believes is a fine vintage is his pleasure, though that pleasure would be spoiled if he knew that he was deceived. But there is nothing irrational about basing his decision on the pleasures he will enjoy if he is well informed. My decision to purchase "fair-trade" coffee is a rational decision based, not on the maximization of my own utility, but on maximization of (some positively responsive function of) the utilities both of myself and the producer, relying on my belief that "fair-trade" coffee really is more beneficial to the producer. The producer's utility from his increased income is a quale consequent partly on *my* state of belief. Any "warm glow" is a symptom of my decision but not an influence on it. Again, if I am rational, I will do my best to assure myself that my belief is not based on fraud.

From one point of view, this is a comfortable conclusion. We need not be concerned about the impossibility of a Paretian liberal nor about the logical consistency of the "warm glow" explanation of philanthropy. We are not just authorized but required to ignore busybody preferences and desires for a fairer world as influences on the utility of individuals. This is not to say that busybody preferences and desires for a fairer world are not relevant to the evaluation of public policy. In the political process, we may call for a more equal distribution of income on the grounds that it will increase utility, or in a more Rawlsian vein, for a more equal distribution of utilities; and we may advocate for public policy constrained by deontological values such as the prohibition of alcohol. But the utilities used for those arguments, or for weighing the opportunity cost of prohibitions, are utilities based on the qualities of individual experience.

From another point of view it is a less comfortable conclusion. Since states of belief may influence the decisions of rational and well-informed decision makers, the individual willingness to pay will correspond to the marginal utility relevant to welfare economics only in the special case that it is not (on average) influenced by states of belief. My willingness to pay for "fair-trade" coffee simply deviates from my marginal utility of drinking the coffee, because it is based on my belief that "fair trade" is more fair. This admits a new class of exceptions to the optimality of perfect competition. In doing so it dilutes the coherence of neoclassical economics, and this coherence is a major point in favor of neoclassical economics.

2.5 Concluding summary

By the beginning of the present century, the use of utility concepts had become common in economics, as the basis of a theory of supply, demand and equilibrium. Some economists followed Mill and made this an aspect of a general utilitarian understanding of ethics and public policy, while others resisted this as unscientific. Despite some acknowledged mathematical difficulties with the concept, even those who resisted "utilitarianism" could do little better than to postulate the existence of a functional relation of utility to the array of quantities of consumption goods, and this was to be the case well into the twentieth century. The utilitarianism that Pigou inherited from Marshall was neither Benthamism nor the "ordinal" preference utilitarianism of modern microeconomics but a satisfaction utilitarianism, that is, a utilitarianism that associated a quantity of subjective utility with the satisfaction of a want. To use a terminology that would not be available until well into the twentieth century, they regarded utility as the qualia associated with the satisfaction of wants or desires.

Notes

1 Further discussion of Sidgwick is less relevant to the topic of this chapter and so is reserved to a brief appendix to the chapter.
2 Cooter and Rappoport (1984) attribute essentially this view to Marshall and Pigou, but they seem to go too far, as this chapter and the next will argue.
3 In what follows, WW will refer to *Wealth and Welfare*, 1912 and EW will refer to *The Economics of Welfare*, 1920. Unless indicated otherwise, it is the 1920 edition referred to.
4 This certainly is close to Pigou's position, as we read in WW, p. 24:

> If we assume all members of the community to be of similar temperament, and if these members are only two in number, it is easily shown that any transference from the richer to the poorer of the two, since it enables more intense wants to be satisfied at the expense of less intense wants, must increase the aggregate sum of satisfaction.

5 A full-text search of JSTOR for the word "qualia," limited to economics journals, yielded four references, two of which seem to have used it more or less correctly, while a search of EconLit for records in which the word "qualia" appears anywhere produced one. Yew-Kwang Ng (2003, p. 309), in a discussion of cardinal utility, refers to "The problem of qualia in philosophy," but only in passing.
6 Or perhaps indeterminate. What follows has no authority of scholarship in philosophy or economics, so far as I know, and that is why it is relegated to a footnote. Suppose, however, that we follow Roger Penrose (1989) into quantum mechanics. As Schrödinger's famous cat illustrates, quantum indeterminacy may be observed in a highly sensitive macroscopic system. The human brain is a highly sensitive

system, and Penrose argues that its states may be indeterminate in a quantum sense. He uses this idea primarily to explain mathematical creativity, but remarks in passing that freedom of will might also be a consequence. So when I decide not to scratch my itch, a wave function collapses, and the quale of freedom of decision is simply the way I experience the collapse of the wave function. The account in the main text is, I believe, sufficient for welfare economics; but it may be remarked that the philosophers' physicalism often seems quite Newtonian, even in the twenty-first century.

Appendix: Sidgwick's *Principles of Political Economy*

Sidgwick's *Principles of Political Economy* (1883) displays the work of a powerful mind but one little adapted to the direction of change in economic theory in his time. Sidgwick's caution about imprecise categories and complicating factors – "the structure of these works" in Schultz' phrase – has the result that we find flashes of ideas that will become influential generations later, such as efficiency wages (p. 97), human capital (pp. 81, 126) knockout competition (p. 408) and secular stagnation (pp. 156, 383.) Sidgwick's *Principles* bears comparison with Cairnes' *Some Leading Principles of Political Economy, Newly Expounded* (1878), in that both are aimed at continuing the classical tradition of Smith, Malthus, Ricardo and Mill at a time when marginal analysis was rapidly developing toward the neoclassical economics that would reach its maturity in Pigou's writing. Sidgwick deviates from Cairnes in two important ways. First, where Cairnes rejects Jevons' ideas as without substantive content, Sidgwick adopts Jevons' analysis and describes it as the most important contribution to political economy in a generation. Second, following Mill but contrarily to Cairnes, Sidgwick decisively rejects the wages fund theory of wages (p. 302). But it is not clear that either of these departures is an improvement. Like Cairnes, Sidgwick remains committed to a cost-of-production theory of normal price (p. 57). This modifies Ricardo's embodied-labor theory of value by adjusting the labor value to allow for differences in the capital intensity of production in different industries, that is, treating "abstinence" or (in Sidgwick's preferred phrase) delay as a cost of production along with labor. The same adjustment defines the "transformation problem" in Marxian economics. But this means that Jevons' theory of demand really plays little role in Sidgwick's economics. In the place of the wages fund, Sidgwick adopts what is essentially a residual theory of wages (p. 308. Needs it be said that a residual theory is no theory at all?) This is not to say that Sidgwick is quite unaware of the influence of marginal utility on wages. On the contrary, he dismisses the idea that a market wage is *just* precisely on the ground that it reflects "final," not average or total, utility (p. 505). In his theoretical treatment of international trade, Sidgwick's commitment to a cost-of-production theory of normal price (together with his breadth of focus and a certain cosmopolitanism that regards nations as minor inconveniences) seem to lead him into a confusion of relative and money price (p. 208). Sidgwick rejects Mill's clarification of Ricardo, in which Mill argues that prices in international trade would be determined by the equality of quantities demanded and supplied. Sidgwick instead relies on costs of shipment as determining prices in international trade. What Sidgwick seems to lose sight of is that settlements of prices in international trade are made in money terms, and that the "value of money," that is, the money remuneration of labor and of "delay," would differ from country to country. Unlike Ricardo and Mill – it is true – Sidgwick allows for costs of shipment and for international migration. Ricardo, in his model, had assumed them away. We may give Sidgwick credit for greater generality and care for complications, but his discussion remains confused. In short, where Ricardo gives us a model, Sidgwick gives us a muddle. And this is unfortunately rather typical of Sidgwick's economics: again and again, he points out the difficulty of balancing the complicated opposing tendencies and finally relies not on his economic theory but on his own subjective judgment of the utility consequent on government policies or economic causes. Unlike Pigou, he does not use the *tools* of marginal analysis in his discussion of public policy. This is a good illustration of the reason why economists rely on models, and also, I think, clear enough reasons why it was Marshall, not Sidgwick, who brought marginalism into the mainstream of English political economy.

References

Andreoni, James (1990) Impure Altruism and Donations to Public Goods: A Theory of Warm-Glow Giving, *Economic Journal* v. 100, no. 401 (June) pp. 464–477.

Cairnes, J. E. (1878) *Some Leading Principles of Political Economy, Newly Expounded* (New York: Harper).

Chalmers, David (1996) *The Conscious Mind: In Search of a Fundamental Theory* (New York: Oxford University Press).

Cooter, Robert and Peter Rappoport (1984) Were the Ordinalists Wrong about Welfare Economics? *Journal of Economic Literature* v. 22, no. 2 (Jun) pp. 507–530.

Dietrich, Eric and Anthony Gillies (2001) Consciousness and the Limits of Our Imaginations, *Synthese* v. 126, no. 3 (March) pp. 361–381.

Edgeworth, F. Y. (1881) *Mathematical Psychics* (London: C. Kegan Paul).

Edgeworth, F. Y. (1893) Irving Fisher, *Mathematical Investigations in the Theory of Value and Prices*, *Economic Journal* v. 3, no. 9 (March) pp. 108–112.

Fellner, William (1967) Operational Utility: The Theoretical Background and a Measurement, *Ten Economic Studies in the Tradition of Irving Fisher* edited by William Fellner (New York: J. Wiley) pp. 39–75.

Fisher, Irving (1892) Mathematical Investigations in the Theory of Value and Prices, *Transactions of the Connecticut Academy of Arts and Science* v. 9 (July).

Fisher, Irving (1918) Is "Utility" the Most Suitable Term for the Concept It Is Used to Denote? *American Economic Review* v. 8, no. 2 (Jun) pp. 335–337.

Jackson, Frank (1982) Epiphenomenal Qualia, *Philosophical Quarterly* v. 32, no. 127 (April) pp. 127–136.

Jevons, William Stanley (1866) Brief Account of a General Mathematical Theory of Political Economy, *Journal of the Royal Statistical Society* v. 29 (June).

Jevons, William Stanley (1871) *The Theory of Political Economy* (London: Macmillan & Co.).

Kind, Amy (2015) Qualia, *Internet Encyclopedia of Philosophy*, available at: www.iep. utm.edu/qualia/, as of January 19, 2015.

Malthus, Thomas (1800) *An Investigation of the Cause of the Present High Price of Provisions* (London: Printed for J. Johnson, in St. Paul's-Church-Yard, by Davis, Taylor, and Wilks, Chancery-Lane).

Marshall, Alfred (1948 [1890]) *Principles of Economics* (New York: Macmillan).

McCain, Roger A. (2012) Cairnesian Economics: A Road Not Taken, May, available at: www.researchgate.net/publication/269409820_Cairnesian_Economics_-_A_Road_Not_ Taken.

McCain, Roger A. (2015) *Game Theory and Public Policy*, 2nd Edition (Cheltenham: Edward Elgar).

McCain, Roger A. (2017) *Approaching Equality: What Can Be Done about Wealth Inequality?* (Cheltenham: Edward Elgar).

Morsella, E., C. Godwin, T. Jantz, S. Krieger and A. Gazzaley (2016) Homing in on Consciousness in the Nervous System: An Action-Based Synthesis, *Behavioral and Brain Sciences* v. 39.

Nagel, Thomas (1974) What Is It Like to Be a Bat? *Philosophical Review* v. 83, no. 4 (Oct) pp. 435–450.

Ng, Yew-Kwang (2003) From Preference to Happiness: Towards a More Complete Welfare Economics, *Social Choice and Welfare* v. 20, no. 2 pp. 307–350.

Pareto, Vilfredo (1971 [1906]) *Manual of Political Economy* (New York: A. M. Kelley).

Penrose, Roger (1989) *The Emperor's New Mind* (Oxford: Oxford University Press).

Pigou, A. C. (1912) *Wealth and Welfare* (London: Macmillan).

Pigou, A. C. (1920) *The Economics of Welfare* (London: Macmillan).

Pigou, A. C. (1951) Some Aspects of Welfare Economics, *American Economic Review* v. 41, no. 3 (Jun) pp. 287–302.

Samuelson, Paul A. (1950) The Problem of Integrability in Utility Theory, *Economica, New Series* v. 17, no. 68 (Nov) pp. 355–385.

Schultz, Bart (2017) *The Happiness Philosophers: The Lives and Works of the Great Utilitarians* (Princeton, N.J.: Princeton University Press).

Sen, Amartya (1970) The Impossibility of a Paretian Liberal, *Journal of Political Economy* v. 78, no. 1 (Jan) pp. 152–157.

Sen, Amartya (1983) Development: Which Way Now? *Economic Journal* v. 93, no. 372 (Dec) pp. 745–762.

Sen, Amartya (2009) *The Idea of Justice* (Cambridge, Mass.: Belknap Press).

Sidgwick, Henry (1874) *The Methods of Ethics* (London: Macmillan).

Sidgwick, Henry (1883) *The Principles of Political Economy* (London: Macmillan).

Sinnott-Armstrong, Walter (2012) Consequentialism, *Stanford Encyclopedia of Philosophy*, available at: http://plato.stanford.edu/archives/spr2014/entries/consequentia lism/, as of January 14, 2015.

Speaks, Jeff (2014) What Are Debates about Qualia Really about? *Philosophical Studies* v. 170, no. 1 pp. 59–84.

Stalnaker, Robert (2004) Comparing Qualia across Persons, New York University Department of Philosophy, available at: www.nyu.edu/gsas/dept/philo/courses/gra dmind01/newpapers/Comparing%20Qualia.htm, as of January 18, 2015.

Strotz, Robert Henry (1956) Myopia and Inconsistency in Dynamic Utility Maximization, *Review of Economic Studies* v. 23, no. 3 pp. 163–180.

Tye, Michael (2011) Qualia, *Stanford Encyclopedia of Philosophy*, available at: http://plato.stanford.edu/archives/fall2013/entries/qualia/, as of January 18, 2015.

Volterra, V. (1906) Review of Pareto's Manuale, *Giornale degli economnisti* v. 32, pp. 296–301.

Waddington, C. H. (1977) *Tools for Thought* (New York: Basic Books).

3　Pigou and the founding of welfare economics

Arthur Cecil Pigou (1877–1959) was a student and protégé of Alfred Marshall, and Marshall's successor as professor of economics at Cambridge. He came to economics through an interest in moral philosophy. Of his first book-length work, he writes (1905, p. 3) "The question raised is not, What have Arbitration and Conciliation done? nor yet, How have they done it but rather, What ought they to do, and how ought they to do it?" Nevertheless, he hoped to avoid controversies in ethical theory in that book, and later he regarded economics, in his own words, as a "positive science of what is and tends to be, not a normative science of what ought to be" (EW, p. 5). But he took this position because he saw economics as a practical study, a policy science, and (as we shall see) did not hesitate to make policy recommendations. Perhaps the same could be said of Milton Friedman (1953), with whom that definition of economics as a positive science is more often associated. What we see here is a tension in any policy science, since policy recommendations must arise from verified facts but at the same time draw their force from the values that supply the "ought to." In both cases those values are those of the theorist. For Pigou, those value judgments were discussed systematically in Chapter 2.

3.1　Becoming A. C. Pigou

Executive summary of the section: Pigou's early work focused on the refinement of Marshall's ideas, especially on consumer surplus, and on wage arbitration.

In a 1903 paper, Pigou explicitly addresses the measurability of utility, following Fisher's definition without noting Fisher's qualification that the measure presupposes that a utility function is additively separable. He notes the wide range of influences on the individual's utility that may be hidden under the phrase "ceteris paribus." He defends the concept of consumer surplus against a criticism of Patten (1893). He then goes on to consider cases in which utility is interdependent in the sense that the utility that a person gets from one additional unit depends on the distribution of the commodity over the population, and notes that one cannot aggregate demand curves by horizontal addition in that case.[1] This in turn means that consumer surpluses cannot be aggregated additively, but Pigou argues that this can be ignored for practical problems as the practical problems will involve only small changes in price.

In 1904, Pigou reports, without proof, several propositions on the incidence of taxation (Pigou 1904a). He returns to this topic, considering in particular duties on imports and on domestic production, in 1907 (Pigou 1907b). These discussions make use of the Marshallian conception of increasing and decreasing returns to the scale of the industry, which will be discussed below. In 1910 he clarifies those concepts, using his own terminology, which he will continue to use in WW and EW. In 1904, also, Pigou discusses monopoly pricing strategy (Pigou 1904b) and in 1908 bilateral monopoly, in this case using Edgeworth's concepts of indifference curves and the box diagram. A non-economic essay, "The Ethics of the Gospels" (Pigou 1907a) is of interest for present purposes only insofar as it seems to argue that utilitarianism does not conflict with Christianity.

3.2 *The Economics of Welfare*

Executive summary of the section: In a series of editions over 25 years, Pigou explored the harmony and disharmony of considerations of productivity and distribution in economics.

In WW (1912) and EW (1920), Pigou sets out the ideas that were to form the field known as welfare economics. Pigou tells us in the preface to EW that it was begun as a revision of WW, and extensive tracts are repeated from WW. Some new material can be traced to the occurrence of World War I between the two books: a good deal of discussion of the implications of war finance for economic welfare appears in the second book that is not in the first. (In later editions of EW these are largely omitted and shifted to Pigou 1921.) At the same time, there are some new topics that reflect Pigou's refinement of his ideas. The famous remark about the failure of the telescopic faculty, which was discussed in Chapter 2, occurs in EW (p. 25) but not in WW. Some of the terminology is new in EW, and some criticisms are answered. The organization of the second book is different, and EW is somewhat repetitive as a result. Later editions of EW (1924, 1928, 1932) clarify some points. A few examples in the earlier book are more persuasive than the more well-known, later book. All in all, though, EW is the definitive book.

In both books Pigou begins by defining economic welfare essentially as satisfaction utility, insofar as it can be brought into correspondence with "the measuring rod of money." Pigou will analyze economic welfare in terms of the "national dividend" and its distribution and variability. In EW he writes (p. 30):

Generally speaking, economic causes act upon the economic welfare of any country, not directly, but through the earning and spending of that objective counterpart of economic welfare which economists call the national dividend or national income. Just as economic welfare is that part of total welfare which can be brought directly or indirectly into relation with a money measure, so the national dividend ... is that part of the objective income of the community that can be measured in money.

Pigou gives rather extensive discussion of the problems of actually calculating the real national income in terms that are familiar from modern textbooks.

Pigou concedes that an increase in economic welfare could be offset by a decrease in non-economic welfare. Thus, arguments for policies on the grounds that they increase economic welfare could be defeated by the counterargument that they decrease non-economic welfare to a larger degree. Social interactions that arise among co-workers and the satisfactions of family life are mentioned in WW (p. 8) as sources of non-economic welfare, and along with them, another example of reduction of non-economic welfare, environmental degradation in the form of destruction of scenery. In EW (p. 32), the destruction of scenery is mentioned as a shortcoming of the concept of a national dividend. This seems to be no more than a difference of expression. In any case Pigou takes the position that an increase in economic welfare will *usually* correspond to an increase in overall welfare and that if a change in policy is shown to increase economic welfare the burden of proof is on those who would argue that it would reduce overall welfare through its effect on non-economic welfare.

In WW he then puts forward three propositions, the first two of which he will reiterate (Pigou 1951) from time to time over the next 40 years: (1) (p. 20) "The first of these is that, if a cause is introduced, which makes for an increase in the aggregate size of the dividend, provided that the absolute share of no group of members, in terms of the commodities which that group is accustomed chiefly to consume, decreases, the economic welfare of the community as a whole is likely to be augmented." (2) (p. 24) "[E]conomic welfare is likely to be augmented by anything that, leaving other things unaltered, renders the distribution of the national dividend less unequal." (3) (p. 32) "[I]f a cause is introduced which diminishes the variability, or inequality in time, of the dividend, and especially of that part of it which accrues to the poorer classes, the economic welfare of the community as a whole is likely to be augmented." In EW he proceeds a bit more cautiously, preceding the statements of the propositions with examples and arguments (pp. 47, 53, 67). And there is a certain shift of orientation and a fourth proposition. Proposition (2) becomes more specific: "Any cause which increases the proportion of the national dividend received by poor persons, provided that it does not lead to a contraction of the dividend and does not injuriously affect its variability, will, in general, increase economic welfare." The fourth proposition is (4) (p. 68) "Any cause which diminishes the variability of the part of the national dividend accruing to the poor, even though it increases in corresponding measure the variability of the part accruing to the rich, will, other things being equal, increase economic welfare." There seems here to be an increased sensitivity to the conditions of the poor in particular, and (writing in England in the period before 1920) he identifies the poor with the working class. Propositions (2) and (3) are deduced from the diminishing marginal utility of income, while proposition (4) requires in addition that the second derivative of utility with respect to income decreases as income rises.

It is worthwhile to observe that in proposition (3), Pigou anticipates Modigliani and Brumberg's (1954) argument that utility is increased by consumption smoothing, though Pigou does not suppose that private decisions will lead to optimal consumption smoothing, and a considerable part of EW is devoted to what we would now call macroeconomic policies that tend to smooth consumption, particularly of the working class. This is taken up in Part VI, and leads Pigou into theories of the business cycle that do not arise in WW. Here, again, much of this is deleted in later editions and finds its way into Pigou 1927. In a similar vein, we may note that Pigou is well aware that diminishing marginal utility of income leads to risk aversion (EW, p. 898, Appendix 1, pp. 915–924).

For Pigou, the "factors of production" are labor, waiting and uncertainty bearing. In identifying capital with disembodied "waiting" rather than with concrete capital goods, Pigou is in the tradition of Nassau Senior (1850, p. 58) and John Bates Clark (1899). He insists on the distinction of uncertainty bearing from waiting (EW, p. 348) and argues that public control of industry will reduce uncertainty bearing. This, he suggests, will in turn reduce the rate of technological innovation. His argument that uncertainty bearing is a resource runs along the following lines: consider a set of projects, each of which offers an expected value rate of return above the average, but each individually quite risky. When they are aggregated, the expected value rate of return is the same, but the risk much less. Thus, to the extent that risk aversion causes these projects to be avoided, the national income is less than it would be (with very little risk), and conversely, an increase in the willingness to bear risk increases the national dividend (EW, p. 915).

Given the three propositions in WW, the outline of the book is not surprising. Part II discusses the determinants of the magnitude of the national dividend, though the first two chapters of the part defend the idea that distribution and the volume of production can be considered separately. The defense is particularly against Pareto's argument that the distribution of income is immutable. Part III explores the distribution of the national dividend. Here distinct chapters largely consider distinct forms of redistribution or policies to raise wages. Part IV explores the variability of the national dividend, and chapters that consider means of reducing the negative impact of this variability on the poor or the working class are mixed with chapters that discuss causes, i.e. some theory of business cycles, money and price levels. In the first edition of EW, Part II is followed by parts on the national dividend and labor and on the national dividend and government finance. Part III partly returns to the subject matter of *Principles and Methods of Industrial Peace* (1905) but also incorporates topics from Part III of WW. Again, Part IV recurs to Pigou's contributions on tax incidence. The next part, Part V in the 1920 edition of EW, is a discussion of the distribution of the national dividend, but rather different from Part II of WW. Here we see the refutation of Pareto from Part II of WW. A rich menu of redistributive measures is evaluated. Finally, Part VI is a somewhat rearranged version of Part IV of WW. By the 1932 edition of EW, parts IV and VI have disappeared, the material of those parts shifted (EW, 1932 edition, Preface to the Third Edition) to Pigou's more specialized books, *Industrial Fluctuations* (1927) and *A Study in Public Finance* (1928). The appendices consider, as noted, risk aversion, statistical measurement of elasticities and what are now called externalities. Since externalities, the subjects of Part II and Appendix III, are most influential in the twentieth century and are still only partly understood, they will be reserved and considered last.

Nevertheless, throughout the book, Pigou explores the impact of public policies on the size of the national dividend. For this purpose his key tool is the marginal net product of a resource. He writes (EW, p. 116):

> The value of this marginal social net product is the money value of the economic satisfaction due to it. When there is no element present other than the direct physical addition made to output in the industry directly concerned, this money value is identical with the marginal increment of product multiplied by the price per unit at which the product is sold when the given volume of resources is being employed in producing it.

Then (EW, p. 117),

> On the basis of this definition it can be shown that, provided there are no costs of movement between different occupations, and provided conditions are such that only one arrangement of resources will make the values of the marginal net products in all occupations equal, that arrangement must make the national dividend larger than it would be under any other arrangement.

However (EW, pp. 119–121):

> The foregoing analysis rests upon the assumption that there is only one arrangement of resources which makes the values of marginal social net products everywhere equal ... But, when the law of increasing returns is acting strongly, it is evident that even our condition may very well not be fulfilled ... if several arrangements are possible, all of which make the values of the marginal social net products equal, each of these arrangements does, indeed, imply what may be called a relative maximum for the dividend; but only one of these maxima is the unequivocal, or absolute, maximum.

Nevertheless, Pigou argues that a change in public policy that moves from equal to unequal values of the marginal social net products of a resource in different uses will *probably* decrease the national dividend.

In appropriate circumstances this leads to:

> the highly optimistic theory of Adam Smith, that the national dividend, in given circumstances of demand and supply, tends "naturally" to a maximum ... The theoretical ground of this view may be stated in the form of two propositions. The first is that the dividend necessarily stands at the maximum attainable amount when the marginal net products of resources is equal in all uses, the second that self-interest, if not interfered with, tends to make these marginal net products equal.
>
> (WW pp. 104–105)

The language of EW is less compact and colorful, but equivalent. Part II will address some cases in which the circumstances are not appropriate. Before discussing those, we consider how Pigou uses the tools of marginal social net productivity in the later parts.

In most of these chapters the key point is that the national dividend is largest when the marginal net social product of a resource is the same in all uses of it, and different chapters are often devoted to different obstacles to this equality. Pigou's discussion of monopsony wages will serve as an example of Pigou's approach in general. Pigou treats this as an instance of "unfair" wages in a sense that he borrows from Marshall.

> Real wages in any occupation are fair, according to this definition, when, allowance being made for differences in the steadiness of the demand for labour over a year in different industries, "they are about on a level with the payment made for tasks in other trades which are of equal difficulty and disagreeableness, which require equally rare natural abilities and an equally expensive training."
>
> (EW, p. 505)

Pigou distinguishes two cases:

> On the one hand, wages may be unfair in some place or occupation, because, though they are equal to the value of the marginal net product of the labour assembled there, this is not equal to the value of the marginal net product, and, therefore, to the wage rate, of the labour assembled elsewhere. On the other hand, wages may be unfair in some place or occupation, because workpeople are exploited, in the sense that they are paid less than the value which their marginal net product has to the firms which employ them. The effects of interference with these two kinds of unfairness are by no means the same, and the discussion of them must be kept sharply separate.
>
> (EW, p. 506)

The second of these is the case of monopsony power:

> if any employer, or body of employers, exploits the workpeople in his service, he will, in general, not be able to hire as much labour as would have been available for him otherwise, and, consequently, the value of the marginal net product of such labour as he does hire will be indirectly raised.
>
> (EW, p. 512)

This is illustrated with demand and supply curves for labor in a footnote at p. 512. However, Pigou does not produce a monopsony equilibrium model such as we will later see from Joan Robinson (1933). Rather, he treats it as a case of bilateral monopoly. "Consequently, there is created a range of indeterminateness, within which the wages actually paid to any workman can be affected by individual 'higgling and bargaining'" (p. 513). Thus, "exploitation" is not inevitable but depends on bargaining power. Organization on either side can enhance bargaining power on that side (EW, pp. 513, 514). But in many circumstances, the strategic advantages and wealth of the employer give him the advantage in bargaining power (p. 515). (The greater wealth of the employer implies not only that he may have reserves, but also that his marginal utility of income is less, so that a failure to arrive at a bargain is a lesser cost to him.)

> Thus, it appears prima facie that, though the abolition of this type of unfairness would presumably benefit economic welfare as a whole by preventing the relatively rich from taking money from the relatively poor, it would make no difference to the magnitude of the national dividend. [However,] the forcing down of wages in particular places or occupations, though it does not reduce the labour supply sufficiently to compel employers to refrain from it, does reduce it to some extent. When this happens, the quantity of labour employed there will be so far contracted that the value of the marginal net product of labour there is greater than it is elsewhere. This involves injury to the national dividend.
>
> (EW, pp. 516–517)

In addition, the reduction of wages may reduce the incentives to innovation (EW, pp. 517–518) and permit relatively incompetent businessmen to continue in business who would be eliminated in a competitive equilibrium (p. 519), which will reduce the national dividend now or in the future. Thus, measures to raise exploitative wages will (on the one hand) improve the distribution of the national dividend and (on the other hand) increase its magnitude, so "external interference to prevent that type of unfair wages which I have described as exploitation is desirable in the interest of the national dividend as well as upon other grounds" (EW, p. 519). Pigou then goes on to consider women's wages in particular, and moderates this conclusion somewhat, though he confirms (EW, footnote p. 526) that the removal of all traditional barriers to women's entering labor markets, together with higher wages, would again benefit both the distribution and magnitude of the national dividend. In any case, Pigou rejects *one-size-fits-all* policies and holds (p. 526) that each case of potentially "unfair" wages should be considered separately on the balance of advantages.

In this example, as in some other cases considered, there is harmony between the considerations based on the magnitude and distribution of the national dividend. Some of these instances are also founded on a recognition of what more modern economics calls human capital. He conjectures (WW, pp. 353–356, EW, p. 547–9) that in some industries, higher wages may result in an increase in the productivity of labor, reinforcing the case to raise wages reduced by monopsony. However, in many cases there is "disharmony," that is, proposed policies in which the influence on the size of the national dividend is opposite to its influence on distribution. These policies have to be considered on the balance of their advantages, in principle, but Pigou is generally reluctant to support policies that would reduce the incentive to work or to save, however favorable the prospects for improved distribution. There are exceptions, and here, again, disincentives may be offset by formation of human capital that would increase productivity, as in the cases of trade schools (EW, p. 777), free medical care (EW, p. 779), child care (EW, p. 779) and even perhaps a rise of wages above the equilibrium or "fair" wage (EW, p. 549).

3.3 Externalities

Executive summary of the section: Pigou's ideas on externalities are better remembered. While Pigou seems to have meant mainly to defend Marshall's ideas, his own ideas were more novel than he realized and more correct than is widely supposed.

Those discussions are little remembered. In the later twentieth century, and in the twenty-first, the concept of externalities came to be the one thing that Pigou seems most to be remembered for. In the earlier twentieth century, however, these ideas were among the ones most criticized by many other economists and were generally rejected. To assess Pigou's discussion of externalities we require a careful examination of six interrelated, but distinct concepts:

I.a. economies of scale (of the firm)
I.b. diseconomies of scale (of the firm)
II.a. external economies of scale (of the industry)
II.b. external diseconomies of scale (of the industry)
III.a. positive externalities to third parties
III.b. negative externalities to third parties.

Categories I and II are Marshallian, and Pigou follows Marshall in applying and defending them. Conversely, these concepts have had little influence on the further development of welfare economics. On category II.b Marshall is never quite unequivocal but Pigou arguably goes beyond Marshall's ideas. This category was central to the controversy over Pigou's discussion of externalities in the early twentieth century. Categories III, by contrast, remain influential and have been central to controversies throughout the later twentieth century.[2] However, Pigou does not always clearly distinguish II and III, though the distinction is, if anything, a little clearer in WW than in EW. That is, Pigou treats both II and III as causes of deviations of the market returns to resources from their marginal net products, and in that sense categories II and III have similar implications.

Category I refers to the ways in which costs vary with the scale of the individual firm. Marshall discusses economies to the scale of the individual firm extensively and attributes them (following Mill 1985 [1848], p. 85) to the fact that larger enterprises can adopt a more complex division of labor, and also to some extent on the indivisibility of machinery (Marshall 1948 [1920], pp. 250–263, 278–283). Diseconomies of the scale of the firm are a bit more mysterious, and were to be a subject of some controversy, but Marshall seems to attribute them to the increased difficulty of managing larger enterprises (Marshall 1948 [1920], pp. 284, 289).

For Category II, the costs of each firm in an industry or product group depend not only on the output of the individual firm, but also on the output of the entire group. Here, again, Marshall suggests that increasing the complexity of the division of labor in the larger *industry* would decrease the cost for a representative firm producing a certain amount; and on this score, he stresses the increased flow of business-related information as "external economies" (Marshall, 1948 [1920], pp. 284–253). This is sometimes expressed in other words by saying that the larger industry may be able to support a trade journal and a trade school (Ellis and Fellner 1943). I have one further instance to offer, based on something I was told by a person with experience in the Mississippi plywood industry. I have not been able to find print documentation for it, and offer it only as a hypothetical story. The plywood industry in the United States had first been established in the Pacific Northwest, but plywood plants began to be built in Mississippi after the Second World War as abandoned agricultural land began to yield pine softwood. At first each plant had to maintain an inventory of replacement parts, but after the industry attained a certain size, a company was established in Jackson (Mississippi's largest and central city) that promised overnight delivery of spare parts, reducing the cost of the inventories by merging them.

For external diseconomies, however, Marshall says little more than that they are attributable to the action of nature, while economies are attributable to the actions of man (Marshall, 1948 [1920], p. 418). The examples Marshall gives are consistent with the idea that, in industries subject to decreasing returns, costs rise as a result of the rise in rent, the Ricardian explanation. However, Marshall does observe that in the presence of external economies or diseconomies, the conditions for efficient allocation conflict with those for free entry equilibrium (Marshall, 1948 [1920], pp. 811–812). This will be Pigou's launch point. Marshall does not seem to make any reference to categories III.

In WW (pp. 144–168), Pigou distinguishes two cases in which marginal social net product diverges from private: certain incomplete lease contracts and "third-party" impacts, when some of the benefit or cost of a decision falls on people other than producers or consumers of the good produced. Third-party impacts are categories III. The particular examples he gives are rather modern:

> Such services are rendered, when resources are invested in private parks in cities; for these, even though the public is not admitted to them, improve the air of the neighbourhood … It is true, and this is a matter of growing importance, of resources devoted to the prevention of smoke from factory chimneys … It is true of resources and activities devoted to the perfecting of inventions and improvements in industrial processes, since these cannot in practice be kept secret, and may not legally be patented for an indefinite length of time.
>
> (WW, pp. 158–160)

"Incidental uncharged disservices are rendered to the general public, in respect of resources invested in the running of motor cars that wear out the surface of the roads" (WW, p. 163). Pigou is also concerned with negative third-party effects from the sale of alcoholic beverages and wasteful persuasive advertising.

However, Pigou goes on to discuss externalities of category II in a more Marshallian way. He affirms that for both categories II.a and II.b, there is a conflict between the zero-profit free entry equilibrium and the efficient allocation of resources. The supply price curve – which, for any quantity supplied, gives the price just high enough that the quantity will be offered by competitive firms – does not agree with the curve of *marginal* supply prices, "the difference made to the aggregate expenses of the industry concerned by the production of the OM^{th} unit of output" (WW, p. 173). For a case of external economies, this would be the long-run marginal cost of the firm that produces the OM^{th} unit *minus* the reduction of costs to other firms because of the growth in industry output (supposing, for simplicity, that output could only be produced in discrete units). For a case of external diseconomies, it would be the long-run marginal cost of the firm that produces the OM^{th} unit *plus* the increase of costs to other firms because of the growth in industry output. Pigou writes (WW, pp. 174–175),

> This result, it should be noted, is not inconsistent with the ordinary doctrine of rent, because, in the present argument, various numbers of pounds' worth of resources, including land, are supposed to be employed in an industry, whereas, in the accepted treatment of rent, various numbers of pounds' worth of capital and labour are supposed to be applied to a given area of land.

Pigou notes that this is generally accepted in the case of external economies but not in the case of external diseconomies. Nevertheless, in dismissing these doubts, Pigou remarks that "This objection, however, ignores the fact that an increase in the output of any industry may involve an increase in the price of the raw materials employed in it. When account is taken of that fact, [the criticism] is easily seen to be invalid" (WW, pp. 175–176). Pigou is mistaken in this (and the mistake will be discussed in the appendix to the chapter), and his comment sets the table for Allyn Young's dismissal of external diseconomies in his review of the book (Young 1913). Young's critique and dismissal of external diseconomies became part of the canon of twentieth-century economics. And that is unfortunate because on external diseconomies per se Pigou was right, Marshall was confused, and the canon of economics was quite wrong.

3.4 Young's critique

Executive summary of the section: Allyn Young criticized Pigou's (1912) ideas on externality as confused. Pigou's discussion evolved, largely in response. It is not widely understood that Pigou was correct, as a matter of theory, though his ideas were less useful as policy science.

Young (1913, p. 683) writes:

The significance of the curve of marginal supply prices consists, it will be remembered, in the fact that the expense of producing x + Δx units exceeds the expense of producing x units by more than the amount of expenses specifically incurred in producing the additional Δx units. This excess cost is due to the fact that increased production is only possible at an increased price per unit for the product, which makes possible and necessary an increased annual price for the land (and, under some conditions, for other resources) used in production. This is not a case, it is important to note, in which the money measure of a given quantum of resources can, in order to simplify the analysis, be supposed a constant. Changes in the prices of product and of resources are the very essence of the situation. Increased prices for the use of land and the other factors in production do not represent an increased using up of resources in the work of production. They merely represent transferences of purchasing power.

Pigou, anticipating this criticism, carefully distinguishes his marginal supply price curve from Marshall's *particular expenses curve* (WW, p. 934). Marshall had used this construct to explain cases in which the producers' surplus derived from the supply price curve might correspond to rent (Marshall 1948 [1920], p. 811). Pigou writes (WW, p. 176), "This reasoning derives its plausibility from an implicit assumption that the curve of marginal supply prices employed here is equivalent to Dr. Marshall's particular expenses curve." Young has made just this assumption. In EW Pigou responds directly to Young's criticism, writing:

> This criticism is, undoubtedly, very important. Furthermore, if it were directed against an attempt to apply my duplex system of curves to the output of the whole body of a country's resources lumped together, as it were, into a single industry, it would, no less evidently, be just. For the land available for all the industries collectively in a country is fixed; any increase in the money paid for it is, therefore, merely a transference of purchasing power; and a large part of the additional money costs per unit resulting from an increase in output generally might consist in money so paid. But my analysis is not designed for application to the output of the whole body of a country's resources lumped together into a single industry. Its purpose, on the contrary, is to provide machinery for studying the distribution of resources among a great number of different industries and occupations, each one of which is supposed to make use of only a small part of the aggregate resources of the country. Because every occupation is thus relatively small, the price per unit of the several factors of production in each occupation is determined by general market conditions, and is not affected to any appreciable extent by variations in the quantity of them that is employed in that occupation.[3]
>
> (EW, p. 935)

Pigou, in other words, treats the land input as a variable input for each distinct industry, even though it would have to be treated as a fixed input for the economy as a whole. In the economics of 2019 the fashionable way to express this would be to model the economy as a continuum of infinitesimal industries, and derive the demand for land by integral calculus, then setting that definite integral equal to a constant. Pigou instead takes the (perhaps more honest) tack of confessing that the large-numbers assumption on industries is at best an approximation. Still another way of accommodating the finite number of industries in the economy would be to treat the rental price of scarce land as one dimension of a Nash equilibrium among industries.

Now, all of this is a matter of mathematics, not necessarily of economic policy, and it will be helpful to distinguish between two things: first, the implications of external diseconomies for the mathematical relation between zero-profit free entry equilibrium and the efficient allocation of resources, and plausible reasons why external diseconomies might or might not occur. These will be taken in order.

First, the analytic model. In the appendix to the 1920 edition of EW, Pigou treats demand and supply symmetrically, in a certain sense. On the demand side, we are familiar with the elementary idea that the marginal utility, the demand price if no exotic assumptions are incorporated into the utility function, lies below the average utility curve. Pigou then treats the long-run supply price under free entry as an average cost curve, and notes that the marginal supply price, that is the industry marginal cost curve, will differ from the supply price as the marginal and average utility disagree. By the third edition, he partly abandons this approach, taking as the general case one in which the cost to firm r is

1. $$C_r = F_r(x_r, y)$$

where x_r is the output of firm r, y the industry output, and F_r the cost function of firm r. Pigou does consider two simpler cases, first where costs are separable as

2. $$C_r = F_r(x_r) + \frac{x_r}{y}\psi(y)$$

and, second, a case of no external effects,

3. $$C_r = F_r(x_r)$$

He adopts a representative firm approach, and after some plausible reasoning to justify it, he also adopts a large-numbers approximation so that, for the general case, the individual firm regards its marginal cost as

4. $$MC_r = \frac{\partial F_r(x_r, y)}{\partial x_r}$$

neglecting $\frac{\partial F_r(x_r, y)}{\partial y}$. At this late date there is no reference to the second order of smalls.

Pigou returns to the treatment of the supply curve as an average cost curve for the simplified case of (2), separability, but concedes that these curves cannot be uniquely defined in the general case. Nevertheless, given a value for y, he observes, the curves can be drawn (with some ceteris paribus conditions) and demonstrate a difference between the supply price and the marginal cost (Liberty fund PDF version of EW, 3rd Edition, pp. 529–537).

This probably will not persuade those who do not want to be persuaded, and it does not seem to have persuaded many at the time. But the cost function really had not been defined at that time, Pigou did not make reference to a production function, which lends itself more readily to expressions about returns to scale, and such mathematical tools as the Kuhn-Tucker conditions and the concept of the cost function as a mathematical dual of the production function did not yet exist. The appendix to this chapter revisits external economies and diseconomies using some of those tools and concludes that while Pigou was confused on some minor points, he was right – external economies and diseconomies can be defined and when they are present the industry marginal cost will, in general, diverge from the free entry equilibrium price roughly as Pigou predicted.

On the score of plausible reasoning, however, Pigou does not do so well. There is one point in EW at which Pigou does offer something we might take as a plausible reason for diseconomies of the scale of the industry. At p. 194 he defends the idea that differential taxation could increase efficiency by the analogy to two roads between the same destinations. He notes that the shorter may become more congested in such a way that its advantage is offset, and says that in that case shifting some traffic to the longer road could improve the situation. He writes, "In these circumstances a rightly chosen measure of differential taxation against road B would create an 'artificial' situation superior to the 'natural' one. But the measure of differentiation must be rightly chosen." Perhaps then we may say that external diseconomies could arise because of some phenomenon akin to congestion. But that remains distressingly vague.

3.5 Empty boxes

Executive summary of the section: Pigou's ideas on externalities continued to attract criticism more or less along Young's lines, and were dismissed by Clapham as "empty boxes." The free-market position of Ellis and Fellner would remain the orthodox position for many years into the twentieth century.

In his review of WW, Young sets a tone that (despite Pigou's attempts to respond in EW in its first and later editions) later critics of Pigou also would strike and that ultimately entered the consensus of the profession (e.g. Frischmann and Hogendorn, 2015, p. 194). The key point of attack is the absence of plausible reasons to suppose that any particular industry is subject to external diseconomies nor, in some cases (and despite Marshall's reference to information provision) external economies. It is worthy of notice that Young twice refers to his imagination in justifying his criticisms:

> I imagine, however, that cases of increasing returns in this sense (i.e., diminishing aggregate expenses per unit of product as production increases) must be rare, if not altogether lacking, in competitive industry, unless an increase in the size of the representative establishment be taken into account as a natural concomitant of increased production in the industry in question …
>
> Professor Pigou says (p. 177): "Provided that certain external economies are common to all the suppliers jointly, the presence of increasing returns in respect of all together is compatible with the presence of diminishing returns in respect of the special work of each severally." I cannot imagine "external economies" adequate to bring about this result.
>
> (Young, 1913, p. 678 n)

Is this any more than a failure of imagination on Young's part? But in fact, Pigou provided nothing, in the case of external diseconomies at least, that might have stimulated Young's imagination.

If Young's review sounded the keynote for the critics of Pigou, a paper of Clapham provided the refrain, "Of Empty Economic Boxes" (Clapham, 1922a). Clapham argues, seemingly quite correctly, that Pigou has offered no basis to say that one industry displays external economies and another industry displays external diseconomies. Indeed he does not distinguish external economies and diseconomies from returns to the scale of the industry in general. He says that the boxes labeled "increasing returns," "constant returns" and "decreasing returns" are empty boxes, and that the study of economics would be better off without them. Further still, he cavils at the whole conceptions of "an industry" (p. 306), "a commodity" (p. 309, Clapham, 1922b, p. 561) and of a "unit of resources" (Clapham, 1922a, p. 311). Perhaps Clapham would admit "units" of labor inputs and of 64's Botany hats, so that some sort of marginal analysis could be done, but clearly a concept of factor-neutral productivity would be impossible in the world Clapham envisions. From a scientific viewpoint, Clapham is on shaky ground, as Pigou observes in his reply. "Absence of evidence is not evidence of absence,"[4] and it is one thing to say that there is nothing in the boxes and quite another to say that we do not know what is in the boxes, or even that we can never know. The three categories are exhaustive: logically, every aggregate that we choose to call an industry must belong to one of them. Clapham may go too far when he says that Pigou's "empty boxes" have no practical implications. Even if we can never know what is in the boxes, there is one practical implication that follows: that we can never know how the equilibrium position of a free market compares with the efficient allocation of resources among the boxes. That is an important "known unknown." But does that mean that every government intervention in the market system is admissible? Certainly not. Pigou would certainly have said not (EW, pp. 296–7). From a point of view of policy science in particular, however, Clapham's position is stronger. A set of logical categories and a corresponding proposal for differential taxation can guide policy only if there is a correspondence between the categories and actual taxable entities. This Pigou does not give us, and to that extent, Clapham's critique has its point.

Pigou's position is of course that the development of economic statistics will fill in the boxes in time (Pigou 1922, p. 495) and contemporaneously, some progress on that point was being made (Secrist 1922, 1931; Taussig 1923; Hess 1922).

Clapham (1922a, p. 311, 1922b, p. 562) also stresses that changes in productivity coincident with changes of the scale of the industry may be the consequences of invention, rather than of the change in scale, and that the two cannot readily be distinguished. D. H. Robertson (1924) took that as his central criticism. Taking first increasing returns industries (Robertson prefers to say "decreasing cost industries"), Robertson gives two plausible arguments that might account for their trends. One is indivisible inputs, and he seems to allow that this might be influential even in the long run and for the industry as a whole (p. 18). The other is that the growth of the industry may be accompanied by a reorganization that results in greater productivity, but this – Robertson tells us (p. 19) – is not a result of the increase in the scale of the industry, since with time it would have come about in any case. The first of these seems to confuse returns to the scale of the industry with those to the scale of the individual firm, especially as Robertson goes on to discuss Pigou's examples of railroads. The second is nothing more than an assertion that Marshall's plausible arguments for external economies are wrong. Robertson then observes (rightly) that Pigou is on even weaker grounds in the case of external diseconomies, but he says (p. 26), "the employment of an additional unit of resources in an industry may modify unfavourably the general organisation of the industry, so as to make each unit of resources there employed yield a smaller net product than it would otherwise have done." That would be a puzzle – we can hardly think that an increase of the scale of an industry would reduce its scope of division of labor, for example. Robertson refers back to Pigou's (EW, pp. 190–191) comment that:

> But, in consequence of the addition of the extra unit, the general organisation of the industry may be modified in such wise that each unit of the flow directed towards it yields a different net product from what it would have done had the addition not been made. ... In an industry working under conditions of diminishing returns, an increment of resources yields a negative indirect net product; hence marginal trade net product is less than marginal individual net product.

While there is room for interpretation here, it seems to me that what Pigou is saying is that even with the most efficient organization of the industry to produce the increased output, the industry will nevertheless experience higher unit costs, not that the reorganization of the industry is the cause of the increase in unit cost. But (as Robertson notes, 1924, p. 26) Pigou gives us no alternative explanation for the increase in costs. Here, again, the question is not about the mathematical logic, but about the plausible reasons why the mathematical logic might be applied, and if they exist, whether they are reliable.

In his review of the second edition of EW, Frank Knight (1926) is also critical of external economies. Knight accepts Young's critique of external diseconomies, as he says Pigou does in the second edition (p. 55), and dismisses external economies on the grounds that tendencies to increasing returns will lead to monopoly and so are inconsistent with Pigou's large-numbers analysis. Knight's review, which describes EW as "economics at its best," is worth reading for itself, both as a piece of splendid writing and for its deep skepticism of assumptions still central to economic theory.

Two decades later, Ellis and Fellner (1943) revisited the controversy and articulated what became the consensus of the profession on the controversy. As to external economies, they concede (p. 504) that conditions such as "the appearance and progress of professional and trade associations and journals, and the like, are not to be dismissed as unrelated to output in every case." However, they will have the consequences Pigou supposes only if they are "reversible," meaning that contraction of the industry would make them non-viable. Otherwise they are dynamic phenomena, and their implications for the allocation of resources, if any, are quite different. And Ellis and Fellner regard reversible economies of this sort as really quite rare. As to external diseconomies, they essentially repeat Young's assertion that the only case of costs rising with expansion of the industry are traceable to land rent or similar rents on limited resources.

3.6 Concluding reflections

As a matter of policy science, the critics have a strong point about Pigou's external economies and diseconomies. If indeed we can suggest no cases in which we might observe relevant diseconomies and can reasonably judge external economies to be rare and unpredictable, then those concepts are hardly likely to be useful, as Pigou hoped, for a coherent economics of policy. But because the controversy focused on this Marshallian construct, Pigou's discussions and examples of third-party externalities fell into the background and seem for some decades to be ignored – although, ironically, Clapham cites the overexploitation of forest due to human carelessness (1922a, p. 308) as an argument against Pigou, and in passing Ellis and Fellner say (1943, p. 502) "The preceding analysis is not concerned with the genuine diseconomies arising from phenomena such as the smoke nuisance, the wasteful exploitation of natural resources, etc." It is these third-party externalities that better prefigure the role of externalities in the economics of the twenty-first century, and were new in Pigou's writing. And, apart from his attempt to defend the Marshallian categories, Pigou gives them no less stress. All in all, the controversy over empty boxes was a diversion, if not a smokescreen.

Nor were the Marshallian externalities really very central to Pigou's work. His discussion of them from the first is largely defensive. Much more important was his discussion of "harmonies" and "disharmonies" between the impacts of particular policies on the size and distribution of the national dividend – what Okun (1981) would later call "the big trade-off" between equality and efficiency. It will be evident how dependent these judgments are on the assumption of diminishing marginal utility of money, income or consumption expenditure. This assumption would be eliminated in the further development of economic theory. Pigou's discussion of the cases of disharmony between the size and distribution of national income would have no influence. The same is true of his discussion about the variability of national income. The relation of diminishing marginal utility of consumption expenditure to risk aversion would be rediscovered by von Neumann and Morgenstern and by scholars building on their work. The influence of life-cycle considerations on consumption expenditures would be rediscovered by Modigliani. Despite many calls for macroeconomics to be rebuilt on microeconomic foundations in the latter twentieth century, Pigou's microfoundations were never built on in any more modern form.

What did have influence was the project itself – the attempt to build a coherent theory of economics and policy recommendation – and Pigou's ideas on the determinants of the size of the national income, that is, on the efficient allocation of resources. Initially, these had to do with monopoly and the negative impact of many deviations from market equilibrium. In writing that "Its purpose ... is to provide machinery for studying the distribution of resources among a great number of different industries and occupations," he pointed the direction of welfare economics would travel in the following period. The task undertaken by his successors who created the New Welfare Economics was to recreate his discussion of the allocation of resources without numerical utilities. This will be the topic of Chapter 4.

Notes

1 This point has been rediscovered from time to time. See, e.g. H. Leibenstein, (1950), "Bandwagon, Snob, and Veblen Effects in the Theory of Consumers' Demand," *The Quarterly Journal of Economics*, v. 64, no. 2 (May) pp. 183-207.
2 This claim is partly justified by the fact that Ronald Coase (1910-2013) received his Nobel Memorial Prize in 1991. Coase' role will be discussed in a later chapter.
3 It is the novelty of this project that Hicks seems to miss in his 1975 retrospective.
4 Quote attributed to Carl Sagan.

Appendix

In the economics of the later twentieth century, the technology available to production has usually been expressed either by a production function or by a cost function that is the mathematical dual of the production function. Thus, for example, if a firm is producing a single output, using input quantities $x_1, x_2, \ldots x_n$, then Q is the maximum output the technology can produce from these outputs, where

1. $$Q = f(x_1, x_2, \ldots x_n)$$

We might have, in particular, $x_1 =$ quantity of labor of a particular quality, $x_2 =$ index of capital invested, $x_3 =$ quantity of raw materials of a particular type, $x_4 =$ quantity of land of a particular type and quality. For a production target Q, the cost function is the solution to the problem

2. $$\min_{x_1, x_2, \ldots, x_n} \sum_{i=0}^{n} r_i x_i$$

subject to $f(x_1, \ldots x_n) \geq Q$

where r_i is the market price of input i and is a parameter. Thus we form the Lagrangean function

3. $$L = \sum_{i=1}^{n} r_i x_i + \lambda[Q - f(x_1, x_2, ..., x_n)]$$

The necessary conditions for the minimum are

4. $$\frac{\partial L}{\partial x_i} = r_i - \lambda \frac{\partial f}{\partial x_i} \leq 0$$

and, considering only inputs used in positive quantities, we may replace the inequality with an equality, so that

5. $$\lambda = \frac{\sum_{i=1}^{n} r_i x_i}{\sum_{i=1}^{n} \frac{\partial f}{\partial x_i} x_i}$$

The minimized cost, $\sum_{i=0}^{n} r_i x_i$, is a function of Q and of the input prices r_i, written

6a. $$C = g(Q, \{r_i\})$$

For this function, input demand is

6b. $$x_i = \frac{\partial g}{\partial r_i}$$

Returns to scale, however, are more directly expressed in terms of the production function. Returns to scale are, mathematically, a local property of the production function. Let $\{x_{i,1}\}$ be an input vector with $Q_1 = f(\{x_{i,1}\})$. For each i let $x_{i,2} - x_{i,1} = \Delta x_i = \mu x_{i,1}$. Let the corresponding increment $Q_2 - Q_1 = \theta Q_i$. Further, let $\Theta = \lim_{\mu \to 0} \theta$. Then consider the differential

7a. $$\frac{dQ}{d\mu} = \Theta Q_1 = \sum_{i=1}^{n} \frac{\partial f}{\partial x_i} x_i$$

Suppose then that $\Theta = 1$. Then we have

7b. $$Q_1 = \sum_{i=1}^{n} \frac{\partial f}{\partial x_i} x_i$$

This is the case of constant returns to scale. Suppose, however, that $\Theta \neq 1$. Then we have

7c.
$$Q_1 = \frac{\sum_{i=1}^{n} \frac{\partial f}{\partial x_i} x_i}{\Theta}$$

If $\Theta > 1$, then we have increasing returns and the marginal productivity payments more than exhaust the output. This was pointed out by von Wieser (1889), but seems still not to be widely understood in economics. If $\Theta < 0$, we have decreasing returns *to scale*, and the marginal productivity payments are less than the total output. This seems hardly to be understood at all in modern economics.

Returning to the cost function, equation 6a, we can see now where both Pigou's comment about raw material prices and Young's assumptions about rent are mistaken. Let r_3 be the price of raw materials and r_4 rent per unit of land. Then, supposing positive quantities of both inputs are used, then $\frac{\partial C}{\partial r_3} > 0$, $\frac{\partial C}{\partial r_4} > 0$. On the one hand, this involves no change in the *cost function*, and on the other hand, it is true regardless of returns to scale in the underlying production function. Rises in cost as a result of increasing raw material prices or of rising rents cannot be correlated in any way with returns to scale. It is quite possible for an industry with increasing returns to scale to display rising costs over time due to increases in rent and/or raw material prices.

Thus far we have made no distinction between the returns to the scale of the firm and of the industry. The simplest case is that of monopoly, since there are no differences in that case (EW pp. 947-948.) Returns to the scale of the industry are then "internal," and decreasing returns will exacerbate, and increasing returns to some extent offset, the usual monopoly restriction of output. For the competitive case, however, we must allow for the output of the industry to expand or contract by increasing or decreasing the number of firms in the industry. Suppose that each firm in the industry minimizes costs subject to an independent production function

8.
$$Q_j = f_j\left(\{x_{i,j}\}\right)$$

Then, given r_i, let Q° be the output at the efficient scale, that is, the scale at which returns to scale are constant. (If there is no such scale there will be no competitive industry, as both Pigou and his critics realize.) It follows that industry output can always be increased from mQ° to $(m+1)Q^\circ$ by adding one more firm producing Q°, with a proportionate increase in resource use and cost. Using the "large numbers" assumption we suppose that, to a good enough approximation, costs are proportionate to output everywhere. The argument at this point would be that a perfectly competitive industry can only operate with constant returns to the scale of the industry.

The difficulty with this argument is that it is a *petitio principia.* We have excluded external economies and diseconomies by assumption. The basis of Marshall's and Pigou's external economies is that the increasing scale of the industry results in increasing productivity of the resources used by the individual firms in the industry. This is clearly the idea behind the references to trade schools and journals. By symmetry, for external diseconomies the increasing scale of the industry must somehow (perhaps through something akin to congestion?) result in a decrease in the productivity of the resources used by the individual firms in the industry. The independent production functions of the form 8. are inconsistent with these possibilities.

Without abandoning the production function approach, we might proceed as follows.[1] Suppose there are m potential firms and firm j employs $x_{i,j}$ units of input i. Then

9a.
$$X_i = \sum_{j=1}^{n} x_{i,j}$$

9b.
$$Q_j = f_j(\{x_{i,j}\}, \{X_i\})$$

To allow for free entry, we should consider these as potential firms only, in the sense that with a given industry demand, some firms will occupy corner solutions such that for some j, $Q_j = x_{1,j} = x_{2,j} = \ldots = x_{n,j} = 0$. Then, with increasing industry demand, some firms j might shift from corner to interior solutions, "entering" the industry. We might say that the *extended returns to scale* (ERS) for such a function are defined as follows: Consider a multiplier μ. Let $\Delta x_{i,j} = \mu x_{i,j}$ $\Delta X_i = \mu X_i$, and $\Delta Q_i = \theta Q_i$, and then proceed as above with $\Theta = \lim_{\mu \to 0} \theta$. As before, if $\Theta = 1$, then the extended returns to scale are constant, if $\Theta > 1$, increasing, and if $\Theta < 1$, decreasing.

We suppose that each firm that produces a positive amount does so in a way that minimizes its own cost. Denoting the Lagrangean function for firm i as L_i, by analogy with condition 4, we will have

10a.
$$\frac{\partial L_j}{\partial x_{i,j}} = r_i - \lambda_j \left[\frac{\partial f_j}{\partial x_{i,j}} + \frac{\partial f_j}{\partial X_i} \right]$$

Noting in passing that

10b.
$$\frac{\partial X_i}{\partial x_{i,j}} = 1$$

However, denoting two distinct firms, each producing positive output, as j, k, we also have

10c. $$\frac{\partial L_k}{\partial x_{i,j}} = \lambda_k \frac{\partial f_k}{\partial X_i}$$

This influences the cost of firm k but is under the control of firm j according to 10a. – an external effect.

Suppose the cost of producing output Q^* in the industry is minimized. Among the constraints will be

11a. $$Q^* \le \sum_{j=1}^{m} Q_j$$

together with the production functions for the respective firms. We will substitute $\sum_{j=1}^{m} x_{i,j}$ for X_i. Then the Lagrangean function is

11b. $$L^* = \sum_{i=1}^{n} r_i \sum_{j=1}^{m} x_{i,j} + \sum_{j=1}^{m} \lambda_j^* [Q_j - f_j(\{x_{i,j}\}, \{X_i\})] + \varsigma \left(Q^* - \sum_{j=1}^{m} Q_j \right)$$

Necessary conditions for the minimum include

12a. $$\frac{\partial L^*}{\partial Q_j} = \lambda_j^* - \varsigma \le 0$$

12b. $$\frac{\partial L^*}{\partial x_{i,j}} = r_i - \lambda_j^* \frac{\partial f_j}{\partial x_{i,j}} - \sum_{k=1}^{m} \lambda_j^* \frac{\partial f_k}{\partial X_k} \le 0$$

For some potential firms, we recall, there may be a corner solution at $Q_j = 0$
$S = \{j \ni Q_j > 0\}$. We have, for $i \in S$

12c. $$r_i = \varsigma \left[\frac{\partial f_j}{\partial x_{i,j}} + \sum_{k \in S} \frac{\partial f_k}{\partial X_i} \right]$$

12d. $$\varsigma = \frac{\sum_{i=1}^{n} r_i x_{i,j}}{\sum_{i=1}^{n} \left[\frac{\partial f_j}{\partial x_{i,j}} + \sum_{k \in S} \frac{\partial f_k}{\partial X_i} \right] x_{i,j}}$$

We might now proceed in one of three ways. First, in the more modern mode, we might make the approximating assumption that the set of potential firms is a continuum, each using an infinitesimal proportion of X_i and producing an infinitesimal output, and that S is a connected subset of the continuum, so that X_i, industry cost and Q^* would be obtained by integration over S. Second, in the fashion of Marshall and Pigou, we might appeal to the large numbers assumption, and say that, to a good enough approximation, $\frac{\partial f_i}{\partial X_i} \frac{\partial X_i}{\partial x_i}$ is of the "second order of smalls" and can be neglected,[2] so that 10a. becomes

13.
$$\frac{\partial L_j}{\partial x_{i,j}} = r_i - \lambda_j \frac{\partial f_j}{\partial x_{i,j}}$$

Either approach will yield the same condition 13, and each will lead to the conclusion that the free entry equilibrium is inefficient as Pigou's discussion said. The third possibility is to eliminate approximative assumptions and explore the Cournot-Nash equilibrium of the industry.

Following either of the first two approaches, assuming that the representative firm j just covers its costs, then in place of 12d we have

14a.
$$\zeta = \frac{p^* Q_j}{\sum_{i=1}^{n}\left[\frac{\partial f_j}{\partial x_{i,j}} + \sum_{k \in S} \frac{\partial f_k}{\partial X_i}\right] x_{i,j}}$$

Suppose further that the extended returns to scale of the industry are constant; then 14a becomes

14b.
$$\zeta = \frac{p^* Q_j}{Q_j} = p^*$$

This is Pigou's marginal supply price. That is, ζ is the industry marginal cost. Returning to the "large numbers" case, and using instead 13, we have

15a.
$$\lambda_j = \frac{p Q_j}{\sum_{i=1}^{n} \frac{\partial f_j}{\partial x_{i,j}} x_{i,j}} = \zeta\left[1 + \frac{\sum_{i=1}^{n}\sum_{k \in S}\frac{\partial f_k}{\partial x_{i,j}} x_{i,j}}{\sum_{i=1}^{n}\frac{\partial f_i}{\partial x_{i,j}} x_{i,j}}\right]$$

Here, λ_j is the individual firm's marginal cost, and will deviate from the industry marginal cost, ζ, as $\sum_{i=1}^{n} \sum_{k \in S} \frac{\partial f_k}{\partial X_j} x_{i,k}$ is positive or negative. For market equilibrium we must have

15b. $$\lambda_j = p$$

Let p be the price that brings forth Q*, given that 15b holds. If, then, $\sum_{i=1}^{n} \sum_{k \in S} \frac{\partial f_k}{\partial X_i} x_{i,k} > 0$, we see that the industry marginal cost

15c. $$\zeta > p$$

This is Pigou's case of external diseconomies. Suppose instead that $\sum_{i=1}^{n} \sum_{k \in S} \frac{\partial f_k}{\partial X_i} x_{i,k} < 0$. Then similarly

15d. $$\zeta < p$$

This is Pigou's case of external economies.

If the extended returns to the scale of the firm are not constant, then the case is a little more complex. We have

16a. $$\Theta Q_j = \sum_{i=1}^{n} \frac{\partial f_j}{\partial x_{i,j}} x_{i,j} + \sum_{i=1}^{n} \frac{\partial f_j}{\partial X_{i,j}} X_{i,j}$$

16b. $$\zeta = \frac{p^* Q_j}{\Theta Q_j} = \frac{p^*}{\Theta}$$

Here, p* is the average and ζ the marginal industry cost, allowing for the returns to the scale of industry inputs. Suppose $\Theta > 1$. This is the case of external diseconomies, so that the increasing extended returns to the scale of the firm will offset, and if Θ is large enough, possibly reverse the relationship of ζ and the market-clearing price. Suppose $\Theta < 1$. This is the case of external economies, so that the deviation of ζ from the market-clearing price will be exacerbated. To determine the relation of the market-clearing price to the social marginal cost in the industry, both influences would need to be taken into account.

The Cournot-Nash analysis is only a little more complex. In place of 15a. we have

17a.
$$\lambda_j = \frac{pQ_j}{\sum\limits_{i=1}^{n}\left[\frac{\partial f_j}{\partial x_{i,j}}+\frac{\partial f_j}{\partial X_i}\right]x_{i,j}} = \zeta\left[1+\frac{\sum\limits_{i=1}^{n}\sum\limits_{k\in S}\frac{\partial f_k}{\partial x_{i,j}}x_{i,j}}{\sum\limits_{i=1}^{n}\left[\frac{\partial f_j}{\partial x_{i,j}}+\frac{\partial f_j}{\partial X_i}\right]x_{i,k}}\right]$$

and the previous comments will follow pari passu as

17b.
$$\sum_{i=1}^{n}\left[\frac{\partial f_j}{\partial x_{i,j}}\right] >< \sum_{\substack{k\in S\\k\neq j}}\frac{\partial f_j}{\partial X_i}$$

In principle, this condition might differ from one firm to another. If, however, we adopt a representative firm model, then condition 17b is the same for each firm and approaches 15b, 16b in the limit as the number of firms increases without limit.

In short, Pigou was right and his critics were wrong. If p is the price paid by buyers and there are no third-party externalities nor "snob and bandwagon effects" (Leibenstein, 1950) then $p = \zeta$ is an efficiency condition. If, in some industries, external economies prevail and in others external diseconomies, then with free entry, prices will deviate in opposite ways from the social marginal cost, and there is in principle a schedule of subsidies to industries with external economies and taxes on industries with external diseconomies that would support $p = \zeta$ and efficiency – if only we had the knowledge to calculate it.

Notes

1 Compare J. de V. Graaff, 1957, pp. 28-32.
2 This may seem odd, since we have already noted that $\frac{\partial X_i}{\partial x_{i,j}} = 1$ and a finite value for $\frac{\partial f_j}{\partial X_i}$ seems an unavoidable aspect of the problem. It is here that the modern approach using integral calculus seems more transparent. For that approach, supposing that S is a set of positive measure, $X_i = \int_S x_{i,j}$ and deleting a single firm from S does not change its measure, so $\frac{\partial X_i}{\partial x_{i,j}}$ is infinitesimal. Zero is the only infinitesimal real number, so $\frac{\partial X_i}{\partial x_{i,j}} = 0$. (Compare Robinson, 1974). Suppose on the other hand that we increase each $x_{i,j}$ by Δx_i; then $X_i + \Delta X_i = \int_S x_{i,j} + \int_S \Delta x_{i,j}$ and $\Delta X_i = \int_S \Delta x_{i,j}$, and this is applicable when industry costs are minimized.

References

Bates Clark, John (1899) *The Distribution of Wealth* (New York: Macmillan).

Clapham, J. H. (1922a) Of Empty Economic Boxes, *The Economic Journal*, v. 32, no. 127 (Sept) pp. 305–314.

Clapham, J. H. (1922b) The Economic Boxes, *The Economic Journal* v. 32, no. 128 (Dec.) pp. 560–563.

Clark, John Bates (1899), *The Distribution of Wealth* (New York: Macmillan).

Clark, Andrew E and Andrew J. Oswald (1994) Unhappiness and Unemployment, *The Economic Journal* v. 104, no. 424 (May) pp. 648–659.

Friedman, Milton (1953), *Essays in Positive Economics* (Chicago: University of Chicago Press).

Frischmann, Brett M. and Christiaan Hogendorn (2015) Retrospectives: The Marginal Cost Controversy, *The Journal of Economic Perspectives* v. 29, no. 1 (Winter) pp. 193–205.

Graff, J. de V, (1957), *Theoretical Welfare Economics* (Cambridge University Press).

Hess, Herbert W. (1922) *Review of Costs, Merchandising Practices, Advertising and Sales in the Retail Distribution of Clothing*, 6 Vol., by Horace Secrist and The National Association of Retail Clothiers, The Annals of the American Academy of Political and Social Science v. 103, (Sept.) pp. 147–148.

Hicks, J. R. (1975) The Scope and Status of Welfare Economics, *Oxford Economic Papers* v. 27, no. 3 (Nov) pp. 307–326.

Knight, Frank H. (1926) Economics At Its Best, *The American Economic Review* v. 16, no. 1 (March) pp. 51–58.

H. Leibenstein, (1950), "Bandwagon, Snob, and Veblen Effects in the Theory of Consumers' Demand," *The Quarterly Journal of Economics*, v. 64, no. 2 (May) pp. 183–207.

Marshall, Alfred (1948/1920), *Principles of Economics* (New York: Macmillan).

Mill, John Stuart (1987), *Principles of Political Economy* (A. M. Kelley; Reprint of 1909 edition).

Modigliani, Franco and R. E. Brumberg (1954) Utility Analysis of the Consumption Function, *Post-Keynesian Economics* edited by K. K. Kurihara (New Brunswick: Rutgers University Press) pp. 388–436.

Okun, Arthur (1981), *Prices and Quantities* (Washington: Brookings Institution).

Patten, Simon N. (1893), "The Interpretation of Ricardo," *Publications of the American Economic Association* v. 8, no. 1 (Jan) pp. 77–82.

Pigou, A. C. (1903) Some Remarks on Utility, *Economic Journal* v. 13, no. 49 (Mar) pp. 58–68.

Pigou, A. C. (1904a) Pure Theory and the Fiscal Controversy, *Economic Journal* v. 14, no. 53 (Mar) pp. 29–33.

Pigou, A. C. (1904b) Monopoly and Consumer's Surplus, *Economic Journal* v. 14, no. 55 (Sept) pp. 388–394.

Pigou, A. C. (1905), *Principles & Methods of Industrial Peace* (London: Macmillan).

Pigou, A. C. (1907a) The Ethics of the Gospels, *International Journal of Ethics* v. 17, no. 3 (Apr) pp. 275–290.

Pigou, A. C. (1907b) The Incidence of Import Duties, *Economic Journal* v. 17, no. 66 (Jun) pp. 289–294.

Pigou, A. C. (1908) Equilibrium Under Bilateral Monopoly, *Economic Journal* v. 18, no. 7 (Sept) pp. 205–370.

Pigou, A. C. (1910) Producers' and Consumers' Surplus, *Economic Journal* v. 20, no. 79 (Sept) pp. 358–370.

Pigou, A. C. (1912), *Wealth and Welfare* (London: Macmillan).

Pigou, A. C. (1920), *Economics of Welfare* (London: Macmillan).

Pigou, A. C. (1921), *The Political Economy of War* (London, Macmillan).

Pigou, A. C. (1922) Empty Economic Boxes: A Reply, *The Economic Journal* v. 32, no. 128 (Dec) pp. 458–465.

Pigou, A. C. (1924) Those Empty Boxes, *The Economic Journal* v. 34, no. 133 (Mar) pp. 30–31.

Pigou, A. C. (1927), *Industrial Fluctuations* (London, Macmillan and Co.).

Pigou, A. C. (1928), *A study in public finance* (London, Macmillan and Co.).

Pigou, A. C. (1951) Some Aspects of Welfare Economics, *The American Economic Review* v. 41, no. 3 (Jun) pp. 287–302.

Robinson, Joan (1933), *The Economics of Imperfect Competition* (London: Macmillan).

Secrist, Horace and the National Association of Retail Clothiers (1921), *Costs, Merchandising Practices, Advertising and Sales in the Retail Distribution of Clothing* (Northwestern University School of Commerce Bureau of Business Research, in cooperation with the National Association of Retail Clothiers.

Secrist, Horace (1931) Statistical Evidences of Regressive Tendencies in Distributive Costs, *Journal of the Royal Statistical Society* v. 94, no. 4 (4) pp. 591–598.

Senior, Nassau (1850), *Political Economy* (Second Edition, London, Griffin).

Taussig, F. W. (1923) A Contribution to the Study of Cost Curves, *The Quarterly Journal of Economics* v. 38, no. 1 (Nov) pp. 173–176.

Young, Allyn A. (1913) Review: Pigou's *Wealth and Welfare, The Quarterly Journal of Economics,* v. 27, no. 2 (Aug) pp. 672–686.

4 Preference theory and the emergence of the New Welfare Economics

The emergence of what would be called the New Welfare Economics took place within the context of a broader critique of the prior utilitarian approaches in economics. The critics' proposal was to replace utility functions with preference orderings, and thus they are "ordinalists" as against "cardinalists" who would continue to use numerical properties of utility functions in their theory. Pigou's welfare economics was, as we have seen, closely tied to his satisfaction-utilitarian ethical theory. This ethical theory was unacceptable to the ordinalists. Nevertheless, Pigou had provided a theory that was, on the one hand, consistent with a subjectivist value theory – to which the ordinalists were committed – and on the other hand, that supported policy prescriptions which most economists, including the ordinalists, regarded as valid, such as conclusions against monopoly and protective tariffs. For ordinalist economists, it would be important to reconstruct those aspects of Pigou's welfare economics without any reference to utilitarian values as they understood utilitarian values. This was the "New Welfare Economics." While this is a history of welfare economics, not of microeconomic theory broadly, the two new currents of thought are so intertwined in this period that they must be taken together in chronological order for the purposes of this book.

By "cardinal utility" is meant utility that is measurable in numerical terms and, in context, comparable as between different individuals in such a way that it can be aggregated by addition. The first, numerical measurability does not imply the second nor does the second imply the third, but, without the second and the third, Pigou's arguments for redistribution to the poor cannot be made. The term "ordinal utility" means that for purposes of economics it is sufficient to suppose that people can order the alternatives available to them as more or less preferable. In any case the ordinalist project and the New Welfare Economics were not simply the same, as the importance of Abba Lerner (1932, 1934) and Hotelling (1938) in the origins of the ordinalist approach to microeconomics demonstrates.

The project of the New Welfare Economics was then to recover some of the prescriptions of Pigou (and many others) on the allocation or "distribution of resources among a great number of different industries and occupations" without, however, any judgments on the distribution of those resources among individuals or groups. Is there more to this than ideology? Certainly it is ideologically convenient for a free-market ideologue, and for some, this may have been one of its attractions. Considering the developments on the continent of Europe at that time, there would be no shame in supporting a free-market ideological position! But clearly there is more to it than that, as again illustrated by Abba Lerner in his contrast to J. R. Hicks, who acknowledges Lerner as one of the sources of his own ideas (1939/1946, Preface to the 1st Edition). It seems pretty clear that Hicks and Lerner were not in close agreement on ideological matters. There was a real intellectual interest in understanding the economics of prices and markets, of efficiency, on a basis independent of any judgment of distribution. For this, there was no less authority than that of J. S. Mill (1987 [1909]), the second founder of utilitarianism. Further, for many purposes, the analysis in terms of indifference curves is far more powerful and transparent than the cumbersome apparatus Pigou inherited from Marshall. Finally, a committed utilitarian could easily enough derive indifference curves from an assumed cardinal utility function, and so could adopt the ordinalist analysis of the allocation of resources without giving up the cardinalist conclusions on the distribution of income or wealth. These points perhaps account for the cultural victory of ordinalism among economists.

4.1 Ordinal preference and welfare economics

Executive summary of the section: Lerner, Hicks and Allen laid the basis for modern microeconomics, but the rejection of "cardinal" utility concepts was not uncontested.

The New Welfare Economics was to be built on foundations laid by Edgeworth and Pareto, but it did not at first take a revolutionary form. In two contributions by Abba Lerner (1932, 1934), indifference curves and preference systems were tools to increase the transparency and generality of ideas already familiar in economics. In Lerner (1932) the author notes that an analysis attributed to Barone, in which the gains from trade are graphically demonstrated, could be extended. Barone had considered a two-country, two-good model in which, much as Ricardo, the trade-off between two goods differs from one country to the next, but is constant for each country. Lerner adapted Haberler's non-linear "production indifference curves," that is, a production possibility frontier, in place of Barone's linear constant trade-offs (1932, p. 346). The production possibility frontier would be a key tool of the New Welfare Economics. In this paper he also made use of community indifference curves with a qualification that would be lost sight of in some later literature. In Lerner (1934) he addressed monopoly theory. This paper is the origin, of course, of the celebrated Marshall-Lerner conditions. But before restating Marshall's monopoly theory in terms of the elasticity of demand, his objective is to supply "scientific" support for the economist's negative evaluation of monopoly. To do that (Lerner 1934, p. 163) he illustrates monopoly pricing with a diagram of a production possibility frontier (here designated as a "displacement cost curve") and an indifference curve. He shows that beginning from the monopoly position, it is possible to make one person better off without making anyone else worse off – Pareto's criterion for a social improvement. At p. 164, relabeling the "displacement cost curve" as an indifference curve for a second person, he demonstrates that for Pareto optimality it is necessary for any two consumers to face the same price. This is something of a masterwork of theory with economy of means, relying on Paretian concepts to recover and reinforce ideas already well established in economics by means neither equally transparent nor equally general.

The reconstruction of microeconomics on the basis of indifference curve analysis was continued by Hicks and Allen (1934a, 1934b). The substance of these papers has little to do with welfare economics. They develop individual demand theory in terms of indifference curves and their formulation is well known to students who have completed intermediate microeconomic theory. But there is an odd inconsistency that speaks to the cardinal-ordinal controversy. At p. 53, Hicks (Hicks and Allen 1934a) treats the possibility that an indifference map cannot be integrated to form a utility function as a key argument against cardinal utility, though he also treats the possibility that indifference directions may not be integrated to generate indifference curves as a mere curiosum (p. 56 note). Allen, however, assumes that the indifference map can be integrated and uses the integral to justify the representation of an indifference map by an index utility function (a method that again will be familiar to a student in intermediate microeconomic theory, Hicks and Allen 1934b, p. 196). But Georgescu-Roegen was to show (1936) that a non-integrable indifference map could be constructed that would be inconsistent with an index utility function. Integrability had become an ambiguity within the ordinalist framework.

So far as mathematical economics is concerned, Hicks-Allen ordinalism was not uncontested. Lange (1934) pointed out what he described as an inconsistency in Pareto's ideas: Pareto had assumed not only that a person could decide which of two bundles of consumer goods would give her the greater satisfaction, but also which of two transitions from one bundle of goods to another would give her the greater increase in satisfaction. This, Lange showed, would lead to something in the nature of cardinal utility. That is, considering bundles x, y and z, with z preferred to y and y to x, we suppose that a person could tell us that a substitution of y for x would be preferable to a substitution of z for y, or conversely, or that the two substitutions are indifferent. Then adjust y so that the substitution of y for x and z for y are indifferent. It follows that the preference of z over x is twice as great as the preference of y over x. This can be extended to any multiples. For Hicks and Allen, given that one utility function u(x) is an index of a given preference system, any monotonic transformation $\phi(u(x))$ of u(x) also is. To preserve the multiples Lange had derived, only linear transformations of u(x) could be indices. Conversely, given a zero point and a scale, we have a numerical utility function. This is an idea now familiar due to the utility theory of von Neumann and Morgenstern (1944).[1] Lange concedes that the Hicks-Allen apparatus is sufficient to characterize market equilibria, but that some notion of intensities of preference is necessary for welfare economics (1934, p. 224).

Allen (1935) responded, arguing that Lange's multiples are 1) not necessary for the characterization of market equilibria, and 2) not sufficient for welfare economics. Allen has a point here. Given that individual utility functions are determinate only relative to a given zero point and scale, it remains impossible to make interpersonal comparisons, there being no objective scale or zero applicable to all individuals. (As we will see in later chapters, Hildreth 1953 and Harsanyi 1953, 1955 addressed and, in different ways, resolved this issue.) Allen said also that (1935, p. 115) "This assumption refers to changes in the 'intensity' of ... preferences ... The assumption cannot be expressed in terms of the individual's acts of choice; it can only be supported by introspection into one's own experience or by questioning others about their experiences." Zeuthen (1937, p. 238), however, points out that comparisons of finite increments of utility or intensity of preference do enter into "acts of choice [that] appear in valuations of business risk as well as insurance and lottery contracts ... The condition for equilibrium is that at the margin money x marginal utility x probability must be equal in the two cases." This, too, would enter into the von Neumann-Morgenstern utility theory. Zeuthen goes on to point out the role that this plays in his own bargaining theory (1930).

Samuelson (1938) would give what he thought of as a refutation of Lange's argument. However, the refutation rests on the claim that Lange requires a preference field over changes in consumption that shares all the properties of the preference field over consumption vectors, including transitivity. Samuelson shows that no such preference field could exist. However, it is not clear that this is required for the judgment over duals that Lange's argument requires. It seems that it is sufficient for Lange's argument that any two changes in consumption vectors can be ranked, even if triples cannot be consistently ranked. In any case, Samuelson's argument does not seem to have influenced the subsequent controversy over measureable utility.

4.2 Robbins and Harrod

Executive summary of the section: Robbins' program for economics was both ordinalist and hostile to welfare economics on principle. But a controversy of Robbins and Harrod on the role of utility would set the stage for the emergence of the New Welfare Economics.

The ordinalist alternative was not a simple negation, and ordinalist theories had to be built up over more than a decade. The manifesto for ordinalist price and allocation theory came, of course, from Lionel Robbins. Robbins' *Essay on the Nature and Significance of Economic Science* is best known for its proposed definition of economics: "the science which studies human behaviour as a relationship between ends and scarce means that have alternative uses" (Robbins 1932, p. 15). This definition may seem very narrow – and it can be persuasively argued that it is indeed too narrow to encompass modern economics – but the examples and arguments that Robbins gives establish that it defines a far broader field than might appear at first impression. At the same time, it delineates economics clearly from technology (p. 31). These are values of the essay and probably account for its widespread influence on scholars in economics. But Robbins is not really interested in the allocation of resources per se. He would subsume it to value theory, understanding values strictly as relative, not themselves quantities. This he reiterates and underlines in Robbins (1934). And the value theory he proposes is strictly subjectivist, but Robbins is persuaded that it is scientific while utility theory is not.

At the same time, Robbins attempts to exclude normative judgments from economics completely. Thus, Robbins attempts to walk a rather strange tightrope. On the one hand, he contrasts his proposed definition of economics with the definition of economics as the study of the causes of material welfare, which he attributes especially to Cannan (1888, pp. 4, 7), and which he finds inadequate. But in this, Robbins interprets leisure and entertainment as immaterial (pp. 8–9, 12). I suspect that those who define economics as the study of material welfare would perceive a difference of material welfare between John and James, who consume food, clothing and shelter at the same standard but John spends 12 hours at labor while James spends six hours at labor and six in the enjoyment of musical performances. On Robbins' interpretation of "material welfare," their material welfare would be the same. Then Robbins writes (p. 21) "it is not the *materiality* or even the material means of gratification which gives them their status of economic goods; it is their relation to valuations ... The 'Materialistic' conception of economics therefore misrepresents the science as we know it" (emphasis and quotation in the original). But any careful thinking about "valuations" is excluded by Robbins' own materialist, that is scientistic, program for economics. If we are to understand economics as "the science which studies human behaviour as a relationship between ends and scarce means that have alternative uses" we shall need some explicit consideration of "ends." Robbins writes (p. 23) that economics assumes "that human beings have ends in the sense that they have tendencies to conduct which can be defined and understood." In a footnote he adds "Such a definition ... entirely removes the concept of an 'end' from the metaphysical." It also removes the concept of an "end" from any connection with the subjective values of the individual.

On its face, this would seem to conflict with what Robbins has earlier said about the relation of economic goods to valuation. As against this, Robbins insists that the valuations are relative, not absolute. "Valuations" as absolute quantities simply do not exist; rather valuations exist only as ratios of valuation, that is as relative prices (ch. 3). Now, it is not obvious how a relative valuation can be derived from a "tendency to conduct." For this, Robbins relies on the principle of diminishing marginal valuation. Robbins holds that this is not an empirical proposition but an analytic one (p. 76):

> this ... is implicit in the conception of goods which are scarce in relation to the use which might be made of them. The assumption that some specific uses ... must be relinquished so long as the good remains an economic good implies just that hierarchy of uses which underlies the various applications of the Law of Diminishing Marginal Utility.

That is: the "tendencies to conduct" differ in their intensity, but they are relatively satiable. Thus, the valuation of good a relative to good b will be greater the more intense the "tendency to conduct" that it satiates. Additional units of good a will satiate less intense "tendencies to conduct" and so receive a lower valuation relative to good b, so far as the quantity of good b is unchanged. This roundabout language follows the Austrian interpretation of marginal utility, especially Menger (1976 [1871]). Elsewhere (1932, p. 123) Robbins uses a more direct language, referring to individual preferences. And this – the idea that relative valuations can be derived from preferences, and that anything beyond this is unscientific – is the point at which Robbins' writing has had its formative influence on modern economic theory.

This is not to say that Robbins would have economists refrain from giving advice on policy. Whatever the values that inform policy may be, economists would be able to advise the policy makers of the consequences if their policies are imposed, at least on a market economy. Speaking of a minimum wage law (pp. 130–131), "It is a well-known generalization of Theoretical Economics that a wage that is held above the equilibrium level necessarily involves unemployment." (Robbins regards this as an analytic proposition, not an empirical one; considered as an empirical proposition it is not at all clearly true.) "If, in the society imposing such a policy, it is generally thought that the gain of absence of wage payments below a certain rate, more than compensates for the unemployment and losses it involves, the policy cannot be described as uneconomical." But economists, we suppose, can advise the government that there will be unemployment and losses and perhaps estimate how much. Even then, there is a lacuna in this advice. As Robbins points out (p. 55) individual scales of valuation, and thus market equilibria, can only be determined on the basis of a given distribution of wealth. But every change in policy will modify the distribution of wealth. Is, then, Robbins' criterion of valuation really independent of the distribution of wealth? This will prove to be a deeper problem than it may appear prima facie.

Robbins would have us believe that advising on the basis of the consequences in this way is free of value judgments, so that an economics based on ordinal preference theory, unlike that of the English utilitarians, is value free. But to hold that policies ought to be evaluated on the basis of their consequences is a value judgment: it defines Robbins' economics as a species of consequentialism. Utilitarianism is at least another species of consequentialism. And a non-consequentialist normative economics is quite possible (e.g. Nozick, 1974) In advising the political decision makers on certain consequences, and not on the deontological standing of the policies, Robbins is imposing his own value judgments. His defense is, of course, that *he* is not making the value judgments – he is leaving them to the political authorities. And that apology, artful as it is, is one of the most influential points in Robbins' essay.

It should be said that Robbins' understanding of "science" is not quite the standard understanding in the twentieth and twenty-first centuries. He consistently admits introspection as "scientific" evidence (note also Robbins 1938) and seems to treat economics as a deductive science, as his comments on wage regulation suggest. At the same time Robbins seems to regard the relation of economic activity to ethical and political values as simple and transparent, requiring no careful thought. He writes (1932, p. 127) "given the desirability of individual liberty, absence of regimentation, power of continuous initiative, there is strong reason for supposing that conformity to the criteria of free economic equilibrium constitutes a fulfillment of these norms." But (p. 128) "It is clear that society, acting as a body of political citizens, may formulate ends which interfere ... with the free choices of the individuals composing it. There is nothing in the corpus of economic analysis which in itself affords any justification for regarding these ends as good or bad." What seems missing here is any idea that ethical decisions and market preferences might be interdependent or overlapping – that a person who buys fair-price coffee because he has utilitarian or equalitarian ethical values might also want to see those values expressed in public policy (but compare pp. 87–88), and would face an "economic problem" of balancing his preferences in public policy no less than Robinson Crusoe does in economizing on wood (pp. 10–11), and that a coherent welfare economics could help him to do so.

Robbins is not calling for any reformation of welfare economics. Quite the contrary. He never seems to refer to Pigou. He regards welfare economics as "simply the accidental deposit of the historical association of English Economics with Utilitarianism" (p. 125) and regrettable as such. All in all, Robbins assigns no positive value, and perhaps indeed a negative value (p. 125), to coherence in the study of the economics of public policy. But the consensus of economists in the second quarter of the twentieth century was otherwise. Having (on the one hand) adopted Robbins' view that no more than preference orderings should be attributed to individuals as expressions of their individual valuations and (on the other hand) retaining Pigou's aspiration to a coherent economics of public policy, they set out to refound welfare economics on preference orderings. This was the New Welfare Economics.

In his presidential address Harrod (1938) sets out what is pretty clearly an alternative to Robbins' position. He *distinguishes* value theory from the (more or less prescriptive) study of the allocation of resources. With respect to the latter he assures us (p. 390) that most economists have shared a value judgment that Harrod sees already in Adam Smith: that "If an individual prefers a commodity or service X to Y, it is economically better that he should have it." Taking this with a principle that "the complex phenomena of markets and prices might be regarded as the result of the efforts of individuals to inform each other of their preferences" – also attributed to Smith – Harrod assures us that economists can offer meaningful advice even with very little empirical information. On the other hand, he rejects Robbins' claim that economists can inform the political authorities of the consequences of the policies they choose – that would, he says, require empirical knowledge we do not have and not be very useful to them anyway. As to interpersonal comparisons, Harrod, who can never be accused of oversimplifying in the interest of clarity, is a little ambiguous. He considers two arguments against it. We will take them in opposite order. The second, that an economist may have little to add to political arguments that are already fully before the public, he gives some credit and some reservation. The first – Robbins' scientistic argument – he clearly rejects, providing (p. 396) a particularly clear summary of the argument from more and less urgent objectives to diminishing marginal utility, and noting that interpersonal comparisons are no less necessary to support a conclusion in favor of free trade than they are to support a conclusion in favor of redistribution. He concludes that "some sort of postulate of equality [of the capacity to enjoy satisfaction] has to be assumed." Robbins' response (1938) attacks that specific point. He writes (p. 636):

> I well remember ... reading somewhere – I think in the works of Sir Henry Maine – the story of how an Indian official had attempted to explain to a high-caste Brahmin the sanctions of the Benthamite system. 'But that,' said the Brahmin, 'cannot possibly be right. I am ten times as capable of happiness as that untouchable over there.' I had no sympathy with the Brahmin. But I could not escape the conviction that, if I chose to regard men as equally capable of satisfaction and he to regard them as differing according to a hierarchical schedule, the difference between us was not one which could be resolved by the same methods of demonstration as were available in other fields of social judgment.

This exchange, directed as it was to the cardinalist-ordinalist controversy, seems also to have stimulated the emergence of some key points in the New Welfare Economics.

4.3 Compensation tests

Executive summary of the section: The idea of compensation tests as an application of consumer surplus concepts evolved in the ideas of several writers, among whom Hicks contributed both important insights and synthesis.

Hotelling's (1938[2]) address to the Econometric Society is somewhat in the spirit of Lerner's papers, if more explicitly political (pp. 260, 265). Beginning from Dupuit's (1844) discussion, Hotelling's address is a powerful call for marginal cost pricing, through regulation if necessary, in the cases of railroads, bridges and roads especially. That is, he is particularly concerned with industries in which unavoidable fixed costs result in increasing returns and quite likely in a range of zero marginal costs. While Hotelling does not reject cardinal utility approaches in general (p. 247) he notes that the consumer and producer surpluses can be derived from preference relations, without cardinal measurement of utility (pp. 248–245), applies this to the selection of tax systems that least waste resources (pp. 246–7) and advocates the use of surplus measures in cost–benefit analysis to choose among projects (pp. 267–8). In this he relies on what will come to be known as the compensation test for a potential Pareto improvement (p. 267; Kaldor, 1939). Much of the work of the New Welfare Economics from this point on is coloring within the lines of Hotelling's sketch.

Kaldor's (1939) essay takes the form of a response to Robbins (1938) and Harrod (1938), but unlike those papers it is a contribution to welfare economics. Indeed, Kaldor distinguishes the development of welfare economics from the ordinalist controversy, and that may be his most important contribution. He argues that Harrod and Robbins are both mistaken: Robbins mistaken in his view that a scientific welfare economics is impossible and Harrod for his view that welfare economics requires comparability of utility. Kaldor's position (1939, p. 550) is that a scientific welfare economics can be based on a compensation test: if a change in public policy results in gains and losses distributed in such a way that the gainers could in principle compensate the losers and still be better off, then the change can be said to be an improvement in terms of economic efficiency. Kaldor stresses that it does not matter if the compensation actually is paid. Speaking of the repeal of the corn laws – Harrod's test case – he writes (p. 551):

> In order to establish his case, it is quite sufficient for him to show that even if all those who suffer as a result are fully compensated for their loss, the rest of the community will still be better off than before. Whether the landlords, in the free-trade case, should in fact be given compensation or not, is a political question on which the economist, qua economist, could hardly pronounce an opinion.

If we were to designate a "father of the New Welfare Economics," Lerner, Hotelling or Kaldor might be reasonable nominees for different reasons. But a more conventional nominee would be J. R. Hicks, despite the fact that his work within welfare economics largely postdates those three. The two famous papers with Allen (Hicks and Allen 1934a, 1934b) are important for microeconomics, but they contribute nothing to welfare economics aside from clearing away the brambles. *Value and Capital* (1939/1946) was Hicks' Great

Book, a comprehensive statement of economic theory as he conceived it. The first two parts extend his work with Allen and are well established in contemporary intermediate microeconomics. The later and larger two parts are now largely forgotten.

In *Value and Capital* Hicks restates Robbins' case against "cardinal utility" (1939/1946, pp. 18–22). He rejects the "assumption" of diminishing marginal utility in Pigou and Marshall, proposing instead the less restrictive assumption of a diminishing marginal rate of substitution, i.e. the convexity of indifference curves. But diminishing marginal utility is not exactly an assumption in Marshall and Pigou: rather it is a deduction – plausible if not strictly conclusive – from their satisfaction utilitarianism together with the idea that some wants are more urgent than others. Unlike Robbins, Hicks makes no attempt to recover the argument from urgency. Instead, he justifies his assumption that indifference curves are convex on the argument that it is necessary for the stability of market equilibria and that market equilibria would not be observed if they were not stable. Now, this observation may have some Bayesian value (depending as always on one's priors) but it is neither strictly true nor conclusive. It is not strictly true because non-convex indifference curves could give rise to some stable equilibria, and quite possibly to more than one. What convexity gives us is the uniqueness of equilibria, a property not easily observed. It is not conclusive because market equilibria could be stabilized by some other phenomena, such as inertia or fear of the unknown; or, indeed, what we observe and suppose to be market equilibria might be something else altogether. In short, Hicks has added an unsupported assumption to replace one that was at least probable on other grounds in the theory of Marshall and Pigou. Thus his theory is less coherent than theirs, as well as narrower. Now, 1) one often hopes to gain in coherence by narrowing the scope, unlike this case, but 2) in fairness, ordinalism is still a highly coherent theory by comparison, for example, to the economics of Adam Smith. What the narrowing has gained, however, is not coherence but exemption – exemption both from the issues surrounding the measurement of utility and the redistributive implications of it. For Hicks, clearly, that is enough.

For welfare economics, we may limit our attention to the appendix to Chapter 2. Here Hicks gives his interpretation of the consumer surplus (1939/1946, pp. 39–41) as a compensating income variation. However, this is not the compensating variation of a price change, but the compensating variation of the introduction of a new good or the elimination of an industry. In a footnote (p. 41) he acknowledges Hotelling's contribution, which he says he became aware of after the appendix was written. In 1939, however, joining his own "compensating variation" with Kaldor's "compensation test," Hicks has what seems to be something of a road-to-Damascus experience. In his address to the Economic Society of Stockholm,[3] entitled "The Foundations of Welfare Economics," having described Robbins' position, he writes (1939, p. 696) "I must admit that I should have subscribed to it myself not so long ago. But it is rather a dreadful thing to have to accept." Taking the view that the purpose of economic activity is to satisfy wants, he argues that an economic system can be evaluated on the basis of its success in doing that, that is, on its efficiency; and that this evaluation can be scientific. Drawing on Harrod, Kaldor and Hotelling, whom he cites, he gives a synthesis of their ideas. Kaldor's compensation test is a key to it (p. 700). Briefly describing the concept of Pareto optimality, he follows Lerner in introducing the production possibility frontier (substitution curve) in the context of international trade. In a footnote (p. 701) he observes that Pareto optima are not unique. He discusses the marginal conditions for optimality and shows, in a diagram, how increasing returns may invalidate them. For policy in a private enterprise economy, that is, deviations from market equilibria, he relies on Kaldor's test of potential compensation (p. 706) and considers third-party externalities as discussed in Pigou: "The ultimate implications of this exception are indeed very large. Hidden under this heading are some of the gravest philosophical issues about the relationship between the individual and society" (p. 707). He returns to consumer surplus as a measure of the loss due to the complete elimination of an industry (p. 707) and discusses the implication of imperfect competition in the sense of Chamberlin and Robinson.

In 1941 Hicks "rehabilitates" the concept of consumer surplus, noting that although the marginal utility of money is not an objective quantity, constancy of the marginal utility of money is an objective condition. (It corresponds to zero income effects.) Again he relies on the test of potential compensation (p. 111). He notes that a Paretian optimum maximizes the sum of the consumer and producer surplus (p. 113). In this discussion he relies on the Marshallean surpluses: the area between the supply and demand curve. He then considers the consumer surplus from the introduction of a new good, or the loss from the elimination of one (pp. 115–116). At no time in this paper, however, does Hicks discuss indifference curve analysis of the compensating variation of price changes.

In the same issue of the *Review of Economic Studies*, Hicks' position in *Value and Capital* was criticized by Henderson (1941). Henderson's critical point is that Hicks has not recognized how his conclusions depend on the assumption of a constant marginal utility of money (p. 117). Henderson modifies Hicks' diagram from *Value and Capital* (p. 118) to show that Hicks' treatment of the compensating variation due to the introduction or elimination of an industry is ambiguous. If indifference curves are not parallel – that is, if the marginal utility of income is not constant – then the compensating variation for elimination of the industry is not the same as the compensating variation corresponding to giving up the specific quantity purchased at the ex ante market equilibrium. He then goes on (p. 120) to define the compensating variation for a price change – originating in the diagram we all learned in intermediate microeconomics – and argues that, allowing for both increases and decreases in price and for different values based on the two different quantities demanded that may be observed, there are four different quantities that might be relevant to different questions, rather than Hicks' one.

Scitovsky's critique (1941) follows and cites Hicks (1941). It is a criticism of all welfare economic approaches based on the compensation test, with either potential or actual compensation. He first considers the argument from actual compensation – perhaps a straw man but one to be eliminated. "Favouring an improvement in the organisation of production and exchange only when it is accompanied by a corrective redistribution of income fully compensating those prejudiced by it might seem to be a way out of the difficulty, because such a change would make some people better off without making anyone worse off" (p. 79). But this, he tells us, is not a decision free of value judgments. "For, going out of their way to preserve the existing distribution of income, they imply a preference for the status quo." Scitovsky then uses the Edgeworth box apparatus to discuss compensating variations for changes in economic policy that alter the quantities of goods available to the society. His point is that, on the basis of compensation tests, some such changes in policy may be evaluated either as improvements or deteriorations depending on the distribution of income from which they begin. He also (p. 87) relates the different compensating variations to the Paasche and Laspeyres price indices. He concludes with the well-known argument that a change from A to B might be evaluated as an improvement and then, the distribution of income having shifted, the return from B to A would also be evaluated as an improvement. This seems to have been treated by many economists in later years as a curiosum. But that misses the more important point. Scitovsky writes (p. 86):

> Assume next that the members of our first group are rich and those of the second poor. Then the gain of the first group expressed in money (or in terms of any single commodity) will be greater than the money equivalent of the loss suffered by the second group. Therefore, if we so redistributed income as to restore approximately the initial distribution of welfare, there would be a net gain, making members of both groups better off than they were before. Conversely, if the people favoured by the change were poor, and those prejudiced by it were rich, the money equivalent of the former's gain would be insufficient fully to compensate the latter's loss, so that a redistribution of income tending to restore the initial distribution of welfare would result in a net loss of satisfaction for everybody.

The conclusion is that any use of a compensation test, potential or actual, requires a value judgment in favor of the status quo. However, in 1942 (pp. 91–92), in developing a theory of optimum tariffs, Scitovsky suggests the compound test:

> that we make sure whether the people who would benefit by the change could profitably bribe those harmed into accepting it. Secondly, we must make sure that the people who are against the change would be incapable of bribing those in favour to vote against it, without thereby losing more than they would if the change were carried.

Hicks (1942) follows Henderson's diagrammatic representation of the compensating variation for a price change and coins the term "equivalent variation" for the income variation corresponding to the reverse change. He associates the two variations with the Paasche and Laspeyres price indices. This recalls Scitovsky's comments but the Scitovsky paper is not cited. He extends Henderson's discussion to analyze the results of changes in two or more prices. In 1943 he returns somewhat to the position of *Value and Capital*, treating the demand curve as a curve of marginal willingness to pay – the marginal valuation (p. 33) – and argues that the quantity-equivalent variation is significant for the consumer surplus from the introduction of a new product but the price-equivalent variation is not. Here he seems to have realized that Hicks (1942) is inconsistent with *Value and Capital*. In 1945–1946, Hicks returns to the idea of the demand curve as the marginal willingness-to-pay curve and synthesizes the previous two with four concepts of consumer surplus, any of which may be more or less approximated by the areas between demand and supply curves.

Given this confusion of concepts and Scitovsky's critique, what can we make of compensation tests? For theoretical welfare economics, the significance of the compensation test is negative. If, beginning from the status quo at A, it can be demonstrated that a shift to status B would pass a test of potential compensation, then we can validly conclude that status quo A is inefficient. Such a test is very valuable, but it has only diagnostic power. It has no prescriptive power. A test that tells us that status quo A is inefficient poses, but does not answer, the question "what, if anything, ought public policy undertake to remedy the inefficiency?" Nor does such a test assure us that there is a unique efficient status; and indeed by now it is known that there are infinitely many. A test of efficiency can answer no questions of public policy. As to consumer surpluses, they would be a key tool of cost–benefit analysis, as in Griliches' (1958) cost–benefit analysis of the social returns to the introduction of hybrid corn; but the failure of this analysis to allow for distributional effects would remain an acknowledged shortcoming of the analysis. If we cannot compare and add the marginal utilities of different individuals, we can hardly assume that a dollar of benefits to each has the same impact on welfare. This point was stressed by Baumol (1946–1947) in a paper that will be discussed in Chapter 5.

4.4 Armstrong and non-transitive preference

Executive summary of the section: Rejecting the "behaviourism" of the ordinal school, Armstrong proposes an alternative interpretation of preference that leads to a cardinal utility measure and that hints at ideas that would emerge in twenty-first-century behavioral economics.

Armstrong (1939) entered this dialog with some pointed criticisms of preference theory. He rejects the idea that a set can be ordered without assigning magnitudes (p. 458) for reasons that are not very clear and that he describes as metaphysical. He also rejects the "behaviouristic" interpretation of indifference curves in Hicks and Allen, arguing (p. 457):

it is clear that on this behaviouristic view preference is not defined simply as choice, for it is implied by Hicks and Allen that it is possible for an individual to be indifferent to two alternatives even when one is chosen. Yet no indication is given in their theory as to the behaviour-mark which indicates, when choice is made, whether there is preference or indifference. One is forced to conclude that Hicks and Allen assume that there is a form of behaviour corresponding to what the introspectionist calls indifference ... in which case the theory is open to the same criticism as that applicable to the non-behaviouristic form of the theory.

In a footnote he suggests that the "behaviourist" could avoid the criticism by abandoning the language of indifference entirely, with a strategy that would be adopted a decade later by Little (2002 [1950]), as we will see in a later chapter.

The criticism he addresses to "the introspectionist's" concept of indifference curves is that indifference is not transitive. "[I]t is a well-known fact that it is possible to be indifferent as between two alternatives A and B and as between B and C, while there is preference for A over C i.e. the relation of indifference is not transitive." Now, perhaps this possibility is really not so well known. Armstrong offers it as a product of his own introspection, but a problem with introspection is that it may lead different individuals to different opinions. In a footnote, Armstrong supports the argument with an example of the substitution of bread for cheese. But, however little known, non-transitivity of indifference is a logical possibility. The transitivity of indifference is an assumption independent of the transitivity of preference. This can be illustrated simply (Armstrong 1939, p. 461). Assume a conventional utility function and define indifference between x and y as follows: for a given constant ε, x and y are indifferent choices if $|u(x)-u(y)|<\varepsilon$. Introspection may lead the reader to reject this. Armstrong's introspection leads him to affirm it. This possibility can be excluded by assuming that choices are indifferent only if $u(x)-u(y)=0$, and this leads Armstrong to suggest that it is only by assuming a utility function that preference theory could escape from its dilemma. He is mistaken – in the absence of a utility function, it is sufficient to assume that what he calls an indifference class (p. 454) is an equivalence class. In standard modern microeconomic theory the two assumptions – that preference is transitive and that an indifference class is an equivalence class – are slyly compacted into one by defining preference as a weak ordering, like $\geq$, rather than as a strict ordering, like $>$. I know of no justification for this choice of definitions other than introspection. (As we will see in a later chapter, this convention has been reconsidered in some discussion of "behavioral welfare economics"; Fleurbaey and Shokkaert 2013).

Armstrong justifies his choice of definitions with a plausible argument that suggests behaviorism in a more modern sense (1939, p. 463).

There is evidently a confusion on this issue that it is important to clear up, a confusion which has arisen owing to the abandonment by utility-theorists of the earlier pleasure-pain theory. On the latter theory, choice is determined not by pleasure-pain but by estimates of pleasure-plain ... Now this difficulty [with Benthamism] is escaped if we regard utility as the intensity of a want and assume that preference results from an esti-mate of this intensity. This means that it is possible to make an erroneous judgment about a mental state which occurs simultaneously with the judgment about it; in other words, that there is nothing contradictory in the concept of my wanting A more than B and judging that I want B more than A. If this be granted, then a state of indifference means not that the intensities of my wants are equal but merely that they have less than a certain degree of inequality, thus preserving the non-transitiveness of indifference.

He goes on to draw a parallel between estimating the intensity of a want with the intensity and hue of a perceived color (pp. 464–4). Recall the dis-cussion of utilities as qualia in Chapter 2: the language of qualia begins with the philosophy of color perception. Armstrong's comments seem consistent with this. All in all, it seems that Armstrong has two important insights that have unfortunately been neglected by subsequent economics: that indifference could be intransitive and, whether we interpret utility as a quale, a number or a want of variable intensity, decisions can only be based on estimates of the consequences, and a reasonable person might base the choice on these estimates only if the difference of the estimates is great enough.

4.5 Lerner, cardinalism and welfare economics

Executive summary of the section: Despite his contributions to ordinalist microeconomics, Lerner suggested that the utilitarian argument for equal-ization of income could be retained. His argument presages the "veil of ignorance" arguments of later decades.

Abba Lerner's Great Book, *The Economics of Control* (1944) was in many ways a response to the Harrod-Robbins controversy and seems to have been little influenced by the discussion of compensation tests. Lerner was committed to marginal-cost pricing and argues for an economic system that has been called market socialism. However, it is his position in the cardinalist-ordinalist controversy that has been the subject of most controversy. Chapter 3 addresses "The Optimum Division of Income." Lerner argues that, prima facie – that is, in the absence of strong contrary arguments, such as an argument that a too-progressive tax would eliminate incentives and so leave everyone worse off – an equal distribution of income would be ideal. His argument runs as follows (pp. 29–31): consider a shift away from equality in the form of a transfer from A to B. The results of the shift will depend on differences between them as to their respective capacities to enjoy satisfaction; in general we may suppose that they differ. But, because individual utility functions are unknowable, we do not know which is which. Thus there are two possibilities: the redistribution is to the one with the greater, or to the one with the less, capacity for satisfaction. With no knowledge which is which, the probabilities are equal. But, supposing that the marginal utility of income is decreasing, this means that the net loss is greater if the redistribution is to the one with the lesser capacity than the gain if it is to the one with the greater capacity. The expected value of a prospect with a 50 percent probability of a smaller gain and a bigger loss can only be negative. Thus, the expected value of welfare change in any deviation from equality is negative.

Of course, Lerner has to make some assumptions to obtain this result (pp. 23–28). Some of the assumptions are not subject to empirical proof. One of the key assumptions, that differences in the capacity of individuals for satisfaction are unknowable, is also a key assumption for Robbins, as we have seen. Notice, also, that this enables Lerner to eliminate a strong prima facie argument against utilitarianism. If it were in fact known that Robbins' Brahmin has a much greater capacity for satisfaction than the untouchable, then maximization of total utility would require that more income be given to the Brahmin. Any equalitarian and many utilitarians would be uncomfortable with this! But the ordinalist assumption that these differences are unknowable gets Lerner off the hook for that issue. Others of Lerner's assumptions would be contradicted by the ordinalists: as we have seen, diminishing marginal utility of income is one of them (p. 26).

Another assumption is that "people enjoy similar satisfactions" (p. 25). The ordinalist position on these is that the proposition cannot be scientifically confirmed or denied. But do Lerner's conclusions follow from his premises? "People enjoy similar satisfactions" is a bit vague. Here, and in his discussion of diminishing marginal utility of income, Lerner is following precisely Pigou's path, reasoning that to satisfy the same wants must give rise to the same quantum of satisfaction from one person to another; but Lerner has added a term of random deviation to this! But this is plausible reasoning, unless we have a much less ambiguous foundation than "similar satisfactions." There are at least two distinct assumptions packed in here. One is that utility functions have numerical properties that allow them to be multiplied and the multiples added to compute a mathematical expectation. If we have a sufficiently regular preference system, that assumption is satisfied: such a preference system can be represented by any of an infinite family of utility functions, and whichever one we choose to use will have those numerical properties. Nevertheless, second, the utility function might have those properties and still not be comparable between persons. In that case, the expected value, though calculable, would be meaningless. It is the plausible reasoning about satisfactions that gives it meaning.

Is it, then, permissible in "scientific" theory to admit plausible reasoning? (Recall that each of the ordinalists we have considered so far has indulged in plausible reasoning.) For a certain sort of science, such as physics, perhaps it is not. However, Lerner is treating welfare economics as a decision science. In a science like physics it is possible, and might be mandatory, to reserve judgment when there is no decisive evidence one way or another. The case is somewhat different in a decision science. It is not possible to not decide. Not to decide *is to decide*, and, in the practice of economics, almost always to decide for the status quo. Even to postpone a decision to wait for more information is to decide. In a decision science, known unknowns may surely influence the decision. Where evidence is not conclusive, plausible reasoning *must* be brought to bear when the alternative is inability to decide. The position of the ordinalists is that matters of income distribution cannot be decided, because satisfactory information for the purpose is not available. Whatever they are doing, (unlike Lerner) it is not decision science.

Of course, Lerner's discussion was far too clever to convince everybody! Two major book reviews addressed it, by Meade and Friedman. Meade (1945, p. 45) finds it interesting and elegant. Friedman (1947, p. 409) writes "The analysis as given is not rigorous, primarily because of appeal to 'equal ignorance.'" Friedman, who had studied actuarial science, provides an alternative proof consistent with the ideas of statistical inference that were then dominant. But Friedman also criticizes Lerner for using an additive utility concept, arguing that he has not really eliminated the claim of the Brahmin to a greater income, and that that claim discredits utilitarianism as a normative theory of distribution (p. 411). Little attacks Lerner (along with most other welfare economists) root and branch (1949b). He rejects Lerner's equiprobability assumption remarking "from ignorance can come only ignorance." He also seems to miss Lerner's argument from diminishing marginal utility. Otherwise, there was little controversy arising from it at the time, and we will return to it in a future chapter.

4.6 Where we have come

By the mid-1940s, "ordinalist" microeconomics, which became the standard microeconomics still taught today, and a "New Welfare Economics" consistent with that microeconomics, had largely been developed through a series of discussions in which John Hicks was a consistent and persistent participant. Hicks is above all a superb *writer*. It is in part the brilliance of the content, but no less Hicks the writer that makes Hicks the advocate a successful advocate for Hicks the theorist. Together with his skill as a writer, his consistent participation in this reasonable dialog and his ability to synthesize, incorporating the ideas of other creative minds into his own synthesis, justify his reputation as the most important founding father of both modern microeconomics and the New Welfare Economics. The ordinalism he shared with Robbins and others was on the ascendant: from this point on the arguments for cardinal utility are defensive. For the theory of resource allocation, everything is to be traced back to indifference curve analysis (see e.g. Scitovsky 1942).

For welfare economics, the subject is less settled. The Kaldor-Hicks test can be tied, via indifference curve analysis, to the various measures of consumer surplus (and perhaps producer surplus, though this remains in need of some clarification) that can be approximated by areas under demand curves and by similar methods. This is the basis of a huge literature in applied economics in the latter half of the twentieth century. However, the unresolved status of distribution remains a problem for the New Welfare Economics. All of the apparatus of the Kaldor-Hicks New Welfare Economics is contingent on the distribution of income: the compensation and other tests and surplus measures depend on budget constraints or on demand and supply curves derived from them. Thus, faced with the question "Does such-and-such change in public policy increase or reduce welfare?" the new welfare economist can only answer, "First you must tell me from what distribution of income the change will begin." Even then, in some cases the new welfare economist will approve changes that make the rich (who can afford large hypothetical compensations to losers) a good deal better off and that make the poor only a little more miserable. One needs not be a utilitarian to be uncomfortable with that. Adding then Scitovsky's insight that shifts in the distribution of income could render the compensation tests ambiguous, it is little wonder that the controversy in welfare economics was to become more, not less intense.

Notes

1 In a footnote at p. 220, Lange cites critically a paper of Morgenstern. Perhaps Morgenstern was aware of Lange's ideas as Lange was of those of Morgenstern.
2 The address was given orally in December 1937 and published in 1938.
3 This paper seems to be the origin of the phrase "the new welfare economics," p. 698. This book will interpret the term in the narrow sense suggested by Hicks' use of it and by the critique of Stigler (1943), excluding contemporaneous contributions by Bergson (1938), Samuelson (1938) and Lange (1942), which will be taken up in Chapter 5.

References

Allen, R. G. D. (1935) A Note on the Determinateness of the Utility Function, *Review of Economic Studies* v. 2, no. 2 (Feb) pp. 155–158.
Armstrong, W. E. (1939) The Determinateness of the Utility Function, *Economic Journal* v. 49, no. 195 (Sept) pp. 453–467.
Baumol, William J. (1946–1947) Community Indifference, *Review of Economic Studies* v. 14, no. 1 pp. 44–48.
Bergson, A. (1938) A Reformulation of Certain Aspects of Welfare Economics, *Quarterly Journal of Economics* (Feb).
Cannan, Edwin (1888) *Elementary Political Economy* (London: Henry Frowde Oxford University Press).
Dupuit, Arsène Jules ÉtienneJuvénal (1844) De la mesure de l'utilité des travaux publics, *Annales des ponts et chaussées*, Second Series, 8.

Fleurbaey, Marc and Erik Schokkaert (2013) Behavioral Welfare Economics and Redistribution, *American Economic Journal: Microeconomics* v. 5, no. 1 (Aug) pp. 180–205.

Friedman, Milton (1947) Lerner on the Economics of Control, *Journal of Political Economy* v. 55, no. 5 (Oct) pp. 405–416.

Georgescu-Roegen, N. (1936) The Pure Theory of Consumer Behavior, *Quarterly Journal of Economics* v. 50, no. 4 (Aug) pp. 545–593.

Griliches, Zvi (1958) Research Costs and Social Returns: Hybrid Corn and Related Innovations, *Journal of Political Economy* v. 66, no. 5 (Oct) pp. 419–431.

Harrod, Roy (1938) Scope and Method of Economics, *Economic Journal* v. 48, no. 191 (Sept) pp. 383–412.

Harsanyi, John (1953) Cardinal Utility in Welfare Economics and in the Theory of Risk-Taking, *Journal of Political Economy* v. 61, no. 5 (Oct) pp. 434–435.

Harsanyi, John (1955) Cardinal Welfare, Individualistic Ethics, and Interpersonal Comparisons of Utility, *Journal of Political Economy* v. 63 (Aug) pp. 309–321.

Henderson, A. (1941) Consumer's Surplus and the Compensating Variation, *Review of Economic Studies* v. 8, no. 2 (Feb) pp. 117–121.

Hicks, J. R. (1939/1946) *Value and Capital* (London: Oxford University Press).

Hicks, J. R. (1939) Foundations of Welfare Economics, *Economic Journal* v. 49, no. 4 (Dec) pp. 696–712.

Hicks, J. R. (1941) The Rehabilitation of Consumers' Surplus, *Review of Economic Studies* v. 8, no. 2 (Feb) pp. 108–116.

Hicks, J. R. (1942) Consumers' Surplus and Index-Numbers, *Review of Economic Studies* v. 9, no. 2 (Summer) pp. 126–137.

Hicks, J. R. (1943) The Four Consumer's Surpluses, *Review of Economic Studies* v. 11, no. 1 (Winter) pp. 31–41.

Hicks, J. R. (1945–1946) The Generalised Theory of Consumer's Surplus, *Review of Economic Studies* v. 13, no. 2 pp. 68–74.

Hicks, J. R. and R. G. D. Allen (1934a) A Reconsideration of the Theory of Value. Part I, *Economica, New Series* v. 1, no. 1 (Feb) pp. 52–76.

Hicks, J. R. and R. G. D. Allen (1934b) A Reconsideration of the Theory of Value. Part II. A Mathematical Theory of Individual Demand Functions, *Economica, New Series* v. 1, no. 2 (May) pp. 196–219.

Hildreth, Clifford (1953) Alternative Conditions for Social Orderings, *Econometrica* v. 21, no. 1 (Jan) pp. 81–94.

Hotelling, H. (1938) The General Welfare in Relation to Problems of Taxation and of Railway and Utility Rates, *Econometrica* (July) v. 6, pp. 242–269.

Kaldor, N. (1939) Welfare Propositions and Inter-Personal Comparison of Utility, *Economic Journal* (Sept).

Lange, Oskar (1934) The Determinateness of the Utility Function, *Review of Economic Studies* v. 1, no. 3 (Jun) pp. 218–225.

Lange, Oscar (1942) The Foundations of Welfare Economics, *Econometrica* v. 10, pp. 215–228.

Lerner, Abba P. (1932) The Diagrammatical Representation of Cost Conditions in International Trade, *Economica*, no. 37 (Aug) pp. 346–356.

Lerner, Abba P. (1934) The Concept of Monopoly and the Measurement of Monopoly Power, *Review of Economic Studies* v. 1, no. 3 (Jun) pp. 157–175.

Lerner, Abba P. (1944) *Economics of Control* (New York: Macmillan).

Little, I. M. D. (1949) The Foundations of Welfare Economics, *Oxford Economic Papers, New Series* v. 1, no. 2 (Jun) pp. 227–246.

Little, I. M. D. (2002 [1950]) *A Critique of Welfare Economics*, 2nd Edition (Oxford: Clarendon).

Meade, J. E. (1945) Mr. Lerner on the "Economics of Control", *Economic Journal* v. 55, no. 217 (Apr) pp. 47–69.

Menger, Karl (1976 [1871]) *Principles of Economics*, translated by James Dingwall and Bert F. Hoselitz (Auburn, Ala.: Institute for Humane Studies).

Mill, John Stuart (1987 [1909]) *Principles of Political Economy* (New York: A. M. Kelley).

Nozick, Robert (1974) *Anarchy, State and Utopia* (New York: Basic Books).

Robbins, Lionel (1932) *An Essay on the Nature and Significance of Economic Science* (London: Macmillan).

Robbins, Lionel (1934) Remarks upon Certain Aspects of the Theory of Costs, *Economic Journal* v. 44, no. 173 (Mar) pp. 1–18.

Robbins, Lionel (1938) Interpersonal Comparisons of Utility, *Economic Journal* (Dec).

Samuelson, Paul A. (1938) The Numerical Representation of Ordered Classifications and the Concept of Utility, *Review of Economic Studies* v. 6, no. 1 (Oct) pp. 65–70.

Scitovsky, Tibor de (1941) A Note on Welfare Propositions in Economics, *Review of Economic Studies* v. 9, pp. 77–88.

Scitovsky, Tibor de (1942) A Reconsideration of the Theory of Tariffs, *Review of Economic Studies* v. 9, no. 2 (Summer) pp. 89–110.

von Neumann, John and Oskar Morgenstern (1944) *Theory of Games and Economic Behavior* (Princeton, N.J.: Princeton University Press).

Zeuthen, Frederick (1930) *Problems of Monopoly and Economic Warfare* (London: Routledge and Kegan Paul).

Zeuthen, Frederick (1937) On the Determinateness of the Utility Function, *Review of Economic Studies*, v. 4, no. 3 (June) pp. 236–239.

5   Social preference

The New Welfare Economics, as it stands in Chapter 4, is capable of posing questions but not of answering them. Let us not underestimate the importance of posing questions! But the objective of that enterprise was to recover the conclusions of Pigou's welfare economics with respect to the efficient allocation of resources without cardinal utility or other value judgments, and without prescribing the distribution of income. That enterprise, unable to give conclusive answers to questions of efficient policy, was a failure. That, at least, was the position of Abram Bergson. Further, he argued, it could not in principle address policy questions without making value judgments. If one were to reject Pigou's utilitarian value judgments, one must supply for them some substitute. Could we build a welfare economics that acknowledges the necessity of value judgments without limiting the theory to utilitarianism? A logic that could do that was provided by Bergson (1938) in a paper that acknowledged assistance from Samuelson and that was signed Abram Burk, to the permanent confusion of economics graduate students. This was one (and in many ways the central one) of formative contributions by scholars associated with Massachusetts institutions that would, many years later, be the home of "saltwater economics." These will be examined in this chapter, along with a less ambitious attempt to aggregate preferences, the discussion of "community indifference curves," contemporary developments in indifference curve analysis that move away from preference theory, and I. M. D. Little's *Critique of Welfare Economics*.

5.1 The social welfare function

Executive summary of the section: The idea of a social welfare function, an extension of the utilitarian's sum of utility functions, originated with the work of Bergson, Lange and Samuelson.

In his founding paper on the social welfare function, Bergson begins by defining an "economic welfare function" that generalizes the summation of utilities in Marshall and Pigou in two ways. First, where the summation of

utilities is a compound function[1] of the quantities of goods and services consumed by individuals, Bergson dispenses with the compound function and
makes welfare a function of the quantities themselves (Bergson 1938, p. 324).
Second, Bergson allows for some other determinants of welfare, such as the
quantity and type of labor supplied and the place of employment. He also
makes welfare dependent on the allocation of non-human resources among
productive establishments (p. 312). In retrospect, this seems a little odd. Perhaps a proprietor might prefer not only to work in his own establishment but
also to deploy to it any resources to which he owns title, but Bergson gives no
hint as to this or any other interpretation. He excludes externalities for simplicity (p. 311 note) and assumes production functions for the productive
establishments as a constraint on welfare (p. 313).

He then states two sorts of welfare propositions: first, "the Lerner conditions," necessary conditions for a maximum of welfare that are derived from
the preferences and production functions alone (p. 316) and, with some further restrictions on the economic welfare function, an "equal shares" proposition (p. 321). This "equal shares" assumption depends on the further
restrictions, which correspond to the value judgments more or less implicit in
Pigou's welfare economics. Bergson stresses that different value propositions
could lead to different optima: "for each of these sets of propositions there
corresponds a maximum position. The number of sets is infinite, and in any
particular case the selection of one of them must be determined by its compatibility with the values prevailing in the community the welfare of which is
being studied." He dismisses the summation of utilities as being "not useful"
on the grounds that comparisons of utility *require* a value judgment (p. 327):
"Secondly, the evaluation of the different commodities cannot be avoided,
even tho this evaluation may consist only in a decision to accept the evaluations of the individual members of the community" (p. 327). Notice that this
precise value judgment was stated in Harrod's (1938) address, which is not
cited, and was hardly "concealed" in Pigou or Marshall (p. 328). But neither
does he find the pure ordinalist position satisfactory: "unless the Cambridge
Conditions, or a modified form of these conditions, is introduced there is no
reason in general why it is more preferable to have the other two groups of
conditions satisfied than otherwise" (p. 329). Thus, welfare economics cannot
proceed without sufficient explicit value judgments: "the determination of
prevailing values for a given community, while I regard it as both a proper
and necessary task for the economist, and of the same general character as
the investigation of the indifference functions for individuals" (p. 323). This
project, however, never seems to have been seriously undertaken.

In his paper Bergson makes reference to papers of Kahn (1935) and Lange
(1936) as the up-to-date expositions of the Pigovian welfare economics.
Kahn's paper argues that Pigou's externalities can be subsumed along with
imperfect competition as divergences of equilibrium price from marginal cost,
and discusses smoke and congestion (pp. 16–18) in terms that would be little
changed in a twenty-first-century textbook. Lange's paper discusses the

application of the marginal conditions in a socialist commonwealth. In some ways the second part of Lange's two-part paper (Lange 1937) might have better served for Bergson's comparison. In any case it was later Lange (1942) who joined the Paretian New Welfare Economics with a social welfare function in a synthesis that has become standard. (The term Lange uses is "social value function," p. 219.) Initially, treating the welfare of society as a vector of individual utilities, Lange notes that Pareto optimality can be expressed as a problem in maximization, where the utility of one person is maximized subject to lower constraints on the utility of all others, along with the production possibility frontier and some adding-up constraints. This is equivalent to maximizing a weighted sum of the individual utilities with an arbitrary weight λ_i attached to the utility of individual i (pp. 215–216). It is shown (pp. 217–218) that this maximum is independent of any numerical value of the utility of individual i – for a different cardinal utility u_i an offsetting change in λ_i will produce the same result – so that the u_i may be thought of as indices of the level of the preference system for individual i. But as there are infinitely many vectors of weights λ_i there are infinitely many Pareto optima. To choose among these requires a social value function, which for Lange is a function of the utility indices (levels of preference) of the individuals i. The implications of this are discussed, and in an appendix, the analysis is extended to allow different individuals (productive establishments) to have separate production possibility frontiers. This refinement allows some externalities to be treated.

Samuelson's comprehensive statement on welfare economics is chapter 8 in the *Foundations of Economic Analysis*. This book having been "written primarily in 1937" (Samuelson 1953, p. vii) but not published until 1945, it is difficult to say to what extent it preceded, and whether it was influenced by, Lange, who is at one point cited along with Bergson (p. 252). Samuelson begins with some history of economic thought, discussing the formation of the "New Welfare Economics" to which he contrasts the position he shares with Bergson. In developing that position, he begins with a social welfare function even more general than the one that Bergson begins with, simply indicating that social welfare is a function of some variables not otherwise specified (p. 221). At pp. 219–228, Samuelson gives literary expression to a sequence of eight "value judgments" that successively specify the variables and the function, culminating with the maximization of the sum of utilities. But Samuelson of course rejects the last two "value judgments" and summation. Just the first four "value judgments" are sufficient to make social welfare a function of the quantities of goods and services consumed and productive services supplied by individuals in society. The fifth and sixth lead to the compound-function formulation, with welfare a function of the (ordinal) utilities of individuals and makes the utilities functions of the quantities of goods and services consumed and productive services supplied by the individual. He then gives conditions for the derivation of the transformation or production possibility frontier from the production functions of individual productive establishments, noting that Lagrange multipliers play the role of prices ("shadow prices"). This at least was conceived by 1941 (footnote p. 234), and thus independently of Lange. This procedure excludes external economies in production, as noted here in the appendix to Chapter 3; Samuelson's sixth "value judgment" has already excluded externalities in consumption (p. 224). He then separately discusses exchange equilibrium (pp. 236–7). The two are then combined for a full set of optimality conditions. There are many qualifications about such things as corner optima. It is worthy of note that Samuelson wrote before linear and non-linear programming were developed, so that his qualifications rely largely on a powerful mathematical intuition. So far, distribution is indeterminate. For a given (unspecified) social welfare function, the conditions for a full optimum are given. The foregoing production and exchange conditions allow derivation of a utility possibility frontier.[2] The welfare function of the individual utilities is then maximized with the utility possibility frontier as the constraint. This approach has become a standard, of course.

Samuelson rejects the compensation tests that play a key role in the New Welfare Economics, including Scitovsky's compound test, as "'twere better" statements. That is, a compensation test can tell us that "'twere better" for policy to produce situation A than situation B, but cannot exclude the possibility that a third situation C might be better than either, and so is inconclusive. By contrast, a social welfare function could in principle provide a definite optimum, a policy package that "'twere better" than any other. But, in practice, as of mid-century, no specification for a social welfare function had been proposed other than the summation of cardinal utilities, which Samuelson and Bergson reject.[3] Thus, in practice, the social welfare function becomes a defensive barrier for the New Welfare Economics – pending the specification of a social welfare function, "'twere better" to choose policies justified by some version of the compensation test.

Meade (1945) commented on Lerner's *Economics of Control*, bringing forward four criticisms of welfare economics in general (pp. 52–54), without any reference to a social welfare function. Tintner (1946) responded by proposing some adaptations of a social welfare function that he suggests could resolve those criticisms. Further discussion of social welfare functions would arise in response to Arrow's *Social Choice and Individual Values* (1951a) but these will be reserved to Chapter 6.

5.2 Community indifference curves

Executive summary of the section: Concepts of community indifference curves arose originally in a context of compensation tests, and are not uniquely defined at any allocation of resources. They are not, in general, contours of a social welfare function, but those contours have been called "social indifference curves."

Along with the discussion of compensation tests considered in Chapter 4 was some renewed discussion of "community indifference curves." Prior to Samuelson (1956) this seems to have been conducted in ignorance of Lerner's earlier use of the concept. Community indifference curves were primarily applied in the theory of international trade. In this brief discussion only the concepts and critique of community indifference curves will be considered.

Lerner (1932) posits a community indifference curve but defines only its slope, which is the slope common to all members of the community at a trading equilibrium. His explanation is limited to a footnote (p. 347) in which he notes that there may be many community indifference curves through a point, depending on the distribution of resources. Lerner's community indifference curve was for the community of the whole world, that is, both trading countries. Just what Lerner might have meant would remain unclear until Samuelson (1956) pointed out that community indifference curves and utility possibility frontiers could be considered as mathematical duals.

In Kaldor (1940) the author derived a concept of community indifference curves from his compensation test. The community indifference curve is derived on the basis of the potential compensation test: along the curve, exact compensation of losers by winners is possible. Kaldor treats this as a measurement of real income, saying that along the curve, real income is constant (however it may be distributed). But Kaldor's discussion is confused. To actually move along Kaldor's indifference curve the compensations must actually be paid. If compensations are not paid, then the community would clearly be moved to a point off the community indifference curve, and even if more than equivalent compensations could be paid (leading to a point above the curve) the actual movement, without payment of compensation, could leave the community below the indifference curve. If we do assume that the exact compensations are paid, then there are nevertheless many community indifference curves through any point, depending on the distribution of income (as Lerner had observed in his 1932 paper). Scitovsky (1942) uses Kaldor's exact compensation community indifference curves, but does observe that there are infinitely many such curves through any point, and that consequently community indifference curves may intersect. He uses intersecting community indifference curves to illustrate his argument for a double compensation test.

Baumol (1946–1947) criticizes Kaldor's community indifference curves on the ground that Kaldor assumes, in effect, that each person's dollar of income has equal social significance. Baumol asserts that some interpersonal comparison of utility is necessary, and that Kaldor does not avoid that but, in effect, simply uses money as the common and comparable measurement. However, in 1950 Baumol presents a derivation of community indifference curves, using the concept of a utility possibility frontier. Samuelson (1950) makes "social indifference curves" the contours of a social welfare function, but then in 1956 takes up Baumol's (1949–1950) discussion, treating *community* indifference curves (as distinct from the contours of a social welfare function) as mathematical duals of the utility possibility frontier.

Mishan (1952) reconsiders the compensation tests and the construction of community indifference curves from them. In the case of Kaldor's exact compensation, if the compensation were in fact paid, then a movement along a community indifference curve would maintain the welfare level of each person constant – all would be indifferent among the alternatives lying along the curve. Mishan adopts this as definitional (pace Lerner 1932) but also requires that the community indifference curve reflect an optimal allocation of the consumers' goods; that is, a point on the contract curve for an Edgeworth box determined by the total quantities of the two goods. The slope of the community indifference curve is the common slope of the marginal rates of substitution for the individuals in this case. Quite explicitly, then, there are many community indifference curves through any point in goods space and reversals and inconsistencies are possible, even when the Scitovsky test is satisfied. Mishan gives a numerical example to establish this (1952, p. 314). However, he argues (p. 321) that a movement from a non-optimal to an optimal position will always pass both the Kaldor test and the Scitovsky reversal test, without inconsistencies. To this extent, he tells us, compensation tests and community indifference curves continue to be useful. Mishan would return to them from time to time in subsequent work (e.g. Mishan 1973, 1982).

Community indifference curves were, at best, controversial (e.g. Enke 1944; Meier 1949; Little 1949) Vanek (1964) would "rehabilitate" them for trade theory, making assumptions of perfect competition in each trading community. We will return to them in a later section of this chapter.

5.3 The cardinalist-ordinalist controversy continued: revealed preference

Executive summary of the section: Samuelson, with Little and Houthakker, reworked preference theory on a basis that is quite physicalist. This shares the shortcomings of any physicalist theory of individual decisions in that it means nothing for normative economics.

Paul Samuelson, 21 years of age, enters the cardinalist-ordinalist controversy (surprisingly!) with a proposal for an empirical measure of the marginal utility of income. This uses the Bellman equation (Samuelson 1937a, p. 1560) that would later become associated with Modigliani's (Modigliani and Brumberg 1954) lifecycle hypothesis of saving decisions. Samuelson goes on to express some skepticism, in the form of a more general model of lifecycle saving decisions that must somehow be ruled out if utility measurement is to occur (p. 160). In a memoire, he recalls having done early work on the lifecycle hypothesis (Samuelson 1998, p. 1377) and indeed, within months, this essay is extended in directions that have nothing to do with utility measurement (Samuelson 1937b).

From this point on, however, Samuelson's contributions are ordinalist, and definitive. In his *Economica* piece (1938a, p. 65), he proposes that no assumptions need to be made about *preferences*. Using techniques from index number theory, he proposes instead the assumption that *choices* are consistent in a certain sense. This is the first version of the principle of revealed preference. It is extended in the *Econometrica* paper in October (Samuelson 1938b). Samuelson rejects the Hicks/Allen assumption of the increasing marginal rate of substitution (1938a, p. 61) and discards the issue of integrability as irrelevant (1938a, p. 68). He also denies that the theory of consumer demand has any relevance to welfare economics (1938a, p. 71).

In these discussions, Samuelson's principal concern is methodological, but it is somewhat different from the methodological position of the previous ordinalists. Samuelson says little or nothing about value judgments, and seems, without saying, to accept the value judgment that Harrod attributed to Smith: "If an individual prefers a commodity or service X to Y, it is economically better that he should have it." But Samuelson's concern is with "operationalism" (Bridgman 1927). That is, concepts are meaningful only if they are defined in such a way that we can carry out operations that determine that an observation conforms to the definition. Samuelson's point then is that markets routinely stage such operations where preference is concerned, though not for numerical utility. He returns to this theme in the *Foundations* (Samuelson 1953), especially chapters 5 and 6; in chapter 7 he argues against cardinal utility theories on the grounds that they require untestable restrictions on the mathematical form of the preference field. However, his formulation of revealed preference at this stage does not (necessarily) return indifference curves, as the local observations he relies on may not support integration – the integrability problem remains unsolved for indifference curves. In 1949a, Little observes that, while Samuelson's local observations may fail to reveal preferences that are expressed by an indifference curve map, a sequence of two local observations can reveal the preferences in such a case. By the time that Little's paper was published, Samuelson's response (1948) had already been published, adopting Little's extension and providing another proof of it. In 1950, Houthakker extended this approach, demonstrating that an indifference curve between two vectors of goods and services could be approximated to any desired degree by a finite sequence of local observations, providing an operational definition of an indifference curve and sidestepping the integrability problem. Again, Samuelson adopts this innovation (1950, 1953), and from this point forward, Houthakker's assumptions are known as the Strong Axiom of Revealed Preference (SARP), while Samuelson's original assumption is the Weak Axiom of Revealed Preference (WARP). The weak axiom is a necessary but not sufficient condition for Houthakker's construction. Further refinements of this approach by Afriat (1967) and Varian (1982), known as the Generalized Axiom of Revealed Preference (GARP), relax some restrictions on the preference field that the SARP required.

Thanks to Samuelson and the others, we have a hypothesis of preference that is free of any element of introspection or plausible reasoning. But is the hypothesis true? The WARP is the weakest of the family, and is entailed by the others, so if the WARP fails empirically the others cannot be true either. The first attempts to test the WARP seem to be those of Koo (1963; Koo and Hasenkamp 1972; Koo and Schmidt 1974). His results were broadly negative. Sippel (1997), Mattei (2000) and Fevrier and Visser (2004) obtained similarly negative results. Of course, this is not a consensus, and see e.g. Cox (1997) and Diaye et al. (2008) for contrary results. In the present century, the growth of behavioral economics has given rise to many "anomalies" in which revealed preference seems to fail. Among active researchers in behavioral welfare economics, the consensus seems to be that the revealed preference hypothesis is false in general. Behavioral welfare economics will be discussed in Chapter 10.

But suppose Samuelson had been right, the WARP experimentally valid and demonstrably the basis of decisions made by real human beings in real markets. What would it mean? Arguably, very little. To make the argument, recall the literature about qualia. We can imagine a "zombie," in the sense of that literature, whose observed behavior is consistent with WARP (and SARP and GARP), and shows every sign of what modern economics calls rationality, but that feels nothing – no pleasures, no pains, no sorrow, no exhilaration, no anger, no regret. We can imagine a population of such zombies. We can imagine that the social arrangements in that population are such that some zombies could be raised to higher levels of their observed preference systems without any others being forced to lower levels of their observed preference systems. So what? What really would be gained if the social arrangements were to be changed in this Pareto-preferable way? Can we say that some of the zombies are "better off"? Certainly we can, if we identify "better off" with being at a higher level of the observed preference system: but no zombie *feels* better off; no zombie *feels* that its suffering is alleviated; indeed no zombie *feels* suffering that might be eliminated. Why then would we *feel* any motive to change the social arrangements in the population of zombies? If we are reasonable, we would not.

Introspection is not, of course, a source of scientific fact, but it may be a source of insight that gives the scientific facts normative or valuative meaning. As I propose to engage in a bit of introspection, perhaps I can be forgiven another brief lapse into first-person narrative. Careful observation of my behavior over the last few years will establish that I prefer a bagel and two cups of coffee to other commodity vectors I might choose for breakfast. That preference is indeed a part of my subjective experience. But it is not a primitive. This preference is something I have learned through trial and error. There was a period when I bought mini-bagels, but I found myself returning for a second mini-bagel quite often – discovering that the psychic return to want satisfaction from the second mini-bagel more than offset my subjective estimate of the cost (in calories more than money; compare Sen 2009, p. 181). And a preference is a comparison – what am I comparing? I can express the answer no better than Pigou did: the psychic return to want satisfaction. So preferences are a feature of my subjective experience, but they are rather complex constructed and learned states of mind. Psychic returns to satisfaction are also a part of my subjective experience, and if they also are not primitives, they are the raw materials from which experience may construct preferences or utility functions. But are these experiences sufficiently coherent and organized to be expressed as a complete preference system or as a utility function? I cannot affirm that from my own subjective experience.

Should we then abandon preference theory (and with it utility theory) as a basis for economic theory? For some purposes, probably not. When we examine market data, we are seeing data that may largely be produced by habitual behavior, and thus expressive of learned preferences. (This is not to say that there are no deviations from GARP in market data; indeed, Koo's studies used market data. But if the deviations are relatively few, as they were in Koo's study, and if they are unpredictable, then the central tendencies that emerge from that data may reflect approximately consistent preferences. It should be stressed that this is a conjecture, not a fact.) For welfare economics, we may fall back to some extent on the preferences (or utilities) that would be expressed by fully informed choosers, in the hope that an actual shift of policies will be justified by those preferences when the population has had an opportunity to become accustomed to the new status. (We might, however, want to allow a deduction for the cost of learning.) However, when we extend the preference (or utility) hypothesis to suppose that people can express preferences over hypothetical alternatives that they have never experienced, or that people can at 24 know the psychic return to want satisfaction that they will experience from spending retirement income at 80, as the lifecycle hypothesis of saving assumes, we are probably pushing a workable hypothesis too far.

5.4 The Little critique

Executive summary of the section: I. M. D. Little was critical of both compensation tests and social welfare functions, outlining a distinct position that is at once more behaviorist and more subjectivist than his rivals, and which stresses (but does not explain) the importance of distribution.

In 1950 I. M. D. Little's *Critique of Welfare Economics* pointed out the shortcomings both of welfare economics based on compensation tests and of the saltwater school of thought. Little also roundly rejected the idea that real human beings would maximize pleasure or satisfaction, writing[4] (pp. 21–22) "a man may support a wife who makes his life unbearable, and without getting any pleasure from the fact that he may be doing his duty." Nevertheless (p. 37), "Welfare economics, so far as the individual is concerned, is, if it is about anything at all, about states of mind. We therefore must argue from behavior and other objective circumstances to states of mind." Further (pp. 54–55), "No one could 'deny' interpersonal comparisons ... those who 'deny' interpersonal comparisons must deny the existence of other minds." For Little, it seems, economic ideas that are founded on the inability to make interpersonal comparisons of utility, happiness or other states of mind are *only* applicable to a world of zombies! But Little somewhat tentatively identifies individual welfare with happiness. Judgments of happiness are descriptive judgments, not pure value judgments (ch. 4), though they have some valuative aspects or implications. However, these subjective states of mind need have no arithmetic properties that would permit their addition or allow changes in the states of mind to be compared in quantitative terms.

Nevertheless Little rejects the use of preferences and indifference relations along with cardinal utility. Taking Samuelson's "revealed preference" a step further, and assuming that choices are consistent, he refers to the objects constructed via "revealed preference" experiments as proposed by Samuelson, Little himself and Houthakker as "behavior lines" (p. 24). If a change of circumstances allows an individual to move to a higher behavior line, then the outcome he chooses in the new circumstances is chosen over the outcome of the earlier circumstances. This is prima facie evidence that he is happier, i.e. has greater welfare, in the new circumstances. But indifference cannot be observed – if given a choice between two alternatives on the same behavior line, the individual will choose one or another. The behavior line corresponding to a particular point x in the space of alternatives is merely the boundary between alternatives chosen over x and those over which x is chosen.

Little notes (p. 49) that, given the idiosyncrasies of real human beings, we are unlikely ever to be able to say something like "one man is better off and no other man made worse off" quite literally. Rather, he says, economics naturally talks of representative men or representative members of identifiable social groups, such as representative consumers, representative landowners or representative employees in the aluminum refining industry. He suggests that this is as it should be, and a reasonable person might judge the situation improved if representative members of one social group are made better off and no representative member of another social group is made worse off. This seems a valuable point: it does indeed seem that in any case, economics is about representative agents and representative members of particular groups, and this can be no less true of applied than of theoretical economics.

Little pointedly rejects the social welfare function approach, writing (p. 81, note also p. 85) "It is, however, clear that if economists wait for someone to come along and give them a consistent set of value premises they would wait for ever. It is not impossible to anticipate the arrival of such a superman" by investigating the implications of a particular set of value propositions, such as the individualistic value judgment that it is better for an individual to be on a higher behavior line (at a chosen point) ceteris paribus. Pending the arrival of superman, however, an economist who relies on the social welfare function approach can only answer policy questions with "I have no answer until we agree on a social welfare function." Thus, Little will defend what Samuelson called "'twere better" statements as more appropriate for the normative economist. Perhaps indeed "'twere better" for the consulting economist to give answers based on some "'twere better" criterion than to wait for superman before answering at all (note also pp. 114, 123).

But "'twere better" statements based on the compensation tests are not sufficient in themselves either. He notes (p. 87) "In the eyes of utilitarians [a compensation test] amounts to the assumption that £1 yields the same amount of satisfaction to whomsoever it is given, rich or poor. Presumably most people would agree that such an assumption is ridiculous." More generally, no change in policy can be assessed for welfare economics without a value judgment with respect to its impact on the distribution of welfare among the individuals. This leads Little to propose the Little Criterion for an increase in welfare (pp. 108–9; in the 2002 reissue note also pp. viii–ix): "the Scitovsky criterion is sufficient ... for the change to be desirable if the redistribution involved is also good."

Thus, let A and B be two social situations, and a transition from A to B creates a favorable redistribution of welfare and satisfies the Scitovsky criterion, i.e. the losers cannot bribe the gainers to return to situation A and still be better off than they were at B. Then situation B is better than situation A. If only the first test were met, and the Scitovsky test failed, meaning that the losers could overcompensate the gainers for a return to A, then the benefit to those who gain by the transition could be obtained more cheaply by a pure redistribution of purchasing power from the losers to the gainers at B.[5]

All the same, Little seems not quite consistent in this. He never gives us much hint as to how to evaluate the distribution of welfare. Certainly an equal distribution of money income cannot be the criterion (2002 [1950], p. 152). But beyond that we get no positive guidance. Must we wait for superman to come and give us a criterion to judge among distributions of welfare? Many of Little's examples involve the removal of a monopoly. Since removal of the monopoly increases efficiency in these examples, it is quite likely that the Scitovsky test would be passed. The change in distribution could be judged an improvement on either of two grounds, or both: that monopoly profits are "unearned" and so unjust, or that owners of monopoly firms are, on the whole, richer than their customers who pay inflated prices. But is this really any more than anticipating "the arrival of such a superman" by investigating the implications of a particular set of value propositions?[6]

In his committed subjectivism, Little is closer to the utilitarians than to the Kaldor-Hicks or the saltwater school. In the rejection of both utility and indifference fields, however, he is further. There is no inconsistency here – Little's logic is clear enough – but perhaps his view is less coherent. Yet again his admission of happiness as a category for welfare economics, but exclusion of preference and indifference, are suggestive of some incoherence. We shall have to return to the assessment of happiness in a later chapter.

The first edition of Little's critique was received with reviews that ranged from praise to skepticism and even "lampoon" (p. ix). Arrow (1951b) pointed out an error that Little corrected in the 1956 second edition. However, it was the appearance of the second edition that stimulated some further development of Little's ideas. Following a review by Meade (1959), an exchange of comments among some of Little's critics and others contrasted interpretations of Little's criterion and the alternatives to it. In some cases Little's criterion was interpreted in ways that Little himself disagreed with. In the course of this discussion, Mishan (1962) emerged as a defender of "'twere better" judgments in welfare economics, *as Mishan interprets them* (p. 238.) It seems, however, that Mishan gives the Kaldor compensation test a more central place than Little does (Sen 1963). Little tells us (1962a, pp. 229–230) that he gave priority to the Scitovsky criterion in part because it will be satisfied in any case of a move to a Pareto optimum.

5.5 Values: is economics thick?

Executive summary of the section: Little stresses that common terms in economics have both descriptive and valuative meanings. In terms of a later philosophic discussion, they are "thick"; and this discussion reinforces Little's point.

One thing that everyone before Little seems to agree on is that there is a clear dichotomy between judgments of fact and judgments of value, and that it is possible for economics to be kept free of value judgments. Long before Friedman, Pigou had declared economics a "positive science of what is and tends to be, not a normative science of what ought to be" (Pigou 1920, p. 5). Robbins, Kaldor and Hicks advocated for an economics without value judgments, although they believed that such an economics could support advice about public policy. Bergson, Samuelson, Lange and Graaff tell us that value judgments must be explicitly introduced and that they are substantially independent of the economic theory. Little casts doubt on all that. Some subsequent thinking in philosophy supports Little's skepticism and may help us to understand the distinctive ideas of Robbins, Kaldor and Hicks – and the narrow philosophic base of the Saltwater school.

Little dissents from the scientism of both sides in the controversy between the New Welfare Economics and the saltwater school. Particularly in chapter 5, Little stresses the importance of persuasive and valuative language in economics. He considers (2002 [1950], p. 67) a view that "To call someone good is not at all like calling him tall. It [calling him good] does not describe any facts about him." But he rejects it. "The above view is too simple. It may be that I only call a man good when he has certain characteristics, and lacks others. I may have some rough and ready criterion of goodness, and when I say that a man is good, I am, then, partly describing him." "Now, the most important kind of value judgment entering into economics is that which is also descriptive" (p. 69). "Welfare economics and ethics cannot, then, be separated. They are inseparable because the welfare terminology is a value terminology" (pp. 79–80).

The old saw is that "you can't get an ought from an is." Is that indeed true? In a sense no doubt it is: from the viewpoint of modal logic, an "ought," that is an affirmation of a value, is a mode of expression different from an assertion of fact. However, some philosophic discussions of the late twentieth century and the current century have reopened the question. This literature focuses on "thick" concepts. To illustrate a "thick" concept, consider honesty. If we say, "M is honest," we are both describing the behavior of M and evaluating it. Thus, "honest" is a thick concept. (This concept, honesty, has not played any part in the discussions of thick concepts among philosophers, probably because it is rather unproblematic: philosophers understandably tend to focus on more problematic cases.) Let us define "honest behavior" as "behavior that avoids lying and opportunism[7] and keeps commitments and is good and praiseworthy because it does." Thus, a thick concept is one that links an evaluative expression with one that is descriptive or non-evaluative. It is an important aspect of thick concepts that the evaluation is merited *because* the behavior is as it is in non-evaluative terms. The definition needs not be entirely free of ambiguity. If M were a diplomat who tells a lie in order to prevent a war, would we regard him as dishonest or, like other diplomats, "an honest man sent abroad to lie for his country?" And if, having been asked "do my whiskers make me look old?" one were to respond with less than complete candor, might we nevertheless regard him as an honest person? By contrast with "thick" concepts, some valuative concepts are "thin." Terms like "good" and "just" only express a valuation without linking it to the descriptive facts or properties that make the object of praise good or just, and as such they are "thin" evaluative concepts (Eklund, 2011). Other examples in this discussion are adjectives such as "rude" and "chaste." If I say "K is rude," I would be able to inventory his behaviors that I have observed that lead me to describe K as rude. Thus, "K is rude" is a factual and descriptive statement, and if my description of his behavior is mistaken, then it might be false. At the same time, "rude" has a negative valuative loading, and so is a thick term.

Now let us take the definition of "honest" as given, and investigate M's behavior. We find that he does indeed avoid lies and opportunism and keep his commitments. We conclude that his behavior is good and praiseworthy. And it seems, hey presto, we have deduced a value from a fact, gotten an ought from an is. It is this seeming possibility that has attracted much attention to thick concepts and terms that express them. A good deal of the discussion of thick concepts in philosophy has centered on the attempt to show that they do *not* provide any valid way to deduce an ought from an is. A common approach has been to "disentangle" the valuative and non-valuative aspects of thick concepts (e.g. Elstein and Hurka, 2009). This approach treats thick concepts as compounds of a thin evaluation and a non-evaluative description. Suppose, then, that we value honest behavior on rule-utilitarian or social-contractarian grounds, or on the basis of an independent moral intuition. In the first two of these cases, it will be clear that we are not deducing the valuation from the facts of M's behavior. Instead, our deduction is from two premises taken together: one that honest behavior is a kind of behavior that we value, and the second that M's behavior is of that kind. The third possibility, an independent moral intuition,[8] may not be so simply resolved, but if the moral intuition pertains to a definite category that can be described with non-evaluative terms, it can presumably be disentangled from the observation that M's behavior avoids lies and opportunism and keeps commitments.

A response is that we cannot use the word "honest" with linguistic competence without expressing *approval* of the behavior as honest. This will better make the point if in place of "honest" we consider thick terms such as "chaste" and "lewd." If one does not share the restrictive view of permissible sexual behavior expressed by "lewd," is it possible for one to use the word at all? If one cannot use the word without affirming the value, then presumably the answer is no (Gibbard 1992). But perhaps one can nevertheless describe the behavior without expressing any valuation of it by finding a non-valuative term that is equivalent. This might involve such a circumlocution as "behavior that some would consider lewd." The contrary point is that a thick concept cannot even be understood without performing the evaluation to which it refers. That is, one cannot say that a person is or is not chaste without evaluating the person's behavior in terms of the restrictive view of sexual behavior that it expresses – if only in the imagination (Kyle 2017). And it may not be possible to find or define an equivalent, non-valuative term that denotes all those behaviors that are chaste, lewd or honest. The extension of a thick term – that is, to translate from the philosopherese, the set of all those things to which the term refers – may be "shapeless" (Roberts 2011), that is, there may be no finite or even definite series of non-valuative terms that will serve to distinguish it. On this view, the description of the behavior as chaste or honest could be based only on the *evaluation* of it as good and praiseworthy on account of its chastity or honesty. If indeed (at least some) thick terms cannot be disentangled because their descriptive terms are shapeless, this may require us to think of valuation per se in a different way.[9]

Suppose that thick terms can be disentangled. It remains that a person who uses the term "honest" (or "lewd" or "chaste") both makes an assertion of fact and affirms a value that is linked to the facts in that the person sees the facts as meriting the evaluation the thick term evokes, even if he does not endorse the evaluation but performs it only in the imagination or as an act of sympathy. This conveys important information that could be crucial, for example, in deliberation about legislation or to choose a leader. For present purposes it will not matter whether thick terms can be disentangled into compounds of thin evaluations and descriptive clauses: what matters is that in either sense, many terms in economics seem to express thick concepts. It seems that these arguments might indeed be applied to common economic terms such as "efficient," "productive" and "compensation." Can we use these words without performing, if only in the mind, an evaluation that greater efficiency and productivity are good things, ceteris paribus, and some rates of compensation are better than others, in the sense of the thin concept of the good? It seems to have been Little's view that we cannot. It seems pretty clear that Little is saying that terms used in welfare economics are "thick."

Perhaps indeed Little does not go far enough. Consider the following phrase: "I want my breakfast." This is a statement of fact, and may be true or false. On its face, it seems to be incorrigible – that is, it would be nonsense to claim that I am mistaken, and that I don't really want my breakfast. My want is whatever it seems to me to be. "The heart wants what it wants." But this is less clear than it appears,[10] and I might lie about it, and thus the statement might be false. At the same time the statement "I want my breakfast" affirms a value in a certain sense. It says that I would value having my breakfast served, and that there are some things I might give up to obtain it, such as the effort and time to prepare it. To put it another way, "I want my breakfast" asserts as a matter of fact that I affirm a certain value.

Is an expression of a want a "thick" concept? We will see that there are some important differences. "I want my breakfast" is different from "M is honest" in at least three important ways. First, "honest" is an adjective; "want" is a verb. This is why I said above that "I want my breakfast" is factual, not descriptive. Second, "M is honest" asserts a fact about someone else, while "I want my breakfast" asserts a fact about myself. In the thick concepts discussed in the philosophic literature, in general, the non-evaluative part is a statement about something outside the consciousness of the speaker, while in an expression of want the factual assertion is about a subjective state of the speaker. Nevertheless, thick concepts 1) link assertions of fact and values in such a way that the fact is a sufficient condition for the value, and 2) provide information that can be important for coordinated action. Expressions of want share these properties. Thus, it seems appropriate to extend the category of thick concepts to include expressions of want.

But, as we saw in Chapter 2, wants and their satisfactions cannot be separately considered, as a want is a potentiality and the satisfaction is its realization. A want is a statement of a *potential* value: satisfaction is the realization of that potential. Having had my breakfast I may report that my want has been satisfied. The satisfaction is a matter of my own experience that I can report incorrigibly. Now, my neighbor might say, "but all you had was a bagel and coffee – don't you want a nice three-cheese omelet?" But my response, "Oh, a bagel is enough for me – I wouldn't want an omelet this early," if it is not a lie, is an incorrigible expression of both fact and value. A want that seems to me to be satisfied is, just because of the seeming, satisfied. To suggest that I am mistaken in reporting the satisfaction of my want is to say that the way things seem to me is not really the way things seem to me, a bit of patent nonsense. Thus expressions of the satisfaction of want are expressions that are both thick and incorrigible, a powerful contrast to thick terms such as "honest" and "rude." Expressions of want are factual statements that are incorrigible in a way that, for example, an estimate of a market elasticity of demand or of the gravitational constant cannot be.

Could we build a more general system of values on such statements? At the very least, it would appear that something like Pigou's satisfaction utilitarianism could be built up on the basis of want statements and thus share the conjunction of statements of fact and value that we find in "I want my breakfast." The problem then is to put these statements on a scale of more or less, as Pigou notes. It is here that the "psychic return" of want satisfaction – the qualia we experience when the wants are satisfied – are brought into the picture. I leave my armchair to prepare my breakfast because the qualia I experience in satisfying my want for breakfast are qualia I prefer to those I experience when I satisfy my want to continue relaxing in my armchair. For now, we need not claim that these relative values can be measured numerically. What we do observe, which is enough for now, is that these statements of want and of want satisfaction and the judgment that one want is greater than another are all statements of fact that are at the same time affirmation of values both absolute and relative. Perhaps this is what Lord Robbins had in mind in his assertion that (at least some) arguments from introspection are objective. On the other side, everything here seems consistent with the position of Harrod (1938).

Can we find other kinds of statements, not referring to want, that also are in the same way statements of fact and of value? Another candidate would seem to be statements about need. Statements of need are complex statements of fact (McCain 2014, 2017) and often interpreted as also statements of value. Consider, for example, "A human being needs a certain number of calories (depending on individual circumstances) for healthy survival." Every need contains both an objective (in this case healthy survival) and a means of attaining that objective, and both statements are matters of fact. They are not, however, incorrigible – one might well be mistaken about one's needs. If we hold a value that each person's healthy survival ought to be assured, then we may conclude from the statement of need that the calories ought to be provided. But the assertion that each person's healthy survival ought to be assured is not a statement of fact. "Whether human need 'ought' to be met must be established on grounds independent of the 'need' claims themselves" (Taylor 1959, p. 111). To proceed from a factual statement of need to a valuative statement without these independent grounds is precisely the sort of argument that "you can't get an ought from an is" is meant to exclude. The conclusion that the needed calories ought to be provided could be rescued if we believe that, as a matter of fact, all or almost all human individuals want healthy survival and want it more than most other things they want. This is a plausible judgment, but it supports the negative answer to the question we are addressing: no, statements of need do not provide any linking of fact and value without referring also to want. Perhaps some other schema might be found that links fact and value as statements of want do, without any reference to want, but need will not do the job.

So statements of want are statements of value, but whose value? It seems on its face that the only sort of normative system that could be based on such statements would be egoistic and, broadly speaking, hedonistic. But perhaps this prima facie judgment is wrong. Consider in place of "I want my breakfast" the statement "I want world peace."[11] This may be a statement of fact – the phrase "world peace" may need interpretation, but given the interpretation of "world peace," either the heart wants that or it does not. If the phrase "world peace" gives more difficulty than does the phrase "breakfast," there is no difference in our understanding of the "I want" part of the two statements. More relevant to welfare economics would be a statement such as "I want more equality of incomes or welfares among people." To the extent that people want certain values to be realized in the state of the world, it begins to seem that any statement of value is at the same time a statement of fact. But are there crucial differences between "I want my breakfast" and "I want world peace?"

For satisfaction utility, there is a difference. Suppose that international arrangements were changed in such a way that I believe world peace would be assured. (Lord, let it be so!) But my belief might be mistaken. In reporting my belief, I am not reporting my own experience nor values, not reporting any seeming from my experience, but expressing a judgment on the probable consequences of change in international arrangements. It may be that I want world peace because I believe that the utility experienced by many other people as well as myself would be greater in that case, but because their experience is theirs not mine, that can only be a conjecture on my part – however plausible a conjecture – and not a report of my experience. This could provide another dimension of the distinction of economic from non-economic welfare.

Again, statements of want are statements of value, but whose value? They are unavoidably the values of individuals, and so may conflict. Even if they are interpersonally comparable, these experiences cannot be aggregated without some independent value judgment. Utilitarianism provides one such judgment; there may be others. But these individual values cannot be ignored. We may ask what the relative social or ethical significance of one individual's wants is relative to the wants of another individual. However, to assign a social or ethical significance of zero to the wants of any individual seems unavoidably to rule that that individual has no social or ethical significance. A normative economics that ignores individual wants and demands denies that any individual has social or ethical significance. This view may be defensible – it might be defended on theological grounds, perhaps – but in any case it demands a powerful defense, and would clearly be rejected by Pigou and by most other economists.

Now, I submit that thick economic terms such as "efficient," "productive" and "compensation" derive their thickness from their relation to expressions of want. This will be clearest in the case of "efficient" as we understand it in Paretian terms. A change of circumstances is Pareto preferable, increases efficiency, if it enables a person to satisfy wants that would not otherwise be satisfied, while no-one else has wants unsatisfied that would otherwise be satisfied. Thus one cannot use the term with linguistic competence without expressing approval of the change *on the basis of subjective values expressed by some people*. This evaluation may be tentative. To use Pigou's terminology, there may be changes in non-economic welfare that more than offset the benefits to those whose needs are newly satisfied. Nor is this judgment incorrigible. The judgment that no-one has wants that are unsatisfied that would otherwise be satisfied may be a mistaken judgment. As for the term "productive," we recall the extensive literature on the calculation of indices of aggregate production with a view to reliably representing relative want satisfaction. In economics, further, judgments of appropriate rates of compensation will be at least partly based on the need for "incentives." This arises from the following chain of reflections: first, many people will want to limit the efforts they make in productive activity; second, that while a person cannot be mistaken about his wants, he may lie about them; third, that a schedule of compensation may be established that is "incentive compatible" in that it balances the wants of the producer to limit effort against the wants satisfied by the production in a way that will in general be Pareto preferable to compensation schedules that are not incentive compatible. Again, this judgment may be tentative. There may be non-economic values that also enter into the determination of a good schedule of compensation: for example, an independent moral intuition about justice might override the economic evaluation. The fact remains that *there is an economic evaluation*, an evaluation of a compensation schedule that arises from economic reasoning per se, and that is expressed by anyone who uses the phrase "efficient schedule of compensation" or "incentive compatible" with linguistic competence.

One can, of course, deliberately and explicitly use the terms with less than full linguistic competence. That is, a scholar may use a thick term as shorthand for a purely descriptive formal definition or system of axiomata, ignoring the valuative concepts that would be implied if the term were used with linguistic competence. This may be convenient for the investigation of formal properties and consequences of the descriptive content. This is essentially what Samuelson and his followers do (for example) in the theory of revealed preference. But do these conventions give rise to a value-free economics? Or to confusion? It seems that a person committed to the full, thick interpretation of "preference" could without hesitation incorporate what the revealed preference theorists have learned in an economic evaluation of policy based on the thick concept of preference. This will be true just to the extent that the formal definition of preference corresponds validly to the descriptive part of the thick concept of preference. Consider by way of contrast the use of the term "envy" in the literature on ordinal concepts of equity (Foley 1967; Varian 1974). Envy seems a thick term comprising a description of an emotional state that is disapproved. But the definition of "envy" in this literature makes no reference to emotional states. Thus, the use of the thick term "envy" to infer valuations via the formal literature on "envy" would be mistaken. Instead, in this literature valuative conclusions might be, and are, inferred (again) from the thickness of "preference." In the second case, then, formalism arguably produces confusion, but in neither case does it produce value-free "science," and it is hard to see how it could.

It is here that Debbie Roberts' (2011) "shapelessness" might present a problem. If it were not possible formally to define the descriptive behavior as honest until after it had been recognized as valuable for its honesty, then no analysis of the behavior would be possible without explicit normative reference – and presumably that is the point of her argument. But it does not seem likely that thick terms in economics will create any such difficulty. We have, after all, volumes of formal discussion of preference that is criticized, if anything, for being too faithful to thick, intuitive concepts of preference, and a want is a want for something – if the object of a want were shapeless, it would not be a want.

Economic evaluation thus arises from any valid analysis using descriptive terms as conventionally defined for economics. Nevertheless the economic evaluation is tentative and may be incomplete and conditional. It may be incomplete because wants are dependent on the distribution of income, and so without any relative evaluation on distribution, the economic evaluation is indeterminate and as such incomplete. (This we learned inter alia from the criticism of Hicks 1939 and Kaldor 1939 by Scitovsky 1941 and Baumol 1946–1947.) The economic evaluation is tentative because there may be other evaluations, "non-economic values," against which it must be balanced. But this seems no less true of the non-economic evaluations themselves: they must be balanced against one another if they are plural, and in any case must be balanced against the economic evaluation.

5.6 A brief concluding summary

The social welfare function, as developed by Bergson, Samuelson and Lange, is conceptually a step forward from the New Welfare Economics, in that it can in principle give definite answers to questions of better public policies, while the New Welfare Economics in principle cannot. It also subsumes Pigou's utilitarian welfare economics as a special case. However, beyond the special case, it offers no answers in practice, pending the arrival of the superman who can give us the appropriate social welfare function. On the other side, "'twere better" judgments based on compensation tests and community indifference curves could at least give some answers based on an economic evaluation, but these remained inconclusive in the absence of a criterion to judge better and worse distributions of welfare, and that criterion remained at best vague.

Sen (2009, p. 96 et. seq.) distinguishes the "transcendental" approach to social choice theory, that is, an approach that seeks the unique best social state, and a comparative approach, which concentrates on the relative evaluation of a few concrete alternatives, perhaps from more than one (convergent) point of view. It would seem that the social welfare function approach is a transcendental approach, in that sense, while Little and the new welfare economists choose a comparative approach. Sen rejects the transcendental approach. In the context of this chapter, one might argue that both have their shortcomings – that neither is a transcendental best approach.

Notes

1 That is, it is a summation function of the variables determined by the utility functions of individuals, which are in turn determined by the quantities of goods and services consumed by the individuals.
2 In 1950, Samuelson uses the concept of a utility-possibility frontier in an extensive welfare-economic critique of output index numbers, stressing the importance of the concept.
3 Compare the contemporary assessment of Scitovsky (1951).
4 Page numbers refer to the 2002 reissue.
5 While the examples used in discussions of the Kaldor and Scitovsky tests and Little's criterion tended to focus on the removal of monopolies and tariffs, examples continue to arise in ongoing policy debates. Consider, for example, Funt (2017). Funt objects to the pricing of highway use (and in particular to congestion pricing) on the grounds that it victimizes the poor. (He offers no evidence.) He then argues that if highway use is priced, the price should vary according to income, with the rich paying more. The idea that prices should differ by income is of course far from new, and it provides a good illustration of Little's criterion. Suppose we begin with an efficient price for some commodity, and through public policy the price is differentiated by income. We suppose that this improves the distribution of real income, thus passing the first part of Little's criterion. However, once prices are differentiated, the poor who are given low prices can benefit by reselling to the rich who then avoid the higher price. Thus, taking all such "black market" sales together, the rich, having lost by the differentiated price, compensate the poor for a return to uniform pricing: the Scitovsky test, and so also the Little criterion, are failed. This seems to provide a powerful case against policies that lead to "black" and "grey" markets. In Funt's argument, of course, we do not begin from efficient prices, but from an inefficient price, viz. zero. Thus, the imposition of an efficient price or Pigovian tax will generate some revenue, and perhaps a surplus over the ongoing cost of maintaining the facility. This applies also to proposals for a Pigovian tax on carbon emissions (Feldstein et al. 2017; Baker et al. 2017) and possibly to shift the air traffic control system to a fee-based rather than a tax-financed system (Davis 2017). This shift of revenue might be relatively regressive – that would have to be established on the basis of evidence, but is a logical possibility. In the case of user fees for highways, one might expect that it would not increase the burden on the poorest, who would be less likely to travel by car, but also would have little proportional impact on the very richest, while increasing the burden on the lower middle class: in any case, the degree of progressivity or regressivity could certainly differ for different ranges of the income distribution. But it would also depend on the distribution of the surplus. Distribution of the surplus as a social dividend would alleviate and possibly reverse any increase in the regressivity of the revenue system that would be a consequence of the imposition of the efficient price (Feldstein et al. 2017; Baker et al. 2017; Geddes and Nenchev 2013). Thus these proposals would be more likely to pass a compound test such as the Little criterion or especially that of Mishan (which takes efficiency as the first criterion).
6 This is addressed in a more formal way in the appendix to Chapter 8, which uses literature not available to Little in 1949.
7 "Opportunism" is meant here in the sense of the definition in McCain (2015, p. 94).
8 In this section the term "moral intuition" is used uncritically and might be thought of as a brief substitute for the circumlocution "what some report as moral intuitions."
9 Since the resolution of this controversy does not matter for the purposes of this book (and I am untrained in philosophy), I reserve to this footnote my estimation of the arguments made. It does seem to me that "thick" terms can be disentangled.

On the one hand stratagem of "what some could regard as lewd" seems to me sufficient to allow disentangling the thick concept even if the non-evaluative part of the thick concept is shapeless. Just what "some" regard as lewd is, of course, an empirical question. On the other side, if the non-evaluative part of a thick concept is shapeless, it seems to me that it follows that the thick concept has no non-evaluative content – is not thick but, rather, thin and narrow. Non-evaluative "content" that cannot be definitely delimited is not content.

10 Recall the discussion of utilities as qualia in Chapter 2. What Pigou called "the psychic return to the satisfaction" of the wants can be interpreted as particular categories of qualia. The speech act "I want my breakfast" expresses my expectation that my breakfast will give rise to qualia of pleasure, but I could be mistaken in that expectation (compare Armstrong 1939).

11 In a dinner-table conversation, my wife's response to "I want my breakfast" was "Right, and I want world peace and a pony." (In our home the preparation of breakfast has always been my chore.) She has a point: as noted before, it is meaningful to speak of wants that are not likely ever to be satisfied.

References

Afriat, S. (1967) The Construction of a Utility Function from Expenditure Data, *International Economic Review* (Feb) pp. 67–77.

Armstrong, W. E. (1939) The Determinateness of the Utility Function, *Economic Journal* v. 49, no. 195 (Sept) pp. 453–467.

Arrow, Kenneth J. (1951a) *Social Choice and Individual Values* (New York: Wiley).

Arrow, Kenneth J. (1951b) Little's Critique of Welfare Economics, *American Economic Review* v. 41, no. 5 (Dec) pp. 923–934.

Baker, James A., Martin Feldstein, Ted Halstead, N. Gregory Mankiw, Henry M. Paulson, Jr., George P.Schultz, ThomasStephenson and Rob Walton (2017) *The Conservative Case for Carbon Dividends* (Washington, D.C.: Climate Leadership Council).

Baumol, William J. (1946–1947) Community Indifference, *Review of Economic Studies* v. 14, no. 1 pp. 44–48.

Baumol, William J. (1949–1950) The Community Indifference Map: A Construction, *Review of Economic Studies* v. 17, no. 3 pp. 189–197.

Bergson, A. (1938) A Reformulation of Certain Aspects of Welfare Economics, *Quarterly Journal of Economics* (Feb).

Bridgman, Percy Williams (1927) *The Logic of Modern Physics* (New York: Macmillan).

Cox, James C. (1997) On Testing the Utility Hypothesis, *Economic Journal* v. 107, no. 443 (Jul) pp. 1054–1078.

Davis, Julie Hirshfield (2017) Trump Backs Air Traffic Control Privatization, *New York Times* (June 5).

Diaye, Marc-Arthur, Francois Gardes and Christophe Starzec (2008) GARP Violation, Economic Environment Distortions and Shadow Prices: Evidence from Household Expenditure Panel Data, *Annales d'Economie et de Statistique*, no. 90 (Apr–Jun) pp. 3–33.

Eklund, Matti (2011) What Are Thick Concepts? *Canadian Journal of Philosophy* v. 41, no. 1 (March) pp. 25–49.

Elstein, Daniel Y. and Thomas Hurka (2009) From Thick to Thin: Two Moral Reduction Plans, *Canadian Journal of Philosophy* v. 39, no. 4 (Dec) pp. 515–535.

Enke, Stephen (1944) The Monopsony Case for Tariffs, *Quarterly Journal of Economics* v. 58, no. 2 (Feb) pp. 229–245.

Feldstein, Martin S., Ted Halstead and N. Gregory Mankiw (2017) A Conservative Case for Climate Action, *New York Times* (Feb 8) p. 25.

Fevrier, Philippe and Michael Visser (2004) A Study of Consumer Behavior Using Laboratory Data, *Experimental Economics* v. 7, no. 1 (Feb) pp. 93–114.

Foley, Duncan K. (1967) Resource Allocation in the Public Sector, *Yale Economic Essays* v. 7 (Spring) pp. 73–76.

Funt, Peter (2017) Highway Robbery Targets the Poor, *New York Times* (May 17) p. 25.

Geddes, R. Richard and Dimitar N. Nentchev (2013) *Road Pricing and Asset Publicization* (Washington, D.C.: American Enterprise Institute).

Gibbard, Alan (1992) Thick Concepts and Warrant for Feelings, *Proceedings of the Aristotelian Society* v. 66, pp. 267–283.

Harrod, Roy (1938) Scope and Method of Economics, *Economic Journal* v. 48, no. 191 (Sept) pp. 383–412.

Houthakker, H. S. (1950) Revealed Preference and the Utility Function, *Economica, New Series* v. 17, no. 66 (May) pp. 159–174.

Kahn, R. F. (1935) Some Notes on Ideal Output, *Economic Journal* v. 45, no. 177 (Mar) pp. 1–35.

Kaldor, Nicholas (1940) A Note on Tariffs and the Terms of Trade, *Economica, New Series* v. 7, no. 28 (Nov) pp. 377–380.

Koo, Anthony Y. C. (1963) An Empirical Test of Revealed Preference Theory, *Econometrica* v. 31, no. 4 (Oct) pp. 646–664.

Koo, Anthony Y. C. and Georg Hasenkamp (1972) Structure of Revealed Preference: Some Preliminary Evidence, *Journal of Political Economy* v. 80, no. 4 (Jul–Aug) pp. 724–744.

Koo, Anthony Y. C. and Peter Schmidt (1974) Cognitive Range in the Theory of Revealed Preference, *Journal of Political Economy* v. 82, no. 1 (Jan–Feb) pp. 174–179.

Kyle, Brent G. (2017) Thick Concepts, *Internet Encyclopedia of Philosophy*, available at: www.iep.utm.edu/thick-co/, as of July 1, 2017.

Lange, Oskar (1936) On the Economic Theory of Socialism: Part One, *Review of Economic Studies* v. 4, no. 1 (Oct) pp. 53–71.

Lange, Oskar (1937) On the Economic Theory of Socialism: Part Two, *Review of Economic Studies* v. 4, no. 2 (Feb) pp. 123–142.

Lange, Oscar (1942) The Foundations of Welfare Economics, *Econometrica* v. 10, pp. 215–228.

Lerner, Abba P. (1932) The Diagrammatical Representation of Cost Conditions in International Trade, *Economica*, no. 37 (Aug) pp. 346–356.

Little, I. M. D. (1949a) A Reformulation of the Theory of Consumers' Behavior, *Oxford Economic Papers*, pp. 90–99.

Little, I. M. D. (1949b) The Foundations of Welfare Economics, *Oxford Economic Papers, New Series* v. 1, no. 2 (Jun) pp. 227–246.

Little, I. M. D. (1962) Welfare Criteria: An Exchange of Notes: A Comment, *Economic Journal* v. 72, no. 285 (Mar) pp. 229–231.

Little, I. M. D. (2002 [1950]) *A Critique of Welfare Economics*, 2nd Edition (Oxford: Clarendon).

Mattei, Aurelio (2000) Full-scale Real Tests of Consumer Behavior Using Experimental Data, *Journal of Economic Behavior and Organization* v. 43, no. 4 (Dec) pp. 487–497.

McCain, Roger A. (2014) Why Need Is "a Word We Cannot Do Without" in Economics, *Forum for Social Economics* v. 43, no. 2 pp. 181–196.

McCain, Roger A. (2015), *Game Theory and Public Policy*, 2nd Edition (Cheltenham: Edward Elgar).

McCain, Roger A. (2017) *Approaching Equality: What Can Be Done about Wealth Inequality* (Cheltenham: Edward Elgar).

Meade, J. E. (1945) Mr. Lerner on the "Economics of Control", *Economic Journal* v. 55, no. 217 (Apr) pp. 47–69.

Meade, J. E. (1959) Review: A Critique of Welfare Economics, by I. M. D. Little, *Economic Journal* v. 69, no. 273 (March) pp. 124–129.

Meier, G. M. (1949) The Theory of Comparative Costs Reconsidered, *Oxford Economic Papers, New Series* v. 1, no. 2 (Jun) pp. 199–216.

Mishan, E. J. (1952) The Principles of Compensation Reconsidered, *Journal of Political Economy* v. 60, no. 4 (Aug) pp. 312–322.

Mishan, E. J. (1962) Welfare Criteria: An Exchange of Notes: A Comment, *Economic Journal* v. 72, no. 285 (Mar) pp. 234–244.

Mishan, E. J. (1973) Welfare Criteria: Resolution of a Paradox, *Economic Journal* v. 83, no. 331 (Sep) pp. 747–767.

Mishan, E. J. (1982) The New Controversy about the Rationale of Economic Evaluation, *Journal of Economic Issues* v. 16, no. 1 (Mar), pp. 29–47.

Modigliani, Franco and R. E. Brumberg (1954) Utility Analysis of the Consumption Function, *Post-Keynesian Economics*, edited by K. K. Kurihara (New Brunswick, N.J.: Rutgers University Press) pp. 388–436.

Pigou, A. C. (1920) *Economics of Welfare* (London: Macmillan).

Roberts, Debbie (2011) Shapelessness and the Thick, *Ethics* v. 121, no. 3 (April) pp. 489–520.

Samuelson, Paul A. (1937a) A Note on Measurement of Utility, *Review of Economic Studies* v. 4, no. 2 (Feb) pp. 155–161.

Samuelson, Paul A. (1937b) Some Aspects of the Pure Theory of Capital, *Quarterly Journal of Economics* v. 51, no. 3 (May) pp. 469–496.

Samuelson, Paul A. (1938a) A Note on the Pure Theory of Consumer's Behaviour, *Economica, New Series* v. 5, no. 17 (Feb) pp. 61–71.

Samuelson, Paul A. (1938b) The Empirical Implications of Utility Analysis, *Econometrica* v. 6, no. 4 (Oct) pp. 344–356.

Samuelson, Paul A. (1948) Consumption Theory in Terms of Revealed Preference, *Economica, New Series* v. 15, no. 60 (Nov) pp. 243–253.

Samuelson, Paul A. (1950) Evaluation of Real National Income, *Oxford Economic Papers, New Series* v. 2, no. 1 (Jan) pp. 1–29.

Samuelson, Paul A. (1953) *Foundations of Economic Analysis* (Cambridge, Mass.: Harvard University Press).

Samuelson, Paul A. (1956) Social Indifference Curves, *Quarterly Journal of Economics* v. 70, no. 1 (Feb) pp. 1–27.

Samuelson, Paul A. (1998) How Foundations Came to Be, *Journal of Economic Literature* v. 36, no. 3 (Sep) pp. 1375–1386.

Scitovsky, Tibor de (1941) A Note on Welfare Propositions in Economics, *Review of Economic Studies* v. 9, pp. 77–88.

Scitovsky, Tibor de (1942) A Reconsideration of the Theory of Tariffs, *Review of Economic Studies* v. 9, no. 2 (Summer) pp. 89–110.

Sen, Amartya K. (1963) Distribution, Transitivity and Little's Welfare Criteria, *Economic Journal* v. 73, no. 292 (Dec) pp. 771–778.

Sen, Amartya (2009) *The Idea of Justice* (Cambridge, Mass.: Belknap Press).

Sippel, Reinhard (1997) An Experiment on the Pure Theory of Consumer Behavior, *Economic Journal* v. 107, no. 444 (Sep) pp. 1431–1444.

Taylor, Paul W. (1959) "Need" Statements, *Analysis* v. 19, no. 5 (Apr) pp. 106–111.

Tintner, Gerhard (1946) A Note on Welfare Economics, *Econometrica* v. 14, no. 1 (Jan) pp. 69–78.

Vanek, Jaroslav (1964) A Rehabilitation of "Well-Behaved" Social Indifference Curves, *Review of Economic Studies* v. 31, no. 1 (Jan) pp. 87–89.

Varian, Hal R. (1982) The Nonparametric Approach to Demand Analysis, *Econometrica* v. 50, no. 4 (Jul) pp. 945–973.

6 Utility and welfare

Further development

By 1950, many details both of the New Welfare Economics and the social welfare function approach had been clarified, though much remained to be done. This discussion was to continue despite the contemporaneous emergence of issues that posed new questions both about the foundations and the applicability of welfare economics of either school (and which will be considered in Chapter 7). At the same time welfare economics assumed a more influential role within the profession of economics and, to the extent that economic theory is influential beyond its ivory tower, in the wider world of policy. This to a considerable extent reflected events outside economics: the increasing recognition of environmental problems as real problems beyond the competence of the market system. To a considerable extent, though, this golden age was a result of further contributions from saltwater economists, that is, in particular, Paul Samuelson, J. de V. Graaff and Francis Bator. There were refinements also in the "'twere better" approaches founded on Kaldor, Hicks, Scitovsky and Little tests and in the application of community indifference curves. Before turning to those developments, however, we consider the emergence of game theory and revisit the cardinalist-ordinalist controversy.

6.1 Von Neumann, Morgenstern and the measurement of utility

Executive summary of the section: A measure of utility based on probabilistic prospects was proposed by von Neumann and Morgenstern. While it is not clear that their concept is relevant to welfare economics, it made the ordinalist claim that numerical utility has no behavioral consequences indefensible.

In 1944, the first edition of the Great Book that founded modern game theory, *Theory of Games and Economic Behavior*, by John von Neumann and Oskar Morgenstern, appeared. In the first chapter was a proposal for the measurement of utility by probabilistic assessment of alternative risky prospects. Thus, for the purposes of this book, the most immediate and direct impact was on the cardinalist-ordinalist controversy. The max min solution for two-person, zero-sum games also had some impact, as we will see. The influence of game theory on welfare economics more generally is less clear, and will be discussed in a speculative way.

The approach of von Neumann and Morgenstern to measurement of utility is now widely familiar. We consider a choice between a certain payment A and a risky prospect comprising a probability p of payment B and (1-p) of payment C, with C>A>B. (Alternatively A, B and C could be commodity bundles, with C preferred to A preferred to B, but treating A, B and C as money payments gives us the utility of money income, at least ceteris paribus.) Now adjust p so that the person is indifferent between the risky prospect and the certain one. Then p is a measure of the utility of A that is unique up to a linear transformation. That is, von Neumann and Morgenstern write (1944, p. 18),

> If he now prefers A to the 50-50 combination of B and C, this provides a plausible base for the numerical estimate that his preference of A over B is in excess of his preference of C over A. If this standpoint is accepted then there is a criterion with which to compare the preference of C over A with the preference of A over B. *It is well known* that thereby utilities – or rather differences in utilities – become numerically measurable.
>
> (Emphasis added)

It was well known from the arguments of Lange (1934) and Zeuthen (1937) in the cardinal-ordinal controversy discussed above in Chapter 4. Von Neumann and Morgenstern go on to reject the indifference curve approach (p. 19) as implying "either too much or too little." Marschak (1950) would go on to establish that a rational person with consistent preferences over probabilistic prospects could only act as if maximizing the expected value of a utility function that would be unique up to a linear transformation. Alchian (1953) explained all this with extensive numerical examples.

What is not clear is that the utility function derived by von Neumann, Morgenstern and Marschak had anything to do with welfare economics. As we will see in Section 6.2, some cardinalists thought not, as did most ordinalists. The issues are summarized in Harsanyi (1953) which will be discussed in a future chapter. Harsanyi would argue that von Neumann-Morgenstern utility *is* relevant to welfare economics, but on grounds that would have little influence for a generation.

It may be useful to think of risk aversion (and risk loving) in terms of qualia. For this purpose it is important that any risky prospect is extended over time, and more than one distinct qualia may be associated with different periods within that elapse of time. Initially, the risky prospect is contemplated and the decision is made to undertake it. There will be qualia associated with this – what is it like to make the decision? Indeed, even when the alternatives are certain, there will be a quale associated with the commitment to one alternative or the other, and it may be a pleasant or an unpleasant quale. If it is unpleasant we have decision aversion. The possibility of decision aversion or decision loving does not seem to have been considered in economics, but if decision aversion is widespread we might infer some friction or inertia in markets, and perhaps widespread decision loving (shopaholism?) would tend to create instability. If decision qualia are particularly unpleasant when the outcome is uncertain, this could contribute to risk-averse behavior. Following the moment of commitment, there is a period during which the outcome remains uncertain. (In a casino this may be quite brief; in the case of a business decision it might be quite protracted.) Finally there is the moment when the uncertainty is resolved, and the gambler is a winner or a loser. Qualia may be associated with both periods. While the prospect remains uncertain, the person may find it pleasurable to contemplate the possibility of being a winner or unpleasant to contemplate the threat of loss. When the uncertainty is resolved, there may be the elation of victory or depression at a loss. Finally the winnings may be spent to satisfy the winner's wants, or the loss may impair the gambler's ability to do so. It is only the qualia realized or prevented at this last stage that are Pigovian want-satisfaction utilities. Nevertheless, qualia associated with the second stage and the elation of winning or the depression of losing will influence a *rational* decision to take or not take the risk. A decision based only on the want-satisfaction utilities of spending or being unable to spend, ignoring these other experiences of gambling, could be ever so calculating and careful – and nevertheless irrational! This deserves one qualification. Gambling in a casino or a lottery may enable the individual to avoid the unpleasant qualia of boredom, and thus satisfy a want for stimulation (Scitovsky 1976). This qualification does not reverse but reinforces the following conclusion: skeptics about the von Neumann-Morgenstern utility measurement were quite right to doubt that a cardinal utility function relevant to welfare economics could be recovered by observing decisions among risky prospects.

Nevertheless von Neumann and Morgenstern had put the cat among the ordinalist pigeons. They had made it impossible for ordinalists to hold that cardinally measured utility has no behavioral implications without showing themselves out of date. However hesitant we are to identify von Neumann-Morgenstern utility with the utility Pigou had postulated, surely no one familiar with von Neumann and Morgenstern's result could endorse Allen's (1935, p. 115) assertion that numerical utility "cannot be expressed in terms of the individual's acts of choice." It had been known since Pigou that behavior under risk would be influenced by the diminishing marginal utility of money, and Zeuthen had reiterated the point, but these could be overlooked before von Neumann and Morgenstern without seeming backward. But no longer. Further, the independence of events in an expected-value formulation impose a form of additive separability, so that there could be no problem of integration in the determination of the preference function over the uncertain prospects nor, consequently, in the determination of the utility function over certain prospects.

The influence of game theory on welfare economics more generally has seemed to be slight. Perhaps the growing influence of game theory is one reason why welfare economics has receded into the background: in particular, the influence of Nash's (1950) extension of von Neumann and Morgenstern's solution for two-person zero-sum games to general games – that is, non-cooperative game theory – has become something of an all-purpose justification for government action in the economy. The argument is thus: *in given circumstances Nash equilibria are inefficient, thus government action is needed to change the rules of the game or guide individual choices to an efficient allocation, and nothing more needs be said.* But, on the contrary, a good deal more needs to be said. When we say that Nash equilibria are inefficient, we are saying that a non-equilibrium outcome Pareto dominates the equilibrium, thus retracing the steps of the New Welfare Economics. Are we then to substitute a cooperative solution to the game for a social welfare function? Well, which cooperative solution: the von Neumann-Morgenstern solution set, the Nash bargain or some generalization of it, the core or the Shapley value or the kernel or the nucleolus? We see that the indeterminacy of the social welfare function is reproduced. Further, like the Paretian optimum (of which they are refinements) the von Neumann-Morgenstern solution set and the core can have very many members, and the core may be null. In any case, all depend on bargaining power, if only in the form of outside options. McCain (2015, p. 68) argues that in public policy, non-cooperative game theory is useful for diagnosis but not for prescription. Game theory might be more useful for prescription if it absorbed more from welfare economics than the Pareto ordering.

6.2 Utility and all that

Executive summary of the section: Remarkably, in the early 1950s cardinalist economists felt able to declare their victory over the ordinalist school. The discussion that followed displayed the exhaustion of both sides in this venerable controversy.

In the retrospect of more than 60 years, it would seem that the advocates of cardinal utility conceptions were on the defensive in the late 1940s and early 1950s. Nevertheless, it was possible for Dennis Robertson, in his presidential address to the Royal Economic Society (1949), to express confidence that the controversy had been resolved in favor of cardinalism. After being "chastised" by Samuelson (Robertson 1952, p. 26) Robertson presented lectures that would be published in the journal *Manchester School* and subsequently (1952) as the lead essay in a book collecting Robertson's writing. The lectures, the book and this section of the present chapter bear the same title: *Utility and All That*. (I am told that this is a "play" on *1066 and All That*, a satirical history of England published in 1930.)

Robertson begins by declaring himself an idiot, at least where mathematical methods are concerned. It might seem that he was being a bit coy, and while that would fit a writing style that is always pleasant and amusing, some apparent misunderstandings do occur (e.g. 1952, pp. 26–27). Robertson begins by briefly recalling Pigou's ideas, with which his only disagreement is minor and terminological. He then points out the argument of Lange that comparison of the degree of preference of A over B with that of B over C would lead to a numerical measure of utility (p. 18) before reviewing the ordinalist position. He then takes note, with some sympathy, of Armstrong's position (p. 22) which, however, he does not quite accept (pp. 27–28) and which he links, oddly, to the von Neumann-Morgenstern approach (p. 28). With respect to von Neumann and Morgenstern he says they "seem to me to have done as much harm as good to the cause to which they have lent their distinguished aid." That is because risk aversion would confound the measurement of utility by risky prospects. He then criticizes all the "tweedledums and tweedledees" of the ordinalist New Welfare Economics and their ordinalist critics, and recognizing that "the juice of mentality seems to be uncommonly hard to keep squeezed out" (pp. 21–22), he essentially invites all to do the easy and natural thing and rejoin the "cardinal club."

In the discussion that followed, Charles Kennedy (1954) raised issues about the meaning of magnitude and measurement, drawing on the ideas of Bertrand Russell. He writes (p. 13) "Thus we shall hold that utility is a quantity, i.e. has magnitude; that it is indivisible; and that two utilities when added together do not yield another utility." He then goes on to discuss Armstrong's (1939) ideas, with which he expresses some sympathy but suggests that Armstrong has failed to distinguish between magnitudes per se and magnitudes having arithmetic properties; and (p. 15) to reject Lange's argument from the comparability of changes in utility to measurability of utility on the grounds that the differences in utility could be magnitudes that are not susceptible to addition. Further (p. 17), if the increments of utility of one person cannot be added, then it is hardly to be expected that one person's increment of utility can be added to that of another person, or subtracted from it. On this score, Little is not excused (pp. 17–18) for all his skepticism, nor are Bergson and Samuelson for all their care (p. 18.) Despite all this, Kennedy is able to conclude, concurring with Robertson, that Pigou's program can be recovered, redistribution and all (pp. 19–20).

A key to all this seems to be the indivisibility of experience, and here again something like qualia seem to come on stage. Had Kennedy written "Thus we shall hold that utilities are qualia, that qualia are indivisible; and that two qualia when added together do not yield another quale," the same idea seems to be expressed in the different terminology. And if utilities are qualia, Kennedy presents a real problem. Even if commodities are divisible and additive (and exceptional cases where they are not are not hard to find) the experiences they arouse in us are not. If I make my omelet with three eggs rather than two, my experience of it is not 50 percent greater, though it is different and may be better (or worse). But I suggest that Kennedy has missed the point of Pigou's and Marshall's "measuring rod of money." However indivisible experience may be, a "revealed preference" procedure along the lines of Samuelson, Little and Houthakker can supply us with a ranking of *commodity bundles* that is expressible in numbers as an index utility function. (If Little is right, real numbers may not be sufficient: infinitesimals, Robinson 1974, may be necessary to capture the ranking of choices along one of Little's behavior lines.) It is true that this numerical expression is indeterminate. To make it determinate we need a function of the marginal utility of money. Since moreover money is divisible and subject to all manner of arithmetical manipulations, this gives us all we need for meaningful marginal utility and equal increments of utility. Armstrong and von Neumann and Morgenstern give us hints along that line. Increments of utility do not (as Allen 1935 first observed) give us interpersonal comparison, to be sure. For that we return (with Pigou) to the reasonable assumption that the qualia aroused in different persons by the same acts of consumption in similar circumstances are commensurate. It is not necessary that qualia be divisible, since money is.

Lionel Robbins (1953) joined this discussion with a passing concession:

> Professor Robertson ... informs us that to be an ordinalist you must refuse to believe in the possibility of the judgment of differences. That is to say, that while I may say I prefer A to B and B to C, I may not say that my preference for A over B is greater than my preference for B over C, for that involves the possibility of cardinal measurement. I confess that I find this very difficult to swallow. If it is true ... I will cheerfully consent to be called a cardinalist. For I am quite sure that I can and do judge differences. The proposition that my preference for the Rembrandt over the Holbein is less than my preference for the Holbein over, let us say, a Munnings, is perfectly intelligible to me.
>
> (p. 104)

At this point, he (like Kennedy) calls on the indivisibility of experience (and wanders a bit off the question). All the same, Robbins remains firmly subjectivist in a sense that is contrary to behaviorism (p. 102). Indeed, he laments,

> It will surely come to be regarded as a paradox in the history of thought that, just at a period when the problems of economic dynamics were beginning to be successfully tackled by methods which can properly be described as extensions of the subjective theory of value, there should have developed a tendency to restate the statical foundations in terms which deliberately eschew any reference to the subjective at all.
>
> (p. 102)

Many of his passages echo his famous *Essay* clearly. He also is consistent in his narrow conception of economics (p. 111):

I confess that it has sometimes occurred to me that, for students, too exclusive an attention to the subject ... may sometimes run the danger of consequences which we should all agree to be unfortunate – immediately ... a naive belief that most, if not all, of the solutions to modern problems were to be found within its ambit; and later, when disillusionment has super-vened, a habit, most disconcerting to one's fellows, of rediscovering the most crashing truisms of politics and history and leaping from the bath, so to speak, with Archimedean enthusiasm, running naked through the city recommending them stridently to all and sundry.

That might seem prophetic, had he not seen it as a danger in Robertson's approach particularly.

Robbins also (p. 104) invites Hicks to clarify the issue of the comparability of increments of utility. This Hicks did (1954). He asserts (p. 155) that incre-ments of money offered for indivisible items tell us nothing about increments of utility and (p. 157) that "cardinal utility [is] always, of necessity, irrelevant to ... actual behavior." This, ten years after von Neumann and Morgenstern (and 17 years after Zeuthen and 42 years after Pigou).

Contemporarily, Marcus Fleming (1952) reconstructed utilitarian welfare economics based on explicit ethical postulates in a form general enough to encompass hedonism and preference utilitarianism as well as satisfaction uti-litarianism. Fleming relies on the comparability of increments of utility, somewhat along the lines of Lange's argument, though the increments in this case are infinitesimal: that is, Fleming argues backward from comparable marginal utility to comparable total utility. His thinking allows for the passage of time – something of a step forward – but not for uncertainty in any prob-abilistic sense, and there is no reference to von Neumann and Morgenstern nor to Marschak. Fleming's focus is clearly on the quality of subjective experience, and had Kennedy been aware of Fleming's ideas he might well have addressed his doubts based on the indivisibility of experience to Fleming's work as well. Daniel Ellsberg (1954), later to become famous in connection with the Penta-gon Papers, was a Fulbright Scholar at Cambridge when he extracted from his undergraduate senior thesis at Harvard a contrast of "Classical and Current Notions of 'Measurable Utility.'" Relying on concepts of operationalism he argues that they are simply different concepts.

Robertson (1954) rejoins the discussion with remarks that extend as well to some other contemporary writings. As for Kennedy's comments, Robertson renews his offer to welcome Kennedy into the Cardinal Club, but simply dis-misses any issue of magnitudes that do not admit of arithmetic operations (pp. 668–9). He tells us that Robbins has just missed his point, and concurs with Hicks on that (p. 668). But he quite misses the point (that I, at least, find in both of them) about the indivisibility of experience. He reiterates and extends his doubts that von Neumann and Morgenstern have enriched the cardinalist position, giving voice to the common-sense idea that the utility of gambling per se can (and must) be distinguished from the utility of acts of consumption that satisfy wants (p. 674). Perhaps, had he been more attentive to Kennedy and Robbins, Robertson might have appealed to indivisible distinct experiences (qualia) of undertaking risks and consuming goods and services that satisfy wants, and used that indivisibility – with or without addition – to make the distinction needed.

However we score this contest, it is the last hurrah for both sides. From this point on, Pigou's satisfaction utilitarianism will not play much part in the development of economics, nor will Robbins' principled subjectivism. Does this mean that the ordinalist side won? After all, it is the economics of Hicks and Allen that we teach in intermediate economic theory. On the other hand, a modern economist will not cavil to assume a cardinal utility function and the maximization of the expected value of utility if those assumptions are helpful, as in the microfoundations of the dynamic stochastic general equilibrium approach in macroeconomics. (Samuelson had, as we noted in a previous chapter, shown that a lifecycle theory of saving entails measurement of utility.) We make the assumptions that will address the problem we mean to solve, and do it in a mathematically tractable way. Cardinal utility has not quite lost its role in welfare economics, though the direction, as a whole, will be quite different.

6.3 More saltwater contributions to welfare economics

Executive summary of the section: Further writing by Samuelson, Graaff and Bator set the stage for something like a golden age of welfare economics.

In papers published in the 1950s, Samuelson extended ordinal welfare economics to a case largely neglected since Mill wrote:

> it is a proper office of government to build and maintain lighthouses, establish buoys, &c. for the security of navigation: for since it is impossible that the ships at sea which are benefited by a lighthouse, should be made to pay a toll on the occasion of its use, no one would build lighthouses from motives of personal interest, unless indemnified and rewarded from a compulsory levy made by the state. There are many scientific researches,

that similarly merit government support. In two papers Samuelson (1954, 1955) introduces a theory of public or collective consumption goods. Samuelson's (1954) model is highly idealized, in that it assumes there are only two kinds of goods, (pure) private goods and (pure) public goods. The latter are distinguished by the fact that they are non-rival: "each individual's consumption of such a good leads to no subtraction from any other individual's consumption of that good" (1954, p. 387). These are incorporated in a scheme that is otherwise the welfare economics Samuelson had set out in the *Foundations*. The novelty is a set of conditions that, for each collective consumption good, the sum of the individual marginal rates of substitution relative to a private-good numeraire must be equal to the marginal rate of transformation of that public good from the numeraire good. In Samuelson (1955) he gives a more extensive diagrammatic exposition that (as he acknowledges) owes something to Lindahl (1919) and Musgrave (1939). (According to Johansen 1963, Lindahl's conception of the optimum supply differs from Samuelson's.)

In the same issue as Samuelson's diagrammatic exposition, Margolis (1955), in a comment on the earlier paper, raises what would be a key criticism of Samuelson's theory: that the definition of a public good is so strict that few if any such goods are likely to be found, including some government services that most would think of as "public goods" in terms of common language. This was to be a subject of continuing discussion for 20 years, with Mishan (1969) providing a mathematically rigorous account of the optimum conditions for a range of intermediate cases. While Mishan's account assumes maximization of a social welfare function much along the line of Lange or Samuelson (p. 343), he relies mainly on a language of "marginal valuations" reminiscent of Pigou. He identifies the individual "valuation" with the compensating variation for the introduction of the good (Mishan 1969, footnote p. 331).

A comprehensive statement of the Bergson-Samuelson approach to welfare economics came from J. de V. Graaff (1957), in the book *Theoretical Welfare Economics*. He begins with a discussion of "technological" optima, that is, conditions such that it is not possible to increase the output of one product without reducing the output of another. "External effects" are allowed for, but Pigovian taxes rejected as inadequate because of such complications as indivisibilities and corner solutions (pp. 24–32). Graaff stresses that the economic assumptions are derived from "behavioralist" observations, and on that ground excludes any assumption of time preference (p. 40). The utility-possibility frontier is derived (p. 60) and related to technical progress (p. 65) and to the phenomena that would come to be known as efficiency wages (p. 60). A social welfare function is used to derive the global optimum and it is stressed that it is only at this point that the marginal equalities are relevant (p. 60).

Perhaps the most important step forward for Graaff's work is the subject of chapter 5, feasible welfare. Here Graaff defines the feasibility frontier, that is, the outer boundary of all utilities that can be attained from the status quo by policies that are understood as feasible. For example, it had long been understood that lump-sum redistributions are not actually feasible, both because information to base them on would not be available and because only random redistributions or capitation taxes or grants would be perceived by the individuals in the system as lump sum. By contrast, a progressive income tax is feasible, but violates the marginal equalities required for efficiency. Graaff's feasibility frontier takes these inefficiencies implied by feasible policies into account and so is generally below the utility-possibility frontier. But it should be stressed that the feasibility considered here is NOT political feasibility, a concept that is "so flexible" that it would make the feasibility frontier a useless concept (p. 60). In the chapters that follow in Graff's book, applications and limitations of the analysis are considered.

In 1957 and 1958, Francis Bator made two contributions which perhaps more than any others established welfare economics as the standard for normative economics for the decades that followed. In "The Simple Analytics of Welfare Maximization" (1957), Bator gave an exposition of the Bergson-Samuelson-Lange models in terms of two individuals, two products – apples and nuts – and two factors of production. Bator first derives a production possibility frontier from the isoquants for the production functions for the two products, using an Edgeworth box-like construction (p. 24). The exchange Edgeworth box is imbedded in the production-possibility frontier to demonstrate the conditions for a Pareto optimum (p. 25). These conditions are used to derive the utility-possibility frontier as the outer envelope of the utility-possibility frontiers for the different feasible vectors of nuts and apples produced (p. 27). Finally, the utility-possibility frontier is confronted with iso-welfare curves to display the global optimum and (crucially!) to demonstrate visually that apart from the global optimum, a Pareto optimum can be inferior to infinitely many situations that are not Pareto optimal. (Note especially pp. 29, 35.) A variety of complications are discussed, including corner solutions, where Bator is able to draw on linear programming (p. 46).

Externalities had returned to the attention of economists in the form of essays by Meade (1952) and Scitovsky (1954), both of which discussed distinctions among different kinds of externalities. Meade, in particular, distinguishes externalities that arise from unpriced factors of production from externalities that "create an atmosphere" (1952, p. 56). In "The Simple Analytics," neither externalities nor public goods are discussed except in passing. In "The Anatomy of Market Failure" (1958), Bator's objective is "to explore and order those phenomena which cause even errorless profit- and preference-maximizing calculation in a stationary context of perfect (though limited) information and foresight to fail to sustain Pareto-efficient allocation." This is market failure as Bator understands it. He defines (pp. 353–354) five cases of market failure: cases in which no market equilibrium exists ("failure of existence"), cases where the efficient prices do not correspond to profit maxima ("failure by signal"), or do not support positive profits for all efficient producers ("failure by incentive"), cases of monopoly and imperfect competition ("failure by structure") or cases in which some inputs or outputs are not priced ("failure by enforcement"). At p. 358 he writes:

> In its modern version, the notion of external economies ... belongs to a more general doctrine of 'direct interaction.' Such interaction, whether it involves producer–producer, consumer–consumer, producer–consumer, or employer–employee relations, consists in interdependences that are external to the price system, hence unaccounted for by market valuations. Analytically, it implies the nonindependence of various preference and production functions. Its effect is to cause divergence between private and social cost-benefit calculation.

He illustrates this with an adaptation of an example of Meade's, involving "direct interaction" between beekeeping and apple orchards, where the bees pollenate the apple blossoms. Bator considers the account of externalities due to Ellis and Fellner: "'the divorce of scarcity from effective ownership'" (p. 361). While granting that this has a certain logic, he observes that it really refers to only the fifth category of market failure, "failure by enforcement." He then presents another taxonomy, this one of *externalities*. These include cases of an unpriced commodity, with market failure by enforcement, illustrated by the case of apple orchards and beekeepers, cases in which the technical conditions for efficient production cannot be realized, such as increasing returns to scale, and "public good externalities," writing (p. 370) "Here the notion is of relevance because much externality is due precisely to the 'public' qualities of a great many activities." Thus, Bator subsumes Samuelson's public goods to the more general category of externalities, and that in turn to the still broader category of market failure. In subsuming public goods to externality and market failure, Bator neutralized the most pointed criticism of Samuelson's public goods, that it is a polar case and a quite uncommon one.

By making the Bergson-Samuelson welfare economics and its criticism of Pareto optimality accessible to an audience of contemporary trained, but not mathematical economists, and by creating the category of market failure that both incorporates externality and public goods and, potentially, other cases, Bator set the stage for the New Welfare Economics to assume its greatest influence in the latter twentieth century. Another key influence was the emergence of environmental pollution as a key social and political issue. Economists were not particularly leaders in this (though Galbraith 1958 sounded the alarm). However, with environmental issues to address, welfare economics was no longer "a hammer looking for a nail" but a key tool for environmental economics (e.g. Ayres and Kneese 1969). The category of market failure "by signal," briefly as it was mentioned, opens economics to the study of the consequences of asymmetrical information (Arrow 1963; Akerlof 1970), a crucially important market pathology that does not seem to have been imagined by economists before 1960. All in all, Bator's work defines the triumphal moment for mid-century welfare economics.

6.4 Compensation tests and community indifference curves yet again

Executive summary of the section: Ideas based on the compensation tests and community indifference curves were refined in debates that arose following the second edition of Little's critique.

By the late 1950s, it had become generally accepted that lump-sum redistributions would not be feasible in practice. Samuelson (1953) had asserted the infeasibility of lump-sum redistributions, and this point is stressed by

Graaff (1957). This would immediately invalidate a compensation test that relies on *actual* compensation by lump-sum transfers, since indeed the compensations could not be actual. Arguably, though, this would not undermine the Kaldor test, precisely because Kaldor does not assume that compensations actually are paid. On this view, the compensation is wholly hypothetical, and the state following both the shift of government policy and the compensation is a "notional" (Meade 1959, p. 126) state only. On the other hand, Kaldor assures us that, if the government feels compensation is appropriate, then the government will redistribute accordingly. This assurance might be less persuasive if the compensation could not actually be carried out.

These issues arose in the discussion following Meade's (1959) review of the second edition of Little's critique (Robertson 1962; Meade 1962; Little 1962a, 1962b; Mishan 1962, 1963, 1965; Kennedy 1963). In addition to some doubts about the use of compensation tests where compensation is infeasible, it became clear that even where both the Kaldor and Scitovsky tests are used, and a distributional test as Little suggests is also applied, contradictions and cycles can be observed. These problems arise where partial utility-possibility frontiers (that is, frontiers for a given basket of goods available to society as a whole) intersect. Alternatively – following Samuelson's observation that the utility-possibility frontiers and community indifference curves are mathematical duals, the cycles are observed where community indifference curves intersect. Eventually, Mishan (1973) – a steady defender of compensation tests – resolved the issue by a discussion that relied precisely on the intersection of community indifference curves. He writes (p. 755) "In general then, there will be a pencil of exchange-efficient community indifference curves passing through point Q_1, none of which are Pareto comparable inasmuch as each such curve corresponds to a distinct distribution of Q_1 as between persons A and B." Taking an example of two assortments of goods, Q_1 and Q_2, which lie on intersecting community indifference curves that would give rise to a cycle, he demonstrates that a third collection Q_3 can be found such that the distributions that generate the intersecting community indifference curves are both found on the contract curve corresponding to Q_3. Indeed that assortment Q_3 is exactly the assortment of consumer goods at which the indifference curves intersect. But it follows that, since the distributions of Q_1 and Q_2 are found on the same contract curve, they cannot be ranked on the Pareto criterion. They can only be ranked, if at all, on a distributional criterion. What Mishan shows is that the tests of hypothetical compensation are valid as tests of potential Pareto optimality exactly in those cases in which they do not generate cycles. Persistence counts: it seems that Mishan must be given the palm both for sorting out the interpretation of tests of hypothetical compensation and for vindicating the usefulness of community indifference curves – to the extent that infeasible compensations are meaningful at all.

Can compensation tests, in general, be defended by the argument that compensation is merely notional and so needs not be feasible? If we can accept the Kaldor test on that reasoning, can Scitovsky's compound test

(1942) be accepted on the same basis, since the reversal test modifies Kaldor's only in ruling out cases in which a cycle might occur? What about the compensation tests as used by Little and Mishan? Little (1962a, p. 230) assures us that the compensation he envisions in using the Scitovsky test is indeed only notional, but the logic of his argument suffers.

Let S_1 and S_2 be alternative "situations," specifying, as the case may be, the assortment of goods and services, policies, property rights and other economically relevant aspects of the outcomes of two different policy programs. If then S_2 is Pareto superior to S_1 indicate this by writing S_2PS_1. If the transition from S_1 to S_2 passes the Kaldor test it means that there is a third situation S_3 comprising S_2 modified by a set of lump-sum transfers such that S_3PS_1. Suppose then that lump-sum transfers are non-feasible, but there is a set of feasible transfers (a tax-subsidy schema, for example) that might be applied at S_2 that, taking account of all "excess burdens" and other incentive effects, transforms S_2 to S_4 and S_4PS_1, then we might with some confidence argue as Kaldor does – that the decision to pay compensations, choosing S_4 over S_2, is a decision separate from the decision to make the transition from S_1 to S_2, and one that might differently reflect the political preferences of the actual decision makers. In that case we surely would not go as far as Kaldor does, to say that the economist could have nothing to say about the decision to make the transition to S_4 – at the very least the economist will have something useful to say about the incentive effects that determine S_4. Now, if there is no S_3 reflecting zero informational cost, even hypothetically, such that S_3PS_2, then it is unlikely on the face of it that there will be an S_4, differing from the hypothetical S_3 by waste of resources via incentive effects, such that S_4PS_1. [1] Nevertheless, when we identify the Kaldor test with "potential Pareto improvement," the implication is that the transition from S_1 to S_2 can – if the government chooses to enact compensations – be the first step to a Pareto-superior situation. Since however we might have S_3PS_2 but no feasible S_4PS_1, the term "potential Pareto improvement" does not seem apt.

For the Scitovsky reverse test we have situation S_5, comprising S_1 plus a schedule of lump-sum redistributions, such that S_5PS_2. Scitovsky's compound test is the Kaldor test plus assurance that there is no such S_5. If we then consider the feasible S_6, comprising S_1 plus some feasible redistributions, given that there is no S_2 such that S_5PS_2, it seems quite unlikely on the face of it that there is a wasteful S_6 such that S_6PS_2. In this case the hypothetical character of S_5 does not seem a problem – if the test is passed against the hypothetical situation it is likely to pass against any real situation of compensation.

For Little's criteria we need an ordering, perhaps incomplete, that indicates that the distribution at S_2 is no worse than that at S_1. In that case write S_2DS_1. Little's criterion is S_2DS_1 and there is no S_5 as above such that S_5PS_2. Little's reasoning must assume that because of its construction S_5 is distributionally equivalent to S_2; that is S_5DS_2 and S_2DS_5. Little's criterion could be defended on the ground that if S_5PS_2, that tells us that the distributive advantages of S_2 could be obtained more cheaply by a simple redistribution from S_1, and therefore the transition should not be to S_2 but to S_5. If, however, lump-sum redistributions are not feasible, but only "notional," this argument fails. It is difficult to think why a policy change should be ruled out on the grounds that losers by that policy would be better off in an alternative situation that is impossible. If we were to display a feasible S_6 as above with S_6PS_2 and S_6DS_2 then it would be reasonable to argue that, from S_1, the transition should not be to S_2 but to S_6. But this is no more than to say that we should not adopt a policy program if we know of another that is Pareto superior to it and no worse in terms of its distributional consequences. This is a reasonable criterion but it seems a bit different from Little's.

Mishan's criterion is that the transition from S_1 to S_2 passes the Kaldor test, S_2DS_1, and the Scitovsky reversal does not occur – that is, there is S_3 as above with S_3PS_1 but no S_5 as above with S_5PS_2. Thus, the Mishan criterion faces an argument similar to the one just pressed against Little, and further, relying as it does on the Kaldor test, it raises the question why the fact that S_1 is Pareto inferior to an impossible state S_3 be a condition for the substitution of S_2 for S_1. Since the Kaldor test could be passed for infeasible lump-sum redistributions but failed for any feasible redistribution, it seems that Little was correct to put greater stress on the Scitovsky test.

6.5 Assessment of welfare economics after mid-century

Executive summary of the section: All in all, New Welfare Economics, salt-water welfare economics, Little's position and Pigou's welfare economics share more than they disagree on. The use of philosophic concepts of defeasible reasoning helps to bring out the aspects they share. The social welfare function, however, remains problematic.

For all the sometimes warm controversy among the new welfare economists and the saltwater welfare economists, we should not lose sight of what they shared. First, they shared the idea that efficiency in production and exchange could be analyzed in abstraction from the distribution of income or well-being. This is not self-evident. The Benthamite position would be that these are just two aspects of the same thing, and a Marxist would be likely to reject the dichotomy as false. Second, they concur that if the distribution of income or well-being is satisfactory, it is better for people to have what they prefer or choose to have rather than what they do not, and this value judgment they share with Pigou. Further, like Pigou, all are consequentialists, though we see little evidence that any of them see this as the clear value judgment that it is. Indeed, any position that values efficiency is consequentialist: efficiency is a condition on the consequences of a decision. Clearly, the differences among the new welfare economists, and their differences from Pigou, are a family quarrel.

To understand this family quarrel, the ideas of Douglas Walton (1989, 2007, 2011) about informal logic and defeasible reason will be helpful. In particular, the ideas denoted by the term "reasonable dialog" (alternatively "critical discussion") will be helpful in three ways. First, recall, Pigou rarely if ever presents his evaluations of policy as conclusive. Rather, he recognizes that they might be undercut by counterarguments in some cases. In particular, any argument from economic welfare might be undercut by an argument from non-economic welfare. However, Pigou's position is that the burden of proof is on those who assert that considerations of non-economic welfare offset an argument from economic welfare. This is a clear instance of Walton's rules of procedure for a reasonable dialog. Further, for Pigou, an argument from efficiency might be undercut by an argument from income distribution, and conversely. Further discussion, critical arguments and counterarguments would then be necessary to resolve such inconsistencies, and new information might reverse the result.

Second, the evolution of welfare economics in the first half of the twentieth century is at its best *an instance* of reasonable dialog. Pigou's theory, founded as it is on comparisons of incremental utility, is undercut by the Paretian critique of utility theory. Advocates of Pigou's view might respond in one of two ways to undercut the Paretian undercutting argument and restore Pigou's arguments. First, they might argue that the criticism of cardinal utility is itself flawed, as, perhaps, a fallacy of Secundum Quid (ignoring qualifications; Walton 2011, p. 385). As we have seen, defense of cardinal utility theory along these or roughly similar lines was undertaken though, so far as the development of economic theory is concerned, it was unsuccessful. Second, a part of Pigou's arguments – those concerned with efficiency – might be recovered by the argument that they do not depend on the comparison of incremental utilities but can be supported by arguments that do not compare incremental utilities. This was the project of the New Welfare Economics.

But, third, unlike Pigou, the new welfare economists (here partially excepting Little) did not think of the welfare economist's method in ways that resemble a reasonable dialog. Kaldor and Hicks clearly present the compensation tests as conclusive. Scitovsky and the saltwater school alike criticize the Kaldor-Hicks position on the ground that it is *not* conclusive. The saltwater economists also criticize Pareto optimality on those grounds but treat the social welfare function as the condition that admits of a conclusive argument for one policy situation or another. Little in turn criticizes saltwater welfare economics on the ground that their reasoning is inconclusive pending the arrival of Superman. And in every case, the critics are quite right. Welfare economic reasoning is defeasible reasoning (Walton 2011, pp. 378, 385–391). It would seem that in representing their arguments as conclusive, the new welfare economists commit a fallacy that, however we name it, "displays a pattern common to many if not all of the twelve fallacies ... That pattern is for the proponent to press ahead too aggressively to jump to a conclusion uncritically by overlooking the defeasibility of the argument scheme in question" (Walton 2011, p. 404). All this is in profound contrast with Pigou's thought.

What if we reinterpret the New Welfare Economics using reasonable dialog guidelines for the discussion of the impact of a policy change on welfare? Consider first the Kaldor-Hicks compensation test. If we can show that (for example) the replacement of a monopoly by the supply of the product at marginal cost would create sufficient benefits that the beneficiaries could compensate the losers and still be better off, this gives a prima facie case to eliminate the monopoly. Is this sufficient to place the burden of proof on those who would retain the monopoly? Let us grant that it is. If, nevertheless, it could be shown that the Scitovsky test is failed, perhaps because the monopoly internalized what would otherwise be externalities, then the case based on the Kaldor-Hicks test would be undercut. But this could reverse the burden of proof only if there is evidence or information that indicates that the Scitovsky test is failed in this specific case. Facing the burden of proof, the proponents of elimination of the monopoly might make a further argument that the anti-monopoly policy could be accompanied by policies to efficiently remedy the externality, and that these policies would themselves independently satisfy the Kaldor-Hicks compensation test and so ought to be undertaken in any case. The burden of proof would then return to the opponents of the anti-monopoly policy.

If the elimination of the monopoly would also redistribute income in an undesirable way, that too could undercut the argument from a Kaldor-Hicks test. Suppose, for example, the proposal is to privatize a public enterprise that, although it prices inefficiently, uses the profits to subsidize services to the poor. Then a proposal to privatize – or even to require marginal cost pricing, with a consequent reduction of profits – might be rejected on the grounds that the misery of the poor would be increased.

What about the Little criterion? We first notice that it is expressed as a defeasible condition: if the shift from condition A to B results in a better distribution (vague as Little is on the criterion to be used) then the judgment that B should be realized can nevertheless be undercut by the observation that the transition fails the Scitovsky test. This in turn might be undercut by the observation made above that lump-sum redistributions are not feasible. But this point in turn could be undercut, and the negative recommendation on state B restored, by the proposal of a redistributive scheme with a small enough excess burden that both those who gain in the change from A to B remain gainers and those who lose by it are better off than they would be at B.

If our discourse about welfare and public policy were conducted in this way, within the limits of our imperfect knowledge, is it not likely that it would be an improvement?

However, it does not seem that saltwater welfare economics can be rescued in this way. Let us try to see how a social welfare function might enter into a dialog. John says, "Since the move from A to B is a potential Pareto improvement, and our present circumstance is A, we should undertake policies that would realize B." Paul responds, "But that is not true at all. Without a social welfare function, Paretian judgments are inconclusive, and B might well be inferior to A according to the social welfare function." John says, "Well, then, tell me what the social welfare function is, and we will try the experiment." Paul's rejoinder is "Oh, there are infinitely many of them, since the social welfare function depends on value judgments. Evidently your social welfare function is such that the social welfare is increased equally by a one-dollar increase in real income, regardless who receives it. But most people disagree with that, so there is no reason for anyone who disagrees to concur in your conclusion." What this scenario indicates is that the social welfare function argument is a conversation stopper, and conversation stoppers are to be avoided in a reasonable dialog since they not only contribute nothing to the clarification of the issues, but further make it impossible for other participants to make contributions. Nevertheless, as an argument against the Paretian welfare economics, the social welfare function approach has a powerful criticism: *whatever* values a person may affirm, apart from Pareto optimality per se, there can be Pareto-inefficient allocations that are better than a given Pareto optimum. Here, Little's position can be taken as a response, and vague as his criterion of income equality is, it is no more vague (in practice) than those in the writings of Bergson and Samuelson. Mishan's adaptations of Little's compound criterion bear the same interpretation.

On the other hand, such important contributions of the saltwater school as Samuelson's public goods and Bator's market failure can play a more robust role in a reasonable dialog of welfare economics than they might otherwise. Consider Margolis' (1955, p. 347) criticism of Samuelson: "The crowded calendar of the courts certainly implies that the use of this function by A makes it less available to B." In the context of a rational dialog Samuelson might respond "But because of increasing returns to scale, the courts approximate a public good nevertheless; and further the 'atmosphere' of law and order that they create approximates it even more closely, so that the conclusion that courts of law ought to be provided by government from tax revenues stands."

All in all, it seems that Pigou's recognition of the defeasibility of welfare economic arguments, and his openness to undercutting counterarguments, constitute a great advantage for Pigou's discourse by comparison with that of any of the new or saltwater welfare economists. Their failure to consider counterarguments may or may not be thought of as a fallacy, but in either case it is crippling, since their arguments are defeasible – nothing is clearer from their own research! – and without acknowledging that and responding to counterarguments, they are left with nothing. The social welfare function is merely the most extreme instance of this.

6.6 Concluding summary of the chapter

By the mid-1950s, the controversy between cardinalism and ordinalism, properly so called, was over. To a considerable extent it ended in the exhaustion of both sides.

Ordinalism held the key ground in the theory of market equilibrium under certainty. Cardinal utility would continue to play a part in some welfare economic reasoning, but it would not be the cardinal utility of Pigou. The fine points that excited the controversialists and the conviction that one side must be *right* and the other *wrong* no longer commanded much interest in economics. The utility measure of von Neumann and Morgenstern was not clearly helpful to the cardinalists, either.

In many ways the 1950s and the early 1960s could be thought of as something of a golden age for welfare economics, and especially, of course, for the saltwater theorists. Samuelson's public goods and Bator's market failure demonstrated that, with or without a social welfare function or some "'twere better" test, welfare economics could answer questions of crucial interest for public policy. Certainly some questions were left unanswered. Production of public goods would require the imposition of a burden of tax: even if that burden were minimized, how should it be distributed? (Samuelson stressed this point particularly.) And distribution would continue to be discussed. But specialists in policy fields such as environmental economics could take comfort in the conviction that this question was beyond their own specialization, if not, pace Robbins, beyond the competence of economics. Still, the questions of distribution remained unanswered, and are certainly no less central to public policy in the second decade of the twenty-first century than they were in the sixth decade of the twentieth. Perhaps they are more central.

From this point on, the discussions of utility and welfare economics are less intertwined, and indeed discussions of aspects of welfare economics have tended to go on in "silos" among which there has been little interchange. Accordingly, the chronological organization will be abandoned for the chapters that follow.

Note

1   We do need to be a little cautious here. It is possible that a scheme of transfers might have positive incentive effects. Suppose, for example, that compensation to former monopolists were financed by "green" Pigovian taxes on negative externalities. Then the feasible transfers might actually improve on lump sum taxes that would not discourage the negative externalities, and the benefit of this would offset the negative incentive effects of the compensation of former monopolists, if any. But it seems best to treat the Pigovian taxes not as part of the compensation scheme but as a distinct allocative policy, in that it "should" be adopted in any case.

References

Akerlof, George (1970) The Market for Lemons: Qualitative Uncertainty and the Market Mechanism, *Quarterly Journal of Economics* v. 84, no. 3 (Aug) pp. 488–500.

Alchian, Armen A. (1953) The Meaning of Utility Measurement, *American Economic Review* v. 43, no. 1 (March) pp. 26–50.

Allen, R. G. D. (1935) A Note on Determinateness of the Utility Function, *Review of Economic Studies* v. 2, no. 2 (Feb) pp. 488–500.

Armstrong, W. E. (1939) The Determinateness of the Utility Function, *Economic Journal* v. 49, no. 195 (Sept) pp. 453–467.

Arrow, Kenneth J. (1963) Uncertainty and the Welfare Economics of Medical Care, *American Economic Review* v. 53, no. 5 (Dec) pp. 941–973.

Ayres, Robert U. and Allen V. Kneese (1969) Production, Consumption, and Externalities, *American Economic Review* v. 59, no. 3 (Jun) pp. 282–297.

Bator, Francis M. (1957) The Simple Analytics of Welfare Maximization, *American Economic Review* v. 47, no. 1 (March) pp. 22–59.

Bator, Francis M. (1958) The Anatomy of Market Failure, *Quarterly Journal of Economics* v. 72, no. 3 (Aug) pp. 351–379.

Ellsberg, D. (1954) Classic and Current Notions of "Measurable Utility", *Economic Journal* v. 64, no. 255 (Sept) pp. 528–556.

Fleming, Marcus (1952) A Cardinal Concept of Welfare, *Quarterly Journal of Economics* (Aug) pp. 366–384.

Galbraith, John Kenneth (1958) *The Affluent Society* (New York: New American Library).

Graff, J. de V. (1957) *Theoretical Welfare Economics* (Cambridge University Press).

Harsanyi, John (1953) Cardinal Utility in Welfare Economics and in the Theory of Risk-Taking, *Journal of Political Economy* v. 61, no. 5 (Oct) pp. 434–435.

Hicks, J. R. (1954) Robbins on Robertson on Utility, *Economica, New Series* v. 21, no. 82 (May) pp. 154–157.

Johansen, Leif (1963) Some Notes on the Lindahl Theory on the Determination of Public Expenditures, *International Economic Review* v. 4, no. 3 (Sep) pp. 346–358.

Kennedy, Charles (1954) Concerning Utility, *Economica, New Series* v. 21, no. 81 (Feb) pp. 7–20.

Kennedy, Charles (1963) Welfare Criteria – a Further Note, *Economic Journal* v. 73, no. 290 (Jun) pp. 338–341.

Lange, Oskar (1934) The Determinateness of the Utility Function, *Review of Economic Studies* v. 1, no. 3 (Jun) pp. 218–225.

Lindahl, Erik (1919) *Die Gerechtigkeit in der Besteuerung* (Lund: Lund University Press).

Little, I. M. D. (1962a) Welfare Criteria: An Exchange of Notes: A Comment, *Economic Journal* v. 72, no. 285 (Mar) pp. 229–231.

Little, I. M. D. (1962b) Welfare Criteria: An Exchange of Notes: A Rejoinder, *Economic Journal* v. 72, no. 285 (Mar) pp. 233–234.

Little, I. M. D. (2002 [1950]) *A Critique of Welfare Economics*, 2nd Edition (Oxford: Clarendon).

Margolis, Julius (1955) A Comment on the Pure Theory of Public Expenditure, *Review of Economics and Statistics* v. 37, no. 4 (Nov) pp. 347–349.

Marschak, Jacob (1950) Rational Behavior, Uncertain Prospects, and Measurable Utility, *Econometrica* v. 18, no. 2 (Apr) pp. 111–141.

McCain, Roger A. (2015) *Game Theory and Public Policy*, 2nd Edition (Cheltenham: Edward Elgar).

Meade, J. E. (1952) External Economies and Diseconomies in a Competitive Situation, *Economic Journal* v. 62, no. 245 pp. 54–67.

Meade, J. E. (1959) Review: A Critique of Welfare Economics by I. M. D. Little, *Economic Journal* v. 69, no. 273 (March) pp. 124–129.

Meade, J. E. (1962) Welfare Criteria: An Exchange of Notes, *Economic Journal* v. 72, no. 285 (March) pp. 231–233.

Mishan, E. J. (1962) Welfare Criteria: An Exchange of Notes: A Comment, *Economic Journal* v. 72, no. 285 (Mar) pp. 234–244.

Mishan, E. J. (1963) Welfare Criteria: Are Compensation Tests Necessary? *Economic Journal* v. 73, no. 290 (Jun) pp. 342–350.

Mishan, E. J. (1965) The Recent Debate on Welfare Criteria, *Oxford Economic Papers, New Series* v. 17, no. 2 (Jul) pp. 219–236.

Mishan, E. J. (1969) The Relationship between Joint Products, Collective Goods, and External Effects, *Journal of Political Economy* v. 77, no. 3 (May–Jun) pp. 329–348.

Mishan, E. J. (1973) Welfare Criteria: Resolution of a Paradox, *Economic Journal* v. 83, no. 331 (Sep) pp. 747–767.

Musgrave, Richard A. (1939) The Voluntary Exchange Theory of Public Economy, *Quarterly Journal of Economics* v. 53, no. 2 (Feb) pp. 213–237.

Nash, John (1950) Equilibrium Points in n-Person Games, *Proceedings of the National Academy of Science* v. 36, pp. 48–49.

Robertson, D. H. (1952) *Utility and All That* (London: Macmillan).

Robertson, D. H. (1954) Utility and All What? *Economic Journal* v. 64, no. 256 (Dec) pp. 665–678.

Robertson, D. H. (1962) Welfare Criteria: An Exchange of Notes: A Note, *Economic Journal* v. 72, no. 285 (Mar) pp. 226–229.

Robbins, Lionel (1953) Robertson on Utility and Scope, *Economica, New Series* v. 20, no. 78 (May) pp. 99–111.

Robinson, Abraham (1974) *Non-Standard Analysis* (Amsterdam: North-Holland).

Samuelson, Paul A. (1953) Consumption Theorems in Terms of Overcompensation Rather than Indifference Comparisons, *Economica, New Series* v. 20, no. 77 (Feb) pp. 1–9.

Samuelson, Paul A. (1954) The Pure Theory of Public Expenditure, *Review of Economics and Statistics* v. 36, no. 4 (Nov) pp. 387–389.

Samuelson, Paul A. (1955) Diagrammatic Exposition of a Theory of Public Expenditure, *Review of Economics and Statistics* v. 37, no. 4 (Nov) pp. 350–356.

Scitovsky, Tibor de (1942) A Reconsideration of the Theory of Tariffs, *Review of Economic Studies* v. 9, no. 2 (Summer) pp. 89–110.

Scitovsky, Tibor de (1954) Two Concepts of External Economies, *Journal of Political Economy* v. 62, no. 2 (Apr) pp. 143–151.

Scitovsky, Tibor de (1976) *The Joyless Economy* (New York: Oxford University Press).

von Neumann, John and Oskar Morgenstern (1944) *The Theory of Games and Economic Behavior* (Princeton, N.J.: Princeton University Press).

Walton, Douglas (1989) *Informal Logic: A Handbook for Critical Argumentation* (Cambridge: Cambridge University Press).

Walton, Douglas (2007) Evaluating Practical Reasoning, *Synthese* v. 157, no. 2 (July) pp. 197–240.

Walton, Douglas (2011) Defeasible Reasoning and Informal Fallacies, *Synthese* v. 179, no. 3 (April) pp. 377–407.

Zeuthen, Frederick (1937) On the Determinateness of the Utility Function, *Review of Economic Studies* v. 4, no. 3 (June) pp. 236–239.

7 Loss of coherence

In the 1950s and 1960s, the New Welfare Economics was to face a series of challenges. In this chapter we consider first the Arrow "general possibility theorem," second the "general theory of the second best" and third the problems related with other-regarding preferences – that is, altruism and such motives incorporated in individual preferences.

7.1 The general possibility theorem

Executive summary of the section: Arrow's famous "impossibility theorem," that a social welfare function realizing five standards of rationality might not exist, depending on the preferences in the population, is summarized with its context.

In 1951, in *Social Choice and Individual Values*, Kenneth Arrow argued that a *rational* social welfare function could not in general be derived from individual values. Arrow understands a social welfare function as a function with the individual levels of preferences as arguments and an ordinal evaluation of social welfare as the dependent variable. Like individual utility index functions, the social welfare function would be defined only up to a monotonic transformation. We could then think of such a function as being maximized subject to material constraints. In that application, any monotonically increasing transformation of a particular social welfare function would yield the same conditions at the maximum. The aggregate social welfare, then, would be determined by individual welfares in the same way that the welfare of an individual in contemporary economic theory would be determined by maximization of her preferences. There is no doubt that such a function could exist. If all decisions should be referred to a dictator, and the dictator a rational homo economicus (1951a, p. 2), the rationality of the dictator would assure the rationality of the social welfare function. But the question is whether the preferences of two or more people can meaningfully be composed (whether through voting, markets or any other approach that "are methods of amalgamating the tastes of many individuals in the making of social choices," p. 2) with any assurance of a similar rationality. And the answer is no.

After introducing the idea of alternative modes of social choice and the issues they raise for a social welfare function, Arrow gives a set-theoretic discussion of *individual* preference theory. Arrow notes that set-theoretic notation is "not customarily employed in economics" (p. 11). It has become much more familiar since. In particular, Arrow focuses on the sense in which contemporary economic theory understood choice according to one's preferences as "rational" (pp. 12–13). Axiomatically, preference is understood as a weak ordering (a is no worse than b) and as transitive (if a is no worse than b and b is no worse than c, then a is no worse than c). From this weak ordering, as Arrow notes, both preference (the strong ordering) and indifference can be derived using the formulae of symbolic logic. A choice function from a given set of alternatives to the chosen alternative is defined via these ordering relations. For the choice function, it is deduced (p. 16) from these axiomata that the choice between any two alternatives is determined strictly by the individual's preference between the two alternatives themselves. This is the condition known as "independence of irrelevant alternatives." Using an equivalence of the choice and preference functions for two alternative choices, this condition is deduced also for the preference function. (Arrow does not state these conclusions quite explicitly.) These axiomata and this conclusion define the standard of rationality that Arrow demands of the social welfare function (p. 19).

Arrow's following chapter states five conditions that a social welfare function should meet. The first is a condition on the range of alternatives to which it applies. Arrow allows for some restriction on the preference systems to which the social welfare function can be applied (for example, it might apply only to preferences over the vector of goods consumed and productive services supplied). However, the first condition is that there must be at least three alternatives over which all possible preference rankings are admissible (p. 24). The second condition is that the social welfare function be positively related to individual preferences (p. 25). The third is the independence of irrelevant alternatives (pp. 26–27). The fourth is a condition that the social welfare function is not imposed, that is, there are no two alternatives whose ranking in social welfare is independent of the individual preferences (p. 28). The final condition, condition 5, is non-dictatorship, that is, there is no one person whose preferences determine the social welfare evaluation of any pair of alternatives. Of these, the third, the irrelevance of independent alternatives, has attracted the most attention, so we will return to it below. At this point we might note, though, that if transitivity had been assumed for social welfare rankings, as for individual rankings, the independence of irrelevant alternatives would have been a theorem rather than an assumption. The first condition opens the possibility of non-transitive social orderings.

Arrow's chapter 4 revisits the compensation tests. He argues that none of them provides a satisfactory social welfare function. That is hardly surprising, since they were not intended to; but no doubt it is important for completeness. Chapter 5 then addresses the general possibility theorem. It is shown that a social welfare function can exist if there are only two alternatives. For illustrative purposes, it is shown that a social welfare function for a case of two individuals and three alternatives results in a contradiction. This is then shown for the general case. The form of the argument is well known: using the first three assumptions that define rationality for a social welfare function, Arrow establishes that the social welfare function must be either imposed or dictatorial – that is, either depends strictly on the ranking of one individual, or depends on the ranking of none (pp. 56–58).

At several points Arrow identifies the social welfare function with the *process* by which the ranking of social states is derived. This seems to have caused some confusion, and it seems best for me to say explicitly how I interpret it in this essay. It seems to me that Arrow was speaking mathematically in identifying the function with a process of mathematical operations that calculates or approximates it. An analogy may be helpful. If our objective is to estimate a demand function for potatoes, we will proceed at two stages. First we will obtain data on the prices, corresponding quantities sold, and some other variables that will help to identify the demand relationship. Having obtained the data, we will carry out a process of calculations with it, involving such things as addition, multiplication and inversion of a matrix. (In this century these operations will be expedited by a computer.) I submit that for Arrow, voting, buying and selling correspond to the gathering of data in the demand-function example, while the process he refers to corresponds to the addition, multiplication and inversion of matrices in the demand-function example. It is a "process" of calculation taking as given the data produced by voting, buying and selling, while voting, buying and selling are supposed to give us data on people's preference systems as envisioned by the revealed preference theory.

As is well known, Arrow's argument rested importantly on the "paradox of voting," that, if decisions were to be taken by majority voting, it could be that one alternative, let us say alternative a, would be preferred by the majority to alternative b, b to c, and in turn c to a. It is important, however, to keep in mind that *Social Choice and Individual Values* is not *about* voting, but about economic decisions in general. At p. 5 Arrow writes "In the following discussion of the consistency of various value judgments as to the mode of social choice, the distinction between voting and the market mechanism will be disregarded, both being regarded as special cases of the more general category of collective social choice." At chapter 6 he restates the general possibility theorem under restrictive assumptions so that it applies to market equilibria in particular. Still, confusion on this score – that *Social Choice and Individual Values* is a critique of majoritarian ideas in particular – is not surprising. An example of voting, with the paradox, comes at pp. 2–3, and Arrow returns to majority-rule examples again and again: the Borda count is used at p. 27 as an example to illustrate how some of Arrow's rationality constraints can be violated; at pp. 46–47 it is shown that majority voting gives rise to a rational social welfare function in case there are just two alternatives; and at pp. 74–79 Arrow revisits Duncan Black's (1948) discussion of voting with single-peaked preferences and shows that here, again, majority rule can provide a rational social welfare function. Further we may observe that there are (limited) positive results for majority voting, but none for market allocations. Indeed, as Arrow follows Bergson and Samuelson in the view that efficient market allocations are significant only at the maximum of social welfare, it is hard to envision any special case in which market allocations per se could be evaluated as optimal.

As noted, the assumption of the independence of irrelevant alternatives was especially the target of doubts about the general possibility theorem. The reason is not hard to find. In his discussion of a social welfare function in the case of two individuals and three alternatives, at p. 50, Arrow derives consequence 3 from the conditions on a social welfare function: "CONSEQUENCE 3: *If x' P_1 y' and y' P_2 x', then x' I y'.*" Here, P_1 expresses the preferences of individual 1 and P_2 of individual 2. That is, if the positions of the two individuals are opposed, then the social evaluation must be indifferent between them. Now, this is not an assumption but a theorem; however, the independence of irrelevant alternatives plays a key role in the proof, and is invoked again and again. Suppose, then, that we invoke a basic needs consequentialism, such as Cooter and Rappoport (1984) attribute to Pigou and Marshall (compare Bergson 1954, p. 244). This reasonable value system may not resolve all questions, since needs are satiable (McCain 2017, pp. 152–53) so the basic needs criterion would have to be supplemented by some other principle, such as majority rule, where considerations of basic need do not determine a decision. Formally, then, letting V be the population and v a proper subset of V, let the rule of social choice be

a   in case alternatives x and y are such that in x, $i \in V \Rightarrow i$ meets basic needs, while in alternative y, $i \in v \Rightarrow i$ does not meet basic needs, $i \in V \backslash v \Rightarrow i$ meets basic needs. Then xPy, where P is the social welfare preference function.
b   Otherwise, if a plurality prefer x to y, xPy, and conversely; and if the vote is equally divided, xIy.

Further suppose that $i \in v$ prefer to meet their basic needs, so that $xP_i y$, and consider a preference system in particular in which for $j \in V \backslash v$, $yP_j x$. In the two-person case, there is just one individual each in v and V\v, so that by consequence 3, xIy. However, by the augmented basic needs criterion xPy. Thus, the basic needs criterion, which seems quite reasonable, is irrational by Arrow's standard.

Indeed, for the two-person case, consequence 3 seems to rule out any redistributive judgments whatever (compare Mishan 1957, pp. 450–451). For the n-person case, there is no comparable "consequence" that clearly addresses redistributive judgments. However, the hybrid "basic needs" value system given above may still give us some insight. Consider the following example with three individuals, 1, 2, 3, and three alternatives, x, y, z. As before, at y, individual 1 does not meet basic needs and starves, but does meet basic needs at x and z. Thus we consider cases in which xP_1y and zP_1y. (We need not exclude cases in which yP_1x or yP_1z – death before disgrace, for example – as they will not be relevant to the argument.) Any possible preference ordering over x, y and z can be attributed to individuals 2 and 3. Now, depending on their preferences, the social ordering of x and z may be either before the other; but it must be clear that individual 1 is decisive for x over y and for z over y. However, for Arrow by consequence 5 (p. 56) a single individual cannot be decisive for any pair of alternatives. Broadly, Arrow's conditions exclude any overriding value, such as basic needs in this case.

Arrow was quite aware of the discussion of utility in von Neumann and Morgenstern (1944) but seems somewhat ambivalent about it. At pp. 9–10 he dismisses the von Neuman and Morgenstern utility measurement; however, at pp. 20–21, he notes that if randomization over alternatives is allowed, as in the theory of zero-sum games, the paradox of social choice might be resolved. At p. 70, further, he notes that cooperative game theory under the assumption of transferable utility escapes the paradox because it is in effect a one-commodity model. The TU condition can be derived from the observation that payoffs can be redistributed by randomization together with the assumption that agents are risk neutral. At p. 32 he again argues that the von Neumann-Morgenstern utility theory would be unsatisfactory. In passing, at p. 19, he dismisses the theory of games of more than two persons or with non-constant sums as "in a dubious state." He is apparently unaware of the contemporary contributions of Nash (1950) to the theory of non-constant sum games. In a footnote at p. 59 he draws a parallel between his paradox and the cyclical nature of dominance in von Neumann and Morgenstern's theory of general games.

Whatever doubts we may entertain, Arrow's result is an extraordinary turn. As against any questions about the independence of irrelevant alternatives or about the von Neumann-Morgenstern utility theory, the response is that Arrow is working within the scope of the theory of the social welfare function as it was understood at the time he was writing. And he showed that no such object could exist.

7.2 The controversy over "social choice and individual values"

Executive summary of the section: The discussion that followed Arrow's monograph ranged from criticism of details and claims that it was irrelevant to welfare economics to extensions and amendments and to suggestion of more or less utilitarian alternative schemes.

Of course, Arrow's monograph gave rise to a large literature; indeed to several. There were critical responses and others that praised or extended the work. Somewhere in between, a large number of papers followed Arrow's reflections on how the paradox might be resolved, and proposing alternative conditions that might (or might not) resolve it. Others interpreted Arrow's monograph as a contribution to the positive theory of voting and other processes of political choice. While it has been asserted here that *Social Choice and Individual Values* was not about voting per se, its conclusions for social choice in general are applicable to voting in particular and constitute a sufficiently important con- tribution to voting theory that the monograph can correctly be described as a founding contribution to the literature that came to be known as public choice or social choice theory (examples include Baumol 1964 [1952];[1]Buchanan 1954a, 1954b; Buchanan and Tullock 1962; Coleman 1966; Tullock 1967; Williamson and Sargent 1967; Zeckhauser 1969; Black 1969). But public choice theory is not welfare economics – it is a set of predictive hypotheses, whereas welfare eco- nomics is normative – and so no more will be said of it here. A third line of dis- cussion focused (as Arrow had at several points in his monograph) on alternative sets of postulates that might eliminate the paradox and lead to a meaningful social welfare function despite the Arrow theorem, or that invalidate the theorem in some other way. An obvious possibility – bringing cardinal utility or intensity of preference back into consideration – will be left for the end of this section.

Among the critical responses that of Little (1952) deserves particular atten- tion. As it happens, soon after the publication of his monograph, Arrow (1951b) had reviewed Little's *Critique*, and had been particularly critical of Little's lack of mathematical rigor. Now, Little might have taken the view that Arrow's con- clusions reinforce his *Critique* – that Arrow had shown that even Superman would be unable to supply a social welfare function. Instead, however, Little's overall critique is that Arrow has misunderstood the concept of a social welfare function. At p. 423 Little argues that a social welfare function presupposes given tastes, while Arrow writes of changing tastes. This is a simple misunderstanding of Arrow's language. In speaking, for example, of a rise in the evaluation of a social state in the preference system of some individual, Arrow is comparing two preference systems, each of which is given as such. As Rothenberg (1953, pp. 390–91) somewhat charitably puts it, "Little may have confused the surface assumptions of typical working procedure with the deeper and more implicit assumptions involved in the very formulation of the social welfare function." Indeed, Bergson had used similar language (1938, p. 331). But, more sub- stantively, Little raises questions about Arrow's first two conditions (p. 425) and points out that Arrow's formulation precludes distributional judgments (p. 426). Most fundamentally Little asserts that only individuals can make value judg- ments, so that only an individual could have a social welfare function – that the notion of a social welfare function for a group is simply nonsense. And he seems to hold that compromise is unthinkable where individual value judgments are concerned. At p. 431 he writes "Where values are concerned, everyone must be a 'dictator' (i.e., the logic of value judgments is such that one cannot consistently *accept* any value ordering which differs from one's own); where decisions are in question, everyone cannot be a dictator, in Arrow's sense, unless there is unanimity" (emphasis in the original). Perhaps this position can fairly be described as remarkable.

Rothenberg (1953) is to some extent a rejoinder to Little. Rothenberg first points out how Arrow's conception of the social welfare function is derived from that of Bergson (1938) and then addresses Little's points. He then argues that welfare economics must become interdisciplinary, using research in such fields as sociology and anthropology to determine the value judgments that would in turn form a social welfare function.

Kemp's (1953–1954) criticism of Arrow follows similar lines to Little's and is if anything more emphatic. Bergson's (1954) is also dismissive. Perhaps surprisingly, Bergson writes (p. 235) "I find myself in general accord with Mr. Little." This is described as surprising since it seems to contradict what Bergson had written in 1938 (p. 323): "the determination of prevailing values for a given community, while I regard it as both a proper and necessary task for the economist, and of the same general character as the investigation of the indifference functions for individuals, is a project which I shall not undertake here." It would seem that what Arrow had shown is that the research project that quotation puts forward is impossible. However, Bergson concedes (p. 250) that "my own ethical thinking has evolved in the course of time." Bergson writes (p. 240) "In my opinion, Arrow's theorem is unrelated to welfare economics." However, he qualifies this (p. 241):

> It is demonstrated that one could not appeal to a rule of collective decision-making to determine the values to be taken as data in the counseling of any individual on social states. As far as I can see, this interpretation is admissible, and my contention that Arrow's theorem does not apply to welfare economics has to be qualified accordingly.

Bergson now thinks of the welfare economist as a consultant: thus, the values to apply depend on who is being consulted. Little's Superman now is everyman. Can the welfare economist be a consultant to some group, rather than (as Little would have it) only an individual? Bergson seems ambivalent on this. At p. 240 he writes "one might wish to counsel some select group, which holds some values in common." But evidently, this can only be done if their social preferences are unanimous. That a group might hold "some values in common" and these might allow them to compromise on others seems reasonable, but that would again raise Arrow's paradox. But then, at p. 243:

> What of the further possibility that he counsel nobody in particular but the community as such? Is not Arrow's theorem more meaningful in this light? ... But a moment's reflection makes clear that such a conception cannot be very meaningful. After all, even if one prefers to think of the community as an 'organic entity,' he must still concede that in the last

analysis all decisions are made by individuals. If one does not counsel individuals, who is there to counsel?

But this leaves Bergson (and Little and Kemp) with the problem that Bergson had in 1938 proposed to solve: how to choose among the infinitely many Pareto optima that can be expected in an economy as conceived in contemporary economic theory. For Bergson and the other critics, there will now be as many answers as there are individuals, and that is to say, no answer. Bergson is no less defeated than he would have been by Arrow's theorem, and indeed perhaps more thoroughly defeated.

Mishan (1957) does not go so far as to say that Arrow's proposition has nothing to do with welfare economics, but (p. 445),

> Here was a parade of unfamiliar symbolism having all the earmarks of high rigour and thoroughness. And it followed – or so we were told by well-meaning colleagues – that welfare economics had ceased to exist. Any endeavour to construct a satisfactory social-welfare function was apparently doomed to dissolve into contradiction ... [but] the alleged contradictions arise ... from the acceptance by Arrow of propositions to which welfare economists have usually taken exception.

But Mishan supports his arguments by reference to the compensation tests, and indeed concedes (at p. 452) that not all social states can be compared, criticizing Arrow's assumption that they can. Here, again, Mishan gives up any hope of choosing one Pareto optimum among the infinitely many, and he seems to make this definitional of welfare economics. These points are stressed in Davis' (1958) rejoinder. Mishan's position is a rejection of the concept of a social welfare function tout court, and like Little, Mishan might have taken Arrow's theorem as reinforcing his view, but chooses not to. Instead, Mishan tries to breath life back into the New Welfare Economics of Kaldor and Hicks – a project that he will continue, as we saw in Chapter 6.

At this time, Little, Bergson, Mishan and Samuelson were among the economists most recognized in welfare economics. It seems fair to describe the responses of Little, Bergson and Mishan as defensive. Samuelson's response to Arrow was rather long coming in print, though both Little and Bergson acknowledge help from him. However, in 1977, responding to a quite different impossibility theorem, Samuelson makes his difference with Arrow clear. At p. 82 he writes "I was concerned to demonstrate the logical difference between a B-S ISWF and an Arrow Constitutional Voting-Machine Function (A CV-MF), a distinction blurred in K. J. Arrow (1951)." In his example of an existing social welfare function, Samuelson gives a two-person example based on "the formula $\omega = (0.5F^{-1}+0.5C^{-1})^{0.5} (0.5f+0.5c)^{0.5}$" (p. 88). Here F, C, f and c are the two consumption goods of the two individuals, so $(0.5F^{-1}+0.5C^{-1})$ and $(0.5f+0.5c)$ are their respective utility functions and the social welfare function is simply the geometric mean of the utilities.

Samuelson assures us that this social welfare function makes no use of "cardinal" utilities, and he is of course right: any monotonic transformation of either utility function or of the geometric mean function would result in the same global optimum. What Samuelson showed is that a social welfare function could be written down. But that surely was never in question. The difficulty is that Samuelson clearly does not mean that this "existent SWF [social welfare function]" has either any relation to the value judgments of any real person or any property of uniqueness, such as might emerge from an Arrow-like process of social choice on the basis of individual values. Thus, we are back to the unresolved infinity of Pareto optima. Samuelson also insists that the introduction of the von Neumann-Morgenstern utility measurement makes no difference. He writes (p. 84) "J. C. Harsanyi (1955) has given reasons why the ethical observer of individualistic type might wish to 'respect' individuals' risk reactions by making the B-S SWF an 'additively independent' ethically-weighted sum of the individuals' respective von Neumann functions. Again, there is nothing nonordinal about all this" since the von Neumann-Morgenstern utility functions are derived from ordinal preferences over risky prospects. But this weakens ordinalism to a degree that would confound both Samuelson and Arrow, as we shall see.

In his 1963 *Notes*, published as chapter 8 of the second edition of *Social Choice and Individual Values*, Arrow interprets his differences from these critics as terminological, and he concedes to them as such, arguing that his theory remains valid with appropriate changes in terminology.

Arguments that Arrow's result should be resolved by reintroducing cardinal utility arose immediately (e.g. Weldon 1952; Hildreth 1953) and would continue to be discussed over the years (e.g. Weirich 1984). Weldon, after offering a more direct proof of Arrow's theorem, suggested that it should be thought of as a reductio ad absurdam of ordinalism (1952, p. 462). Vickrey (1960), in the course of his survey, discusses the reintroduction of cardinal utility from a number of points of view.

Perhaps the most important writing along these lines, however, came from Hildreth (1953). Incorporating ideas from von Neumann and Morgenstern, Hildreth derived a rational social welfare function as well as cardinal utilities. Arrow had acknowledged (p. 20) that

> if conceptually we imagine a choice being made between two alternatives, we cannot exclude any probability distribution over those two choices as a possible alternative. The precise shape of a formulation of rationality which takes the last point into account or the consequences of such a reformulation on the theory of choice in general or the theory of social choice in particular cannot be foreseen; but it is at least a possibility, to which attention should be drawn, that the paradox to be discussed below might be resolved by such a broader concept of rationality.

Substantially this is what Hildreth does. He begins from a comparison of the concepts of a social welfare function in the writing of Bergson and Arrow, arguing that Arrow's approach subsumes that of Bergson but is more general

(p. 82). He introduces risky prospects and expected values of utility (p. 83) but has to make further assumptions in order to characterize a social welfare function. He assumes that each individual's preferences over prospects is a complete order and both that a probabilistic mix of two social states lies between them in the individual's preference and that there is some pair of social states such that one is unanimously preferred to the other (p. 84). These assumptions are sufficient to allow a von Neumann-Morgenstern utility measure that is in some sense interpersonally comparable. As to the third assumption, we might consider a social state in which everyone meets basic needs and another in which no one meets basic needs – in such a case unanimity could be plausible. A further assumption is that interchanging individuals who have the same preference orderings does not affect the social welfare judgment (p. 86). Again Hildreth does not provide any plausible examples, but this assumption would seem to exclude some instances of special treatment for those who are more sensitive to satisfaction of their wants, perhaps including Robbins' high-caste Brahmin. Further, in order to proceed from a social ordering to a social choice, Hildreth assumes that the utility-possibility frontier is closed and convex (p. 85). He concludes (p. 88) that the addition of von Neumann-Morgenstern utilities supplies a social welfare function that satisfies his conditions. (It is, however, not unique as such.) Hildreth points out that his definition of the social welfare function violates Arrow's condition of the independence of irrelevant alternatives by effectively allowing intensity of preference to affect the ordering (p. 89). And Hildreth argues that Arrow was confused on this point, writing (p. 90):

> If we interpret utility as an ordinal preference indicator and if social orderings are to be based on individual preferences, then the latter position really excludes the possibility of ordering social states any more completely than is done by the new welfare economics. For as soon as we say that state X is socially preferred to state Y for two states such that some individuals prefer X to Y and others prefer Y to X, we are thereby saying that the gains to those who prefer X are socially more important than the losses of those who prefer Y. This implies that we have some basis for comparing the relevant gains and losses. Such a comparison is fundamentally an interpersonal comparison of utilities.

That is, *any* social welfare function presupposes interpersonal comparisons (in some sense) of relative quantities. Regardless of this, any consideration of expected values of probabilistic prospects must violate the independence of irrelevant alternatives, since the comparison of two prospects involving different probabilities of the same two certain prospects depends on the evaluation of the certain prospects themselves – a violation of the independence of irrelevant alternatives as Arrow states it.

Some responses proposed extensions of Arrow's study. Weldon (1952) offered an alternative proof that he believes is more direct. Blau (1957) discovered a minor error in Arrow's proof and provided an alternative proof. Arrow acknowledged the error and corrected it in the 1963 *Notes*. There, also (p. 92), he particularly acknowledged Vickrey (1960) for a restatement of the theory, another proof and a discussion of some alternative possibilities. Vickrey puts particular stress on the possibility that a political decision process would create incentives to misrepresent one's preferences (pp. 517–519), an observation that looks forward to work in political choice such as that of Maskin (1999). The large literature of further impossibility theorems will not be further considered here.

As among Arrow's assumptions and conditions, a great deal of doubt was expressed about the independence of irrelevant alternatives. For example, Gorman (1955) primarily addresses the compensation tests, observing that they do not in general provide a complete ordering of social states. For a special case in which compensation tests do provide a complete ordering, however (p. 34), he points out that this ordering process must violate some of Arrow's postulates and argues that it violates the independence of irrelevant alternatives in particular. Blau (1971) and Osborne (1976) weaken the independence of irrelevant alternatives slightly but obtain impossibility theorems nevertheless. Inada (1964) argues that social welfare must be represented by a functional – that is, not just the utility indices of the individuals, but the entire relationship of the states to the utility indices will figure in the determination of social welfare. He observes that this is crucial if we allow for other-regarding preferences (a point that we return to in a future section of this chapter). This violates the independence of irrelevant alternatives, but again Inada derives an impossibility theorem. Campbell (1973) interprets "intensity of preference" in a way that *entails* the independence of irrelevant alternatives for "realistic environment sets." On the other hand, Contini (1966) dismisses Arrow's assumption of positive responsiveness as vacuous when the set of alternatives is connected. That is, in such a set, no one alternative could rise in anyone's valuation while the rest remain unchanged, since that would create a discontinuity. (I conjecture that Arrow's result could be restored by an assumption of positive responsiveness on any finite subset of alternatives.)

Perhaps the most important rescue mission for rational welfare judgments came from Amartya Sen (1966, 1969). In 1966, Sen had extended previous results on the range of preferences for which majority voting would be consistent – really a contribution to public choice theory, but continuing a line of research that Arrow had begun with his discussion of Black's voting model. In 1969, however, he took a different direction. Arrow had discussed choice functions for individual preference systems (pp. 15–17) but never investigates choice functions as they may correspond to a social welfare function. Sen (1969), however, points out that a rational choice function might be obtained without transitivity of the welfare function. Quasi-transitivity is sufficient. Quasi-transitivity essentially is transitivity of *strict* social preferences, and if it is satisfied then a social choice function can be derived, and conversely, Arrow's proof does not apply to the social choice function.

Sen (1970b) restates and extends this finding. Some of his ideas in this book will be considered in a later section of this chapter. Chapters 1 and 3 discuss individual preferences and a social welfare function very much along Arrow's lines and prove an impossibility theorem in chapter 3. In chapter 2, Sen revisits the Pareto ordering for social states and Pareto-inclusive orders and quasi-orders, that is, orders and quasi-orders which rank states that are Pareto-superior higher. Sen extends the Pareto quasi-order by treating as indifferent social states that are unanimously considered indifferent. This is only a quasi-order since it is not complete – some states may not be ordered nor indifferent. In chapter 4, Sen defines a social decision function and demonstrates that a social decision function does exist for any finite choice set that satisfies Arrow's conditions: unrestricted domain, the Pareto principle, independence of irrelevant alternatives and non-dictatorship. The demonstration is by example, but the key point is that the value ordering that generates the decision function is quasi-transitive. The example used to establish the possibility of a social decision function in this case is the Pareto ordering. Sen defines indifference for the Pareto ordering in such a way that the order is quasi-transitive, and this is sufficient for his result.

It may seem that a study very much along the lines of saltwater welfare economics could be built on this basis. However, as Sen writes (1969, p. 388) "Lest we jubilate too much at the disappearance of Arrow's impossibility result for social decision functions ... The SDFs used satisfy these conditions of Arrow ... would appear to be unattractive to most of us, except perhaps to the high priests of 'Pareto optimality and no more.'" Yet that need not be the last word. As Sen also notes (1970a, p. 50), "it is possible to consider more complex but also more appealing examples." (This will be further addressed in the appendix to Chapter 8.) For that matter, if there had been a will to do it, Pigou's welfare economics might have been recovered by building on Hildreth's (1953) approach. But for the most part, economists by 1970 were losing interest in rigorous normative economics. And many of those who retained such an interest – not least Sen himself – would choose different directions.

7.3 The second best

Executive summary of the section: Using quite powerful mathematical methods, Lipsey and Lancaster and others argued that in real circumstances, conditions to characterize efficiency would be much more complex than had been realized.

In 1956, Lipsey and Lancaster synthesized a number of earlier special case studies to what they called the General Theory of the Second Best. Their mathematical model thus is a quite abstract model of constrained maximization, intended to represent the mathematical structure of a number of economic studies – especially, but not only, in welfare economics. Their result was discouraging. As Mishan would put it (1960, p. 245), "if one or more of the optimum conditions could not, in the circumstances, be met in one or more of the sectors of the economy, one did not make the best of a bad job by proceeding blithely to fulfil the remaining conditions." In the words of Lipsey and Lancaster (1956, p. 11) themselves,

> The general theorem for the second best optimum states that if there is introduced into a general equilibrium system a constraint which prevents the attainment of one of the Paretian conditions, the other Paretian conditions, although still attainable, are, in general, no longer desirable. In other words, given that one of the Paretian optimum conditions cannot be fulfilled, then an optimum situation can be achieved only by departing from all the other Paretian conditions.

Lipsey and Lancaster first give an extensive verbal survey of the special cases and a discussion of the implications of their "general theory." The general mathematical model comes last, but here we shall reverse their order. At p. 26 they posit that an otherwise unspecified function $F(x_1, ..., x_n)$ is to be maximized subject to an equally unspecified function $\Omega(x_1, ..., x_n)$. This is "is a formalisation of the typical choice situation in economic analysis." The solution of the maximization program is, however, identified with the Pareto optimum. It is characterized by a set of first-order necessary conditions, again unspecified but presumably, if the application is in welfare economics, the marginal equalities. These marginal equalities are expressed as ratios of partial derivatives of the two functions. At the next stage an additional constraint is added that requires one pair of these ratios to differ from equality by a constant multiple. With that addition, the necessary conditions for the optimum are much more complex, involving second and cross-partial derivatives, and differ from one variable x_i to another. "In general, therefore, the conditions for the second best optimum ... will all differ from the corresponding conditions for the attainment of the Paretian optimum" (p. 27).

In the ordinary-language discussion that precedes the general mathematical model they reconsider a number of longstanding discussions of uniform guidelines from the previous literature, such as the idea that equal degrees of monopoly across industries will result in efficiency. In general they reject rules of "piecemeal" welfare economics along the lines of compensation tests and the proposals of Little and Mishan. This is perhaps not quite fair, though, since the "piecemeal" proposals, including those of Little whom they particularly cite, do not rely particularly on the marginal equalities. Rather, it would seem, the analysis of Lipsey and Lancaster is even less favorable to saltwater welfare economics, insofar as saltwater welfare economics supports even a qualified endorsement of the Paretian marginal equalities. Further, interpreting Lipsey and Lancaster's F as a social welfare function, the principle of the second best implies that the informational costs of attaining a maximum of a given social welfare function are far greater than they would be in the absence of a constraint away from the marginal equalities.

At first there was little discussion following their paper. McManus (1959) criticized some details, suggesting that the Lipsey and Lancaster constraint away from the Paretian equalities must mean that government policy is constrained in at least two sectors, and questioned their assumptions about the numeraire good. Substantially Lancaster and Lipsey (1959) conceded these points. Mishan's (1960) passing mention of it in his *Survey* has been quoted. In 1962 Mishan expanded his "Second Thoughts on the Second Best." Lipsey and Lancaster's paper has, he says (p. 205), "carried just so much farther the process of disillusion with conventional welfare economics." But "the second-best theorem does no more than point out that, if additional constraints are imposed, the necessary conditions for a maximum are in general more complex." Initially, Mishan does make some defense of the compensation tests as independent of the marginal equalities, and criticizes Lipsey and Lancaster for ignoring issues of income distribution, remarking (p. 207):

> we can but conclude that movements to a second-best position, no less than movements to an optimal position, must be subjected to more searching criteria, such as those proposed by Little, before they can be comfortably accepted. Having said all this, however, and recalling that "the Scitovsky criterion" plus a "better" distribution of income in the new position was one of the criteria suggested by Little, we may carry on with the argument on the supposition that a movement to an optimal position is a good thing.

From there, Mishan expresses some doubts about the extent to which the mathematical reasoning in Lipsey and Lancaster, however valid, is appropriate to welfare economics. Unfortunately, his method throughout is ordinary language, without mathematical specifications, and as a result is largely (and frankly) conjectural. Athanasiou (1966) rejects the analysis on the grounds that the additional constraint is unlikely to be permanent. Athanasiou stresses that Lipsey and Lancaster's k may not be a constant, but he seems to confuse the possibility of a static non-linearity with irreversible dynamic change. As Athanasiou notes, the second-best policies would themselves have to change as conditions do, and this generates even more complexity. Somehow this brings Athanasiou to support a piecemeal Paretian policy, but the route to this end point is not at all clear in his writing. Morrison (1965) broadens the maximization criterion to allow for approximate equilibria in cases in which a constraint is an open set, and finds, and corrects, an algebraic error in Lipsey and Lancaster (p. 52).

In 1965, Davis and Whinston returned to the theory of the second best. They observe (p. 2) that if the functions Ω in Lipsey and Lancaster are additively separable as between industries, then only the two industries directly constrained are affected – that is, piecemeal policy of assuring the marginal equalities in the remaining n-2 industries remains sound. Further, they note, separability is plausible in the absence of technological externalities in production (p. 3). Accordingly they adopt a somewhat more complex and less general model, assuming separable production functions in distinct industries. Their mathematical approach is also a bit more sophisticated, allowing for inequality constraints and relying on the Kuhn-Tucker theorem. They then focus on decision rules in the respective industries. If these depend only on prices, then they may be consistent with the Paretian equalities and are designated as trivial. If the decision rules have independent variables other than prices, they are non-trivial. For example, the decision rule of an unregulated monopoly would include the quantity sold or the elasticity of demand and so is non-trivial. They then impose the constraint that at least one decision rule is non-trivial and recover a second-best theorem along lines similar to Lipsey and Lancaster.

Bohm (1967) rejects the second-best theory on the grounds that it assumes constraints on government policy which themselves are not given but aspects of government policy. The message seems to be that the government could bring about universal competitive pricing if only it would. His two-good example seems oversimple, since the theory of the second best is consistently concerned with third industries. He then posits a set of government policies, expressed as real numbers (p. 310), and maximizes over this. The government policies (taxes and subsidies, for example) enter into the decision functions of the consumers and producers. He assumes, or limits his attention to a case, in which welfare is maximized when all of these policy variables are zero. If, however, he constrains some of them away from zero, maximization gives rise to a second-best result similar to those of Lipsey and Lancaster and Davis and Whinston; but Bohm dismisses this as irrelevant on the grounds that the constraints on government policy are not themselves natural but political. Bohm has raised a valuable point – in real policy decisions we will often have to maximize (if we can) over a given and perhaps quite limited set of government policies. But that is a quite different thing than characterizing a Pareto optimum by maximization. Further, to assume that welfare is maximized when all policies are represented by zeros – that is, under pure laissez-faire – is to assume away the very issues that the theory of the second best, and indeed welfare economics, is intended to address.

McManus (1967) also addressed the Davis and Whinston version of the second-best theory. He questions their identification of market prices with shadow prices, but notes that this is valid if market equilibria are assumed (p. 318). This is a matter of simplicity versus explicit complication. He criticizes Davis and Whinston for neglect of distributional considerations and interprets their maximand as a fixed-coefficients social welfare function (p. 320). Nevertheless, once again, he recovers quite complex second-best conditions. In conclusion, he writes (p. 321) "the authorities have at their command a set of policy instruments which enter these functions as arguments. The optimum is then found by maximizing welfare subject to all the constraints over the domain of these instruments. Indeed the whole problem has little practical interest without some such explicit policy formulation." This seems to be the sort of model that Bohm had attempted and, again, seems a reasonable approach to a quite different question.

Davis and Whinston (1967) responded to some critics in the vein that, on the one hand, the second best is an unavoidable problem for piecemeal economic policy and, on the other hand, that piecemeal economic policy is the only sort that can realistically occur. Sattinger (1970) addresses the second best explicitly as a model of piecemeal economic policy. He makes a number of simplifying assumptions but recovers essentially similar conditions. Bertrand and Vanek (1971), explicitly in a context of international trade in a small country with fixed world prices, and assuming that at least one tariff cannot be changed, find that nevertheless (in the absence of complementarities) a movement toward equal tariffs improves welfare. Santoni and Church (1972) correct a mathematical error in Lipsey and Lancaster (1956) with the result that even more complex second-best conditions are returned.

The theory of the second best tells us that the information required for a second-best optimum could be very extensive and costly. Drawing on this point, Yew-Kwang Ng (1980, pp. 228–231) offers an argument, reminiscent of Lerner's argument for income equalization, to the effect that when we have no information on the direction of second-best deviations from the marginal equalities, then we minimize the expected value of welfare losses by imposing the first-best Paretian equalities. Thus the rules to apply depend on the information available to the policy maker. In a first-best world, in which we know that there are no second-best interdependencies, certainly first-best rules (that is, Paretian marginal equalities) are appropriate. In a second-best world, in which there are a few known second-best interdependencies, as in a case in which one of two substitute goods is taxed, second-best rules should be applied. In a third-best world, in which second-best interdependencies are known to be complex but knowledge as to their net impacts is scarce, first-best rules are again appropriate. Thus, third best is first best.

Many of the technical criticisms of Lipsey and Lancaster and Davis and Whinston derive from the ambiguity of the concept of the Pareto optimum itself. In Lipsey and Lancaster, if we interpret F as a Pareto-responsive social welfare function, and this is maximized subject only to a production possibility frontier, then the social welfare optimum is a Pareto optimum and is characterized by the marginal equalities. If, then, an additional constraint is imposed, such as a monopoly markup, there will still be one or more constrained Pareto optima, and there will also be a constrained maximum of F, which will be a member of the set of constrained Pareto optima, but not characterizable by the marginal equalities. In Davis and Whinston, there is some ambiguity in their treatment of the objective function. To characterize a Pareto optimum they maximize a weighted sum of the utility indices, as in Lange (1942, whom they do not cite). However, they posit a specific set of weights. While they are not explicit, if seems that they mean to use the weights that would characterize the realized market equilibrium. (Lipsey and Lancaster's objective function could also be construed in this way.) They would then be contrasting the constrained realized market equilibrium (which might or might not be a constrained Pareto optimum) with the particular unconstrained Pareto optimum that would maximize the weighted sum of utility indices *with the same weights*. While the relaxation of the extra constraint might lead to a market equilibrium with different weights, the weights would in any case cancel, so that the realized market equilibrium would then (in the ideal case) be Pareto optimal and characterized by the marginal equalities. If this interpretation is correct, the theory of the second best is a valid – and daunting – difficulty with the concept of Pareto optimality as a tool of economic policy.

We may grant that, in the absence of Little's Superman endowed with the authority of a Soviet central planning bureau, piecemeal economic policy is the only sort that is likely to occur. But is the theory of the second best really fatal for piecemeal economic policy? First, the theory of the second best only addresses one kind of piecemeal policy, namely realizing the Paretian conditions in one sector while they are not realized in some other sector. Marginal cost pricing is an example. However, Mishan has a point. Piecemeal policy might be based on a judicious use of compensation tests. Suppose, for example, that we claim that the Kaldor test is met on the basis of an estimate of an increment in consumer surplus. It is true that, if there are imperfections in other sectors, the demand price curve estimated for the purpose will be distorted from the one that would correspond to a Pareto optimum. However, the demand curve still expresses the marginal willingness to pay, in the circumstances given by the imperfections in the other sectors. Something similar would apply to the Scitovsky test. (What is missing is a similarly explicit test for an improved distribution of income.) Second, it seems likely that Pigou would have relied on a "large-numbers" assumption to avoid the second-best problem. That is, he would have said that in many practical cases, the constrained industry would be too small relative to the market economy as a whole to have any noticeable impact on the decision rules for other industries. A more modern economist might model this with a continuum of industries. Now, in this case the "large-numbers" approach is questionable, until we consider the limits on information available to us. Instead of saying "the constrained industry would be too small to have any noticeable impact" we might say "the constrained industry would be too small to have any impact detectable with available information." Ng's theory of the third best (Ng 1980) similarly takes into account the information available to decision makers. His contributions will be discussed in a later chapter. And in the exceptional cases in which it does have a detectable impact, we would then incorporate it explicitly in our model. All in all, it seems that the theory of the second best is less subversive of piecemeal policy than it is of the search for a grand optimum of the social welfare function, at which both Paretian optimality and the Paretian equalities would be realized.

7.4 Other-regarding preferences

Executive summary of the section: If the utility of some people depends on the prosperity of others, Paretian optimality may conflict with free markets or other important values or both.

From Pigou's writing onward, it was understood that the welfare of one person might depend on the economic activity of some others: the term "externalities in consumption" was used in reference to this possibility. There was, however, relatively little systematic study of it. Meade (1945) addressed this in passing (pp. 53–54) and stimulated a more extensive response from Tintner (1946). Tintner posited a second-order utility function with utilities of all agents as arguments, including the own utility of the agent whose second-order utility function it is. This expresses a case in which the agent's preferences depend directly on the welfare of others. For this case Tintner derives a marginal equality rule with the sum of the marginal utilities of all agents equated to the marginal cost of each good or service, suggesting the condition that Samuelson was to derive for public goods. Tintner then considers a case in which each person's preferences depend on the consumption of each good by all agents, and again extracts a condition involving the summation of marginal utilities of different agents for a particular good. He does not, however, consider whether these marginal equalities could be realized in a market economy. Bergson (1954, p. 251 note 7) takes note of Tintner's discussion but rejects it as confused similarly as Arrow's later impossibility theorem.

Kemp (1955) returns specifically to this point. He considers three cases (pp. 217–18), where

a   A values B's consumption of X.
b   A values anyone's consumption of X.
c   A values increases in the money income of B.

He explicitly considers only negative externalities, supposing that cases of positive externalities would be symmetrical. He relies on two-person examples for most of the exposition. To begin, as he writes (p. 218), "Let us consider the case where the consumption by individual A of commodity X gives offence to certain other individuals B, C, D, ..." That is, A's preferences are determined only by his own consumption, while B values both goods and A's consumption of one of them. Kemp uses Kaldor compensation tests to construct a preference map for B that reflects both B's taste for X and B's aversion to A's possession of it. A "generalized contract locus" in this adjusted indifference map gives marginal conditions that differ from those that would apply in the absence of the externality (p. 221). If it is aggregate consumption of X that "gives offense" (including consumption of X by agent B who is offended), then deviations from the marginal equalities cancel out and the generalized contract locus is identical with the contract locus without externalities (p. 223). However, this assumes an interior solution – that is, both agents consume positive amounts of both goods, and for this case it seems that a corner solution might be relevant. In any case, the conventional optimum conditions do not extend to production, where a uniform tax on the production of the offensive good is optimal. If it is A's money income that "gives offense" to agent B, then a "marginal income tax" corrects the resulting externality. For this result, however, Kemp considers only wage or work income and does not allow either for unearned income or for a lump-sum tax or subsidy (p. 226). He concedes that these are only efficiency conditions and that distribution must also be considered. Further, he writes (p. 227) "Throughout we have taken individual preferences as sacrosanct. The criterion for an individual 'improvement' has been a movement to a 'higher' indifference surface. There is some truth, therefore, in the remark that analyses such as the above 'make jealousy respectable.'" But he then dismisses this concern. Kemp's paper does not seem ever to have been cited[2] but the issues he raises are important ones, even if his analysis was preliminary.

In a paper that was something of a celebration of Pigou, Mishan (1965a p. 15) notes that interdependence of utilities, which might also be thought of as externalities in consumption, had been little considered in welfare economics. At p. 8 he had suggested that they might better not be considered as externalities at all, and perhaps should not be considered relevant to welfare economics. Nevertheless he takes these externalities as one category to be considered in his survey and cites Duesenberry (1949) who had suggested that interdependent utilities might justify reduction of work effort below its free-market level via an income tax. In Mishan (1965b, p. 231 footnote), however, he notes that externalities in consumption could result in an upward-sloping section of the utility-possibility frontier, although if the frontier were carefully defined, not an upward-sloping section but a discontinuity would be the correct expression of this. Here, again, only negative externalities of others' consumption or income are considered.

Other-regarding preferences would play a renewed part in a discussion that arose from a paper of Hochman and Rodgers (1969). This paper might better be considered as a contribution to public choice theory, since it offers an explanatory theory of redistribution, which is subjected to a preliminary empirical test (pp. 553–4). They write (p. 543) "Our approach ... implies that redistributive activities can be justified without a social welfare function that makes inter-personal comparisons, provided that utility interdependence is recognized and taken into account in formulating social policy." However, the central theoretical concept used is Pareto optimality, and Hochman and Rodgers seem to assume the normative implications often associated with that concept (and criticized) in welfare economics. Accordingly it is explored here. Hochman and Rodgers begin with a two-person model in which one (richer) person prefers that another (poorer) have a greater income. This implies that some transfers are Pareto optimal (pp. 545–546). The model is then extended to an n-person model in which each richer person prefers that the income of each poorer person be larger, with similar results that might, however, only be feasible through government action due to a large-numbers problem. In this paper, other-regarding preferences pertain only the income of others, not to their consumption of particular goods. Discussion by Meyer and Shipley (1970), Musgrave (1970), Goldfarb (1970) and their reply (Hochman and Rodgers 1970), together with comments by Polinsky (1971) and Schall (1972), clarified the relation of their model to other literatures and some limitations and extensions of it. Hochman (1972) revisits all this, noting that interdependent utilities lead to an upward-sloping segment of the utility-possibility frontier (p. 354) and, citing unpublished work by Rodgers, offers utility interdependence as a justification of redistribution in kind. This might be particularly important for the theory as an explanation of the politics of redistribution, since programs of redistribution in kind were and are fairly common.

Thurow (1971), however, suggests that the income distribution itself may be an argument of individuals' utility functions. If so, then the income distribution is a pure public good. He assumes a measure of the income distribution – as usual, quite unspecified – and makes it an argument of utility functions (p. 329). He then applies the Lindahl-Samuelson vertical addition model of optimal public good production and concludes that some redistribution will be necessary for a Pareto optimum (p. 331). Hochman, Rodgers and Tullock (1973) respond quite critically. They focus particularly on an oddity in Thurow's example: if a poor man prefers a relatively unequal distribution of income, he might have to be compensated for accepting a transfer, with the resulting equalization of the income distribution less preferred to him (Thurow 1971, p. 330; Hochman et al. 1973, pp. 213–4). Apart from that, though, their point is that they prefer their own theory. Canterbery and Tuckerman (1973), by contrast, defend the approach via a Bergson-Samuelson social welfare function based on more conventional utility functions, largely on what they see as pragmatic grounds. Brown, Fane and Medoff (1973) correct Thurow's mathematical approach. Thurow's response (1973) concedes much of the case of Brown, Fane and Medoff but differs with the others as one might expect. Brennan and Walsh (1977) argued that Pareto optimality could not explain redistribution in kind, in that the objectives of redistribution in kind could be accomplished by taxes on non-preferred goods coupled with lump-sum redistributions, without redistribution of welfare. Thus, redistribution in kind would not be "required" for Pareto optimality. (This follows the outline of a long-discussed argument that marginal cost pricing would not be required for Pareto optimality in a case of unavoidable monopoly.) Olsen (1980) offered a counterargument to which Brennan and Walsh replied (1980). The differences expressed were largely differences of interpretation.

Sen (1970a, 1970b), however, took other-regarding preferences in a different direction. He argues that any reliance on the Pareto principle conflicts with "liberal" values in that there can be no private sphere – no set of personal choices that an individual can make without any interference from the public sector. Sen uses the example of a busybody neighbor who prefers that he, Sen, not read *Lady Chatterley's Lover* (which was then thought a particularly risqué novel, though one of literary merit). Indeed, Sen's argument was already present in Arrow's *Social Choice and Individual Values*, which in passing showed that there could not be even two alternatives over which an individual could be a "dictator." Writing as avowed "liberals," Peacock and Rowley respond (1972) in the affirmative, concurring that liberals "indeed may have to eschew adherence to Pareto optimality" (p. 476). Sen's "impossibility" does not seem to be technically problematic in the way that Arrow's was. Substantively, however, it is problematic: the Pareto criterion had been regarded as useful in that it reflects value judgments that would be widely accepted. But those who would be inclined to support Paretian judgments are the same people who are inclined to support the liberal value of a realm of individual private choice. In each case, the values supported are in some sense individualistic.

What all these arguments have in common is the reliance on individual preferences as the basis for welfare judgments. If individual preferences as between peanuts and cashews are to count, why not individual preferences between my welfare and thine, between my money income and thine, and preferences as to whether John Doe drinks alcoholic beverages or reads *Lady Chatterley's Lover* or does not? And if these preferences complicate welfare judgments and render them objectionable to values that are widely held, what really can be left of the ordinalist New Welfare Economics?

7.5 Qualia, again

Executive summary of the section: If we think of utilities as one category of qualia, some of these difficulties disappear, though it is not clear that we may recover Pigou's satisfaction utilitarianism.

It has been argued in a previous chapter that, for Pigou, utility comprised what might in a more recent philosophical language be described as qualia of a certain kind. Qualia may or may not have arithmetic properties. The sensation of the color red, like Bentham's pleasure and pain, might be characterized as having dimensions of intensity and duration. For Pigou's psychic return to want satisfaction, the case is less clear. If qualia of this category differ in quality as well as intensity and duration, there may be no direct way to bring them "under the category of greater and less." However, these qualia are results of material causes, acts of consumption and of supply of labor services, that in general do have arithmetic properties – this is the Marshall-Pigou measuring rod of money. Moreover, it is here that revealed preference could come to our aid. When people choose, with full knowledge, between the activities that cause qualitatively different qualia, we may infer that they prefer the qualia that are realized to those that are not; and moreover, as Little suggests, that they are likely to be happier as a result.

But are preference and happiness qualia? Preference is a subjective experience, but is there something *it is like* to prefer one thing to another? I can say, on the basis of introspection, that I prefer coffee to tea, and that is a matter of my experience of the qualia I experience when I enjoy them. (It may also reflect my opinions about the health effects of the two beverages.) But this is a speech act, specifically a comparison of qualia, not a quale per se. There is something it is like to express this comparison aloud – the feeling of moving my jaw, among other things – but these qualia are quite distinct from the preference itself. If I do not say it aloud, the quale associated with the reflection is a more subtle experience of mentally resolving a question, or remembering the resolution. But, again, this quale is not the comparison itself. Suppose instead that I comment that I am happier this year than last. I suggest that this, again, is a comparison of qualia, but of a much more complex kind and one that requires aggregation of a large number of qualia. If, then, happiness is admissible, why not preferences at least equally so?

In Chapter 2, it was argued that other-regarding decisions are based, not on the qualia experienced by the decision maker, but on the decision maker's belief that others would experience better qualia as a result of the decision. This, again, is a speech act, a comparison of qualia, and an expression of a belief that (unlike one's reports of one's own qualia) could be mistaken. What this suggests is that the ordinalists were just on the wrong track in their discussion of other-regarding preferences. We should instead return to Pigou in the following limited sense: welfare economics is about the qualia that people experience. Because of the innate privacy of qualia, the qualia experienced by others cannot affect my welfare in that sense. Preferences are relevant to welfare economics insofar as they are preferences among one's own qualia, but preferences over the experiences of others, or over such abstractions as the distribution of income, need to be treated differently.

On this we might return to the discussion of the social welfare function. In that discussion a criticism often made in passing was that values and preferences are different things; that a social welfare function might better be based on individual values, not private preferences. But value judgments would entail preferences over social states. For an egoist, there would be no distinction between private preferences and values. For non-egoists there might be some balancing of individual preferences and other-regarding values. Perhaps it is too much to ask, in these more complex cases, that the preferences over social states induced by compromised individual value judgments have the properties such as transitivity that economists had come to associate with "rationality": but in that case, a rational social welfare function could hardly be conceived. Thus, Arrow makes the assumptions favorable to the existence of a rational social welfare function, and finds such a construct impossible anyway. In the light of the discussion of qualia, however, what sort of thing is a "value judgment"? Consider the judgment that welfares are too unequally distributed, for example. Once again, to express this judgment is not to report one's qualia, but to engage in a speech act, a comparison based on one's belief as to the experiences of others. On this basis, we might agree with Little that each individual would have her or his own individual social welfare function. This does *not* mean that Arrow's project was empty, as Little would have us believe. Given that we each have a social welfare function – that is, preferences over social states – the question remains whether these can be aggregated for a group, and that is the question Arrow addresses. What it does tell us is that (except in the case of the egoist) individual preferences over assortments of goods and services are, at most, only indirectly relevant to it. Utility and values are two different things. Our values tell us how we ought to incorporate the utilities (qualia) of ourselves and others in our judgments of overall welfare.

7.6 Concluding reflections

The New Welfare Economics was not knocked out by Arrow's impossibility result, but it was staggered and continued to stagger for two decades. All the same, Sen seems to have provided the remedy in his conclusion that, even if a consistent social welfare function could not always be defined, a consistent social choice theory could be. While Sen's proof of existence relies on a strict Pareto ranking, and thus is subject to the criticism that the Pareto criterion neglects distribution, it is not limiting. We might be able to define a quasi-order that would extend Sen's Pareto ordering and take account of distribution, perhaps along lines suggested by Little or Mishan. (That will be addressed in the appendix to Chapter 8.) At the same time, however, the Pareto criterion itself was also staggering. The second-best theorem and the various theories of interdependent utilities demonstrated that Paretian judgments could be more complex, and require more information, than had been understood. However, the second-best arguments bear narrowly on prescriptions that the marginal equalities be enforced in a particular industry when they are violated in other industries. The implication is that the Paretian inequalities are, to use Walton's phrase, defeasible – but that was hardly new: Pigou had conceded it, claiming only that a prescription based on the marginal equalities would put the burden of proof on those who wished to argue that, in the particular application, other considerations would outweigh them. The second-best complications would then be among the "other considerations." Moreover, while second-best arguments could be brought against "piecemeal" welfare economics of that kind, "piecemeal" welfare economics could still be based on the compensation tests (which, to be sure, would have to take second-best conditions into account). After long controversy, these tests had been rationalized by Mishan (1973). The complications that arose from interdependent utilities do seem to imply that Paretian judgments would require yet another qualification and perhaps another compound test, to take account of the liberal value of a private sphere of decision. This is to say, again, that Paretian tests are defeasible. Should we then abandon them?

Perhaps the challenge faced by welfare economics in the latter twentieth century was less internal than external. At mid-century, economics was increasingly subdivided among specializations, each of which demanded distinct technical preparations of its practitioners. Welfare economics was no exception. But welfare economics is distinctive among specialties in that its applications are unavoidably housed in other specialties, such as environmental economics, international trade and such. More, much of the content of welfare economics comprised cautions that applications in the various other specialties carried the hazard of fallacy and confusion – hardly the things the applied theorist wants to hear! At the same time, some important alternatives to ordinalist welfare economics were to arise in the last third of the twentieth century. The debate would no longer be between Pigovian utilitarianism and ordinalism, but among a plurality of systems, some of the most important largely outside economics.

Nevertheless, something had been lost. What had been lost was the coherence of the Pigovian system. Pigou's utilitarianism could support both a Paretian test and a test of income distribution, but these were not independent assumptions. Rather, both were derived from the utilitarian hypothesis – and moreover the welfare gain from smoothing consumption, and so from reducing macroeconomic fluctuations, would arise from the same hypothesis. For Pigou, by contrast, interdependent utilities were a potential complication to be assumed away, but utilitarianism at least contained the potential justification for doing so. Drawing also on Sen's observation (1973) that utilities need not be aggregated additively but might be aggregated by any concave function, allowing for a greater or less weight on equality, Pigou's highly coherent account of the impact of economic activity on welfare contained the seed of an even broader and more coherent theory. By contrast, critics of the New Welfare Economics observed justly that the compensation tests or Pareto optimality had to be qualified by tests of consistency, by an ad hoc judgment of the quality of the income distribution and, at best, by further ad hoc tests of liberal privacy and for second-best distortions. Regardless of Arrow's theory, as Little had noted, social welfare functions offered no practical way out of this jumble of ad-hockery. To the applied economist looking for normative guidelines, this must have seemed more of a muddle than a help.

Notes

1 Baumol's *Welfare Economics and the Theory of the State* (1952b) similarly uses welfare economics as a predictive hypothesis about political choices, but does not seem to have influenced the subsequent development of the theory of public choice. For a retrospective discussion of this work, see McCain (2014), ch. 8, esp. note 1.
2 Searches in JSTOR and Web of Science gave no evidence of any citations to it.

References

Arrow, Kenneth J. (1951a) *Social Choice and Individual Values* (New York: Wiley).

Arrow, Kenneth J. (1951b) Little's Critique of Welfare Economics, *American Economic Review* v. 41, no. 5 (Dec) pp. 923–934.

Athanasiou, L. (1966) Some Notes on the Theory of Second-Best, *Oxford Economic Papers, New Series* v. 18, no. 1 (Mar) pp. 83–87.

Baumol, William (1964) *Welfare Economics and the Theory of the State* (Cambridge, Mass.: Harvard University Press).

Bergson, A. (1938) A Reformulation of Certain Aspects of Welfare Economics, *Quarterly Journal of Economics* (Feb).

Bergson, Abram (1954) On the Concept of Social Welfare, *Quarterly Journal of Economics* v. 68, no. 2 (May) pp. 233–252.

Bertrand, Trent J. and Jaroslav Vanek (1971) The Theory of Tariffs, Taxes, and Subsidies: Some Aspects of the Second Best, *American Economic Review* v. 61, no. 5 (Dec) pp. 925–931.

Black, Duncan (1948) On the Rationale of Group Decision-making, *Journal of Political Economy* v. 56, no. 1 (Feb) pp. 23–34.

Black, Duncan (1969) On Arrow's Impossibility Theorem, *Journal of Law and Economics* v. 12, no. 2 (Oct) pp. 227–248.

Blau, Juliuan H. (1957) The Existence of Social Welfare Functions, *Econometrica* v. 25, no. 2 (Apr) pp. 302–313.

Blau, Juliuan H. (1971) Arrow's Theorem with Weak Independence, *Economica, New Series* v. 38, no. 152 (Nov) pp. 413–420.

Bohm, P. (1967) On the Theory of "Second-Best", *Review of Economic Studies* v. 34, no. 3 (Jul) pp. 301–314.

Brennan, Geoffrey and Cliff Walsh (1977) Pareto-Desirable Redistribution in Kind: An Impossibility Theorem, *American Economic Review* v. 67, no. 5 (Dec) pp. 987–990.

Brennan, Geoffrey and Cliff Walsh (1980) Pareto-Desirable Redistribution in Kind: Reply, *American Economic Review* v. 70, no. 5 (Dec) pp. 1032–1036.

Brown, Charles, George Fane and James Medoff (1973) The Income Distribution as a Pure Public Good: Comment, *Quarterly Journal of Economics* v. 87, no. 2 (May) pp. 296–303.

Buchanan, James M. (1954a) Social Choice, Democracy, and Free Markets, *Journal of Political Economy* v. 62, no. 2 (Apr) pp. 114–123.

Buchanan, James M. (1954b) Individual Choice in Voting and the Market, *Journal of Political Economy* v. 62, no. 4 (Aug) pp. 334–343.

Buchanan, James and Gordon Tullock (1962) *The Calculus of Consent: Logical Foundations of Constitutional Democracy* (Ann Arbor, Mich.: University of Michigan Press).

Campbell, Donald E. (1973) Social Choice and Intensity of Preference, *Journal of Political Economy* v. 81, no. 1 (Jan–Feb) pp. 211–218.

Canterbery, E. R. and Tuckerman, H. P. (1973) Reflection upon the Income Distribution as a Pure Public Good, *Quarterly Journal of Economics* v. 87, no. 2 (May) pp. 304–310.

Coleman, James S. (1966) The Possibility of a Social Welfare Function, *American Economic Review* v. 56, no. 5 (Dec) pp. 1105–1122.

Contini, Bruno (1966) A Note on Arrow's Postulates for a Social Welfare Function, *Journal of Political Economy* v. 74, no. 3 (Jun) pp. 278–280.

Cooter, Robert and Peter Rappoport (1984) Were the Ordinalists Wrong about Welfare Economics? *Journal of Economic Literature* v. 22, no. 2 (Jun) pp. 507–530.

Davis, O. A. and Andrew B. Whinston (1965) Welfare Economics and the Theory of Second-Best, *Review of Economic Studies* v. 32, no. 1 (Jan.) pp. 1–14.

Davis, O.A. and Andrew B. Whinston (1967) Piecemeal Policy in the Theory of Second-Best, *Review of Economic Studies* v. 34, no. 3 (Jul.) pp. 323–331.

Davis, Richard G. (1958) Comment on Arrow and the New Welfare Economics, *Economic Journal* v. 68, no. 272 (Dec) pp. 834–835.

Duesenberry, James S. (1949) *Income, Saving, and the Theory of Consumer Behavior* (Cambridge, Mass.: Harvard University Press).

Goldfarb, Robert (1970) Pareto Optimal Redistribution: Comment, *American Economic Review* v. 60, no. 5 (Dec) pp. 994–996.

Gorman, W. M. (1955) The Intransitivity of Certain Criteria Used in Welfare Economics, *Oxford Economic Papers* v. 7, no. 1 (Feb) pp. 25–35.

Hildreth, Clifford (1953) Alternative Conditions for Social Orderings, *Econometrica* v. 21, no. 1 (Jan) pp. 81–94.

Hochman, H. M. (1972) Individual Preferences and Distributional Adjustments, *American Economic Review* v. 62, no. 5 (Mar) pp. 353–360.

Hochman, H. M. and J. D. Rodgers (1969) Pareto-Optimal Redistribution, *American Economic Review* v. 59, no. 4 (Sep) pp. 542–557.

Hochman, H. M. and J. D. Rodgers (1970) Pareto-Optimal Redistribution: Reply, *American Economic Review* v. 60, no. 5 (Sep) pp. 997–1002.

Hochman, H. M., J. D. Rodgers and Gordon Tullock (1973) On the Income Distribution as a Public Good, *Quarterly Journal of Economics* v. 87, no. 2 (May) pp. 311–315.

Inada, Ken-ichi (1964) On the Economic Welfare Function, *Econometrica* v. 32, no. 3 (Jul) pp. 316–338.

Kemp, Murray C. (1953–1954) Arrow's General Possibility Theorem, *Review of Economic Studies* v. 21, no. 3 pp. 240–243.

Kemp, Murray C. (1955) The Efficiency of Competition as an Allocator of Resources: II. External Economies of Consumption, *Canadian Journal of Economics and Political Science / Revue canadienne d'Economique et de Science politique* v. 21, no. 2 (May) pp. 217–227.

Lancaster, Kelvin and R. G. Lipsey (1959) McManus on Second Best, *Review of Economic Studies* v. 26, no. 3 (Jun) pp. 225–226.

Lange, Oscar (1942) The Foundations of Welfare Economics, *Econometrica* v. 10, pp. 215–228.

Lipsey, R. G. and K. Lancaster (1956) The General Theory of the Second Best, *Review of Economic Studies* v. 24, pp. 11–32.

Little, I. M. D. (1952) Social Choice and Individual Values, *Journal of Political Economy* v. 60, no. 5 (Oct) pp. 422–432.

Maskin, Eric (1999) Nash Equilibrium and Welfare Optimality (Paper presented at the summer workshop of the Econometric Society in Paris, June 1977), *Review of Economic Studies* v. 66, pp. 23–38.

McCain, Roger A. (2014) *Reframing Economics: Economic Action as Imperfect Cooperation* (Cheltenham: Edward Elgar).

McCain, Roger A. (2017) *Approaching Equality: What Can Be Done about Wealth Inequality* (Cheltenham: Edward Elgar).

McManus, M. (1959) Comments on the General Theory of Second-Best, *Review of Economic Studies* v. 26, no. 3 (Jun) pp. 209–224.

McManus, M. (1967) Private and Social Costs in the Theory of Second Best, *Review of Economic Studies* v. 34, no. 3 (Jul) pp. 317–321.

Meade, J. E. (1945) Mr. Lerner on the "Economics of Control", *Economic Journal* v. 55, no. 217 (Apr) pp. 47–69.

Meyer, Paul A. and J. J. Shipley (1970) Pareto Optimal Redistribution: Comment, *American Economic Review* v. 60, no. 5 (Dec) pp. 988–990.

Mishan, E. J. (1957) An Investigation into Some Alleged Contradictions in Welfare Economics, *Economic Journal* v. 67, no. 267 (Sep) pp. 445–454.

Mishan, E. J. (1960) A Survey of Welfare Economics, 1939–1959, *Economic Journal* v. 70, no. 278 (Jun) pp. 197–265.

Mishan, E. J. (1962) Second Thoughts on the Second Best, *Oxford Economic Papers* v. 14, pp. 205–217.

Mishan, E. J. (1965a) Reflections on Recent Developments in the Concept of External Effects, *Canadian Journal of Economics and Political Science / Revue canadienne d'Economique et de Science politique* v. 31, no. 1 (Feb) pp. 3–34.

Mishan, E. J. (1965b) The Recent Debate on Welfare Criteria, *Oxford Economic Papers, New Series* v. 17, no. 2 (Jul) pp. 219–236.

Mishan, E. J. (1973) Welfare Criteria: Resolution of a Paradox, *Economic Journal* v. 83, no. 331 (Sep) pp. 747–767.

Morrison, Clarence C. (1965) The Nature of Second-Best, *Southern Economic Journal* v. 32, no. 11 (Jul) pp. 49–52.

Musgrave, Richard A. (1970) Pareto Optimal Redistribution: Comment, *American Economic Review* v. 60, no. 5 (Dec) pp. 991–993.

Nash, John (1950) Equilibrium Points in n-Person Games, *Proceedings of the National Academy of Science* v. 36, pp. 48–49.

Ng, Yew-Kwang (1980) *Welfare Economics: Introduction and Development of Basic Concepts* (New York: Wiley Halsted Press).

Olsen, Edgar O. (1980) Pareto-Desirable Redistribution in Kind: Comment, *American Economic Review* v. 70, no. 5 (Dec) pp. 1028–1031.

Osborne, D. K. (1976) Irrelevant Alternatives and Social Welfare, *Econometrica* v. 44, no. 5 (Sep) pp. 1001–1015.

Peacock, Alan T. and Charles K. Rowley (1972) Pareto Optimality and the Political Economy of Liberalism, *Journal of Political Economy* v. 80, no. 3 (May–Jun) pp. 476–490.

Polinsky, A. Mitchell (1971) Shortsightedness and Nonmarginal Pareto Optimal Redistribution, *American Economic Review* v. 61, no. 5 (Dec) pp. 972–979.

Rothenberg, Jerome (1953) Conditions for a Social Welfare Function, *Journal of Political Economy* v. 61, no. 5 (Oct) pp. 389–405.

Santoni, G. and A. Church (1972) A Comment on the General Theorem of Second Best, *Review of Economic Studies* v. 39, no. 4 (Sep) pp. 527–530.

Sattinger, M. (1970) A Model for Piecemeal Welfare Policy, *Review of Economic Studies* v. 37, no. 2 (Arp) pp. 298–301.

Schall, Lawrence (1972) Interdependent Utilities and Pareto Optimality, *Quarterly Journal of Economics* v. 86, no. 1 (Feb) pp. 19–24.

Sen, Amartya K. (1966) A Possibility Theorem on Majority Decisions, *Econometrica* v. 34, no. 2 (Apr) pp. 491–499.

Sen, Amartya (1969) Quasi-Transitivity, Rational Choice and Collective Decisions, *Review of Economic Studies* v. 36, no. 3 (July) pp. 381–393.

Sen, Amartya (1970a) *Collective Choice and Social Welfare* (London: Holden-Day).

Sen, Amartya (1970b) The Impossibility of a Paretian Liberal, *Journal of Political Economy* v. 78, no. 1 (Jan) pp. 152–157.

Sen, Amartya (1973) On Ignorance and Equal Distribution, *American Economic Review* v. 63, no. 5 (Dec) pp. 1022–1024.

Thurow, Lester C. (1971) The Income Distribution as a Pure Public Good, *Quarterly Journal of Economics* v. 85, no. 2 (May) pp. 327–336.

Thurow, Lester C. (1973) The Income Distribution as a Pure Public Good: A Response, *Quarterly Journal of Economics* v. 87, no. 2 (May) pp. 316–319.

Tintner, Gerhard (1946) A Note on Welfare Economics, *Econometrica* v. 14, no. 1 (Jan) pp. 69–78.

Tullock, Gordon (1967) The General Irrelevance of the General Impossibility Theorem, *Quarterly Journal of Economics* v. 81, no. 2 (May) pp. 256–270.

Vickrey, William (1960) Utility, Strategy, and Social Decision Rules, *Quarterly Journal of Economics* v. 74, no. 4 (Nov) pp. 507–535.

von Neumann, John and Oskar Morgenstern (1944) *Theory of Games and Economic Behavior* (Princeton, N.J.: Princeton University Press).

Weirich, Paul (1984) Interpersonal Utility in Principles of Social Choice, *Erkenntnis* v. 21, no. 3 (Nov) pp. 295–317.

Weldon, J. C. (1952) On the Problem of Social Welfare Functions, *Canadian Journal of Economics and Political Science / Revue canadienne d'Economique et de Science politique* v. 18, no. 4 (Nov) pp. 452–463.

Williamson, Oliver E. and Thomas J. Sargent (1967) Social Choice: A Probabalistic Approach, *Economic Journal* v. 77, no. 308 (Dec) pp. 797–813.

Zeckhauser, Richard (1969) Majority Rule with Lotteries on Alternatives, *Quarterly Journal of Economics* v. 83, no. 4 (Nov) pp. 696–703.

8 The veil of ignorance

The ideas of John Rawls require some attention. Rawls was not a welfare economist – indeed his ideas are rather distant from economics – but he was influenced by welfare economics and has in turn influenced thinking in economics as well as a wide range of social scientific and philosophic thought. The position in Rawls' *A Theory of Justice* (1971) is in a sense social contractarian. Among the best-known ideas from that work are the "original position" and the "difference principle." Individuals deliberate to arrive at a just social system in an "original position" of equality (p. 62) and behind a veil of ignorance such that each is unaware of what position she or he would occupy once the system is established. The "original position" from which the social contract emerges is not, of course, a historical condition (p. 12). Rather it is a framework of thought, and the restrictions of the original position constrain thought in such a way that self-regarding decisions are nevertheless fair (pp. 136, 516). The influence of Rawls for social philosophy in the latter twentieth century can hardly be overestimated. His influence in economics as a whole has been less pronounced, but one strand that emerged from welfare economics adopted this understanding of fairness and applies it to define a fair distribution of income. Broadly speaking, this conception is social contractarian. For this chapter, we will first review a contribution of John Harsanyi, which precedes Rawls and of which he is critical; Lerner's argument from ignorance for redistribution, then the ideas of Rawls himself and finally a modest literature that has attempted to construct an economics that combines Paretian welfare economics with a somewhat Rawlsian understanding of a "fair" distribution of income.

8.1 Harsanyi's reconstruction of utilitarianism

Executive summary of the section: Drawing on the von Neumann-Morgenstern utility measurement and using the veil of ignorance convention, Harsanyi recovered an aggregate utility social welfare function.

The remarkable biography of John Harsanyi (1920–2000) is fairly well known. Having been a refugee from Nazi and Communist regimes in Hungary, and earning a living as a manual laborer in Australia, studying in the evening for a master's degree in economics – his third field of study – he submitted papers to the *Journal of Political Economy* that became a step toward a career in the United States and a share in the 1994 Nobel Memorial Prize for his work in game theory. It is those early papers that concern us here.

In a two-page paper (Harsanyi 1953) that lists Harsanyi as "Formerly of the University of Budapest," Harsanyi addresses the relevance of the "measure" of utility in von Neumann and Morgenstern to welfare economics. As observed in earlier chapters, this had been intensively discussed and questioned. The von Neumann-Morgenstern measure would reflect the person's attitude toward risk: ought the social significance of a person's expenditure be considered more or less because the person is more or less risk averse? In particular, Friedman and Savage (1948, 1952) had explained gambling behavior by a range of increasing marginal utility of income. Harsanyi (1953, p. 435) argues that this is misleading, writing

> When welfare economists compare the marginal utility of higher and of lower incomes, they have in mind people's habitual incomes. On this basis it is a reasonable assumption that the wealthy derive, from a marginal dollar, less utility than the poor do. On the contrary, gamblers compare the marginal utility of their actual income with the utility they expect from a sudden large increase in their income, which latter is certainly much higher than the utility of this higher income would be for a person long accustomed to enjoying it.

Following this hint that adaptation of happiness to the stable income must be allowed for, Harsanyi also hints at what would later be called loss aversion, the taste for gambling per se, and mentions simple irrationality as yet another confounding factor in relating gambling to utility.

But the central point of Harsanyi's paper is that, with these qualifications, value judgments on social welfare can be interpreted in a way that relies on the von Neumann-Morgenstern theory. The key point is that valid judgments of welfare must be impartial, disinterested, "impersonal" (p. 434). He writes (pp. 434–5):

> Now, a value judgment on the distribution of income would show the required impersonality to the highest degree if the person who made this judgment had to choose a particular income distribution in complete ignorance of what his own relative position (and the position of those near to his heart) would be within the system chosen. This would be the case if he had exactly the same chance of obtaining the first position (corresponding to the highest income) or the second or the third, etc., up to the last position (corresponding to the lowest income) available within

that scheme. This choice in that hypothetical case would be a clear instance of a "choice involving risk."

In 1955 Harsanyi expands on this, citing Marshak (1954) and concluding that

> it has been shown that a rational man (whose choices satisfy certain simple postulates of rationality) must act as if he ascribed numerical subjective probabilities to all alternative hypotheses, even if his factual information is insufficient to do this on an objective basis – so in welfare economics we have also found that a rational man (whose choices satisfy certain simple postulates of rationality and impartiality) must likewise act as if he made quantitative interpersonal comparisons of utility, even if his factual information is insufficient to do this on an objective basis.

His proof of this proposition draws on Fleming's (1952) formalization of the idea in turn traceable to Lange (1934) that people would be able to compare the increase in benefits as between two transitions from one bundle of consumer goods to another. Harsanyi generalized Fleming's model to allow for risky prospects, again using the Marshak theory of choice among risky prospects, and, through a series of theorems, demonstrates that on these postulates of rational behavior together, the social welfare function must be a weighted sum of the von Neumann-Morgenstern utilities (p. 314). Further (p. 316),

> I have argued elsewhere that an individual's preferences satisfy this requirement of impersonality if they indicate what social situation he would choose if he did not know what his personal position would be in the new situation chosen (and in any of its alternatives) but rather had an equal chance of obtaining any of the social positions existing in this situation, from the highest down to the lowest ... More exactly, if the former individual has any objective criterion for comparing his fellows' utilities with one another and with his own ... his social welfare function will represent the unweighted mean of these utilities, while in the absence of such an objective criterion it will, in general, represent their weighted mean, with arbitrary weights depending only on his personal value judgments. In the former case social welfare will in a sense be an objective quantity, whereas in the latter case it will contain an important subjective element.

In other words: any *rational* person will adopt a social welfare that is a weighted sum of cardinal utility functions (as proven in the paper) and rational persons who reason impartially, as if behind a veil of ignorance, will concur on an unweighted mean of utility functions. At p. 319 he discusses (what would seem to be) non-economic determinants of welfare and, like Pigou, suggesting what Walton (1989) calls reasonable dialog, Harsanyi places the burden of proof on those who assert that welfare is influenced by phenomena "unchangeable" through economic policy.

We recall that (two decades later) other-regarding preferences raised issues for Paretian welfare economics. Let us see how this might have been handled in Harsanyi's system. An individual's other-regarding preferences would clearly enter into the determination of her individual social welfare function. That is: they would influence the weights attached to the utility of others in that individual's weighted average of everyone's utilities. For a person who feels no other-regarding preferences, the weight on her own utility would be one, and that on the utility of others zero. Presumably many would weight the utility of others somewhat less than one's own utility, and the weight on others' utility might depend on whether they are kin or personal acquaintances. Impartial consideration would require one to choose equal weights. But that does not mean that the other-regarding preferences of the individuals would be ignored (see esp. note 5, p. 311). Rather, the social welfare function seems to be an equally weighted mean of the individual social welfare functions. Thus (p. 320) Little's (1952) criticism that social welfare functions can only be individual is refuted. On the other hand, impartial considerations demand that we set aside our "subjective" individual value judgments and substitute for them the equal weighting of utility functions. Does that not mean that we must set aside our private other-regarding preferences in doing so? That behind the veil of ignorance we must be ignorant even of our individual, idiosyncratic, other-regarding preferences? Yet – to maximize utility – we must be aware of our preferences among the goods we ourselves enjoy and, indeed, aware of others' preferences among the goods they enjoy. (But reliance on markets for the allocation of private goods may resolve that problem of ignorance.) Harsanyi concedes that to the extent that our knowledge is incomplete we can only rely on personal value judgments, but that as information increases the impartial judgments of rational individuals would converge on an equally weighted average of individual utilities.

Harsanyi's reconstruction of utilitarianism attracted the attention of some important economists and he was to complete a PhD study for the doctorate in his third field – after philosophy and sociology – under the guidance of Kenneth Arrow. However, it seems to have had limited influence in economics. Did it influence the ideas of Rawls? While this question does not admit of an unequivocal answer there is plausible reason to believe that it did.

8.2 Lerner revisited

Executive summary of the section: Samuelson and others revisited Lerner's equalitarian argument. Much of the discussion centered on the possibility that ignorance could explain anything.

We recall that Lerner (1944) had proposed that equalization of income would increase the expected value of aggregate utility. The "veil of ignorance" in this case is very limited: the government is ignorant as to which of its subjects is more and less susceptible to satisfaction. Nevertheless, Samuelson would have it in this group. We also recall that there were a few reviews, with some doubts expressed about Lerner's argument from ignorance, especially by Little.

There it lay until Samuelson's address celebrating Lerner's sixtieth birthday. Samuelson follows Little in dismissing Lerner's postulate of ignorance of the capacities for satisfaction, quoting but not citing Little (Samuelson 1964, p. 174.) However, Samuelson does not miss the argument from diminishing marginal utility. He essentially treats it as a kind of social contract formulation, which he calls a voting model, with the veil of ignorance then taking the place of the ignorance of the capacities for satisfaction. This in turn Samuelson dismisses as unrealistic, calling instead for "Bergson social welfare functions." By 1964, the more common term was "Bergson-Samuelson social welfare functions"!

Samuelson's remarks brought Lerner's argument back to the attention of others, though, including the author of this book. Accordingly I will shift temporarily to a first-person narrative. In the first instance it was my teacher, William Breit, whose attention was engaged, along with that of his collaborator William Culbertson. They revisited Samuelson's "voting model," placing it securely "at the constitutional level of choice" (Breit and Culbertson 1970, p. 438), to use the language they took from Buchanan and Tullock (1962). They argue that, with "log-rolling," some risk lovers may be induced to vote for equality. They then attribute to Lerner two theorems, a "weak" theory that establishes a positive expected value from equalization of distribution, and a "strong" theory that establishes that, for a large group, an increase in total satisfaction is a certainty. (Of these I find only the first in Lerner, and Lerner agrees: Lerner 1970, p. 442). They then provide what they describe as a rigorous proof of the strong theory (Breit and Culbertson 1970, p. 440). Lerner points out some difficulties in it (1970, p. 442.) But perhaps there is a sound intuition in their argument: I conjecture that, as the size of the population increases, the probability that the net benefit from redistribution toward equality is positive approaches 1 in the limit, and that inference had not previously been pointed out. To that extent, "weak and strong" theorems somewhat as Breit and Culbertson proposed might actually be set out, a point that I missed at the time. Lerner, however, did not quite miss it (1970, p. 443).

Breit and Culbertson's piece led to three "further comments," one of them mine. McManus et al. (1972) first give a formal mathematical proof of the Lerner theorem for n persons, treating the equal probability assumption as Bayesian (p. 491). They also argue that the equal-ignorance assumption, problematic as it is, is necessary only because Lerner has followed the utilitarian tradition by maximizing the sum of utilities. They propose instead a maximin aggregation of utility (p. 495). Rawls' *A Theory of Justice* had just appeared in 1971 and is not cited.

I took the opportunity to respond to Breit and Culbertson but my real target was Little and Samuelson and the phrase "from ignorance can come only ignorance." In place of Lerner's "absolute ignorance" I postulated minimum information about the distribution of utility functions and, drawing on Theil (1967) and Shannon-Weaver information theory, I observed that equal probabilities are a condition for minimum information (McCain 1972, p. 489). This provides another, not strictly Bayesian, justification for the equal-probability assumption. I also suggested (p. 499) that Lerner's conclusion should be interpreted as the non-normative first term of a syllogism in which the second term is a value judgment and the third an imperative. The point was that *no* policy recommendations can be made without value judgments. That was pretty clearly Lerner's view, often lost sight of in the discussion, but I have modified my views somewhat in the course of this study.

Amartya Sen joined the discussion (1973) with a claim of priority in the maximin aggregation of utilities and an extension of the theorem that, with the equi-probability assumption, equal distribution is optimal for any concave function aggregating individual utilities. The maximin aggregation would be an extreme special case. This seems to me to be very important. To be a utilitarian is to be a consequentialist who regards subjective pleasures and pains or satisfaction of wants or something like that as the consequences that "count." This does not tell us how they should be aggregated. Summation in itself does not reflect any value judgment for equality, though, as Lerner and many others had argued, such a judgment may on some premises be inferred from it. Sens' concave aggregation functions admit of equalitarian value judgments of any weight. Sen's ideas, of course, have evolved in a complex non-utilitarian direction.

The issue sprang up again as recently as 2002, as Pestieau et al. argue that the central authority could obtain information about the individual utility functions by making randomized offers so that individuals would sort themselves by relative risk aversion. They assume, however (p. 541), that individuals' preference systems do not differ "in a Lerner world." I do not find this assumption in Lerner.

8.3 Rawls' renewal of the social contract theory

Executive summary of the section: Rawls' well-known ideas drew explicitly on the veil of ignorance convention to support a normative social theory regarded by some (but perhaps not correctly) as quite egalitarian.

For Rawls, as noted, decisions are fair if they are made as if behind a veil of ignorance. He supposes, therefore, that the principles of a fair society are determined by this as-if reasoning, and thus form what we may think of as a social contract. As with a conventional contract, that is, the social contract is founded on mutual benefit, and the benefit that we derive from it carries with it an obligation to act in accordance with the contract. For Rawls, this veil of ignorance is extended even to the point that the individual does not know his or her tastes with respect to goods and services, nor, perhaps (though I do not find this in Rawls) the individual's gender – whether he or she is a he or she! In the original position "the parties do not know their conception of the good" (Rawls 1971, p. 142). These restrictions are such that self-interest leads the individual to take the perspective of a representative person. One cannot seek advantage for one's special position because one (hypothetically!) does not know what one's special position is. Moreover, the uncertainty of the original position is so radical that probabilities cannot be used (pp. 169–170). Thus Rawls excludes the probabilistic utilitarianism of Hildreth (1953), and Harsanyi (1953, 1955) discussed above. For such radical uncertainty, Rawls supposes, the max min is the appropriate decision procedure. "The restrictions which would so arise might be thought of as those a person would keep in mind if he were designing a practice in which his enemy were to assign him his place" (Rawls 1957, p. 656). Thus the difference principle: inequalities are tolerable only if they improve the condition of the least favored representative person.

A contrast with Harsanyi's Bayesian veil of ignorance raises the question whether, and in what sense, Rawls' max-min criterion is rational. Rawls' comment suggests the max-min solution in game theory, but in game theory the max-min criterion is applicable primarily in zero-sum games. For social contract theory, surely, variable-sum games are the nearer concept. The max-min criterion may also express extreme risk aversion. But the max-min criterion also generalizes a cake-cutting solution (Dubins and Spanier 1961; Kuhn 1967) in problems of fair division. It is as if the various roles in the realized society were to be chosen by each of the deliberators in turn, with each reasoning as if he would be the last to choose. This is not merely a criterion of rationality but of rational fairness. This (as Harsanyi had argued) gives the argument for fairness a kind of objectivity. A disagreement as to what is fair cannot arise just from a difference of subjective preferences among social arrangements, but must be based on some evaluation of the merits of the reasoning and fact assumed, and in that sense is objective.

But how are individuals in the original position to judge better or worse even for a hypothetical representative individual given the veil of ignorance that extends even to their "conception of the good," their tastes and risk aversion? They are supposed to judge well-being in terms of quantities of "primary goods": that is "things which it is supposed that a rational man wants whatever else he wants" (Rawls 1971, p. 92; note also p. 142). Moreover, the broad categories of these "primary goods," "rights and liberties, opportunities and powers, income and wealth" (p. 92) are lexically ranked (p. 44), with liberties taking first place relative to the others. The role of "primary goods" motivates my observation, above, that Rawls' ideas are distant from economics. For Rawls, rational choices are not the choices of instruments to attain some given wants, but rather the wants themselves are rational, and rationality is goodness (Rawls 1971, ch. 7).

Further, the difference principle is not as equalitarian as it may appear. Large rewards for entrepreneurs may benefit the least favored of non-entrepreneurs (p. 78) and it is assumed that a competitive economy will not create increasing inequality (p. 158) and this, together with other details of economic theory, is known at the original position despite the veil of ignorance. On the other hand, "both the absolute and the relative differences allowed in a well-ordered society are probably less than those that have often prevailed. Although in theory the difference principle permits indefinitely large inequalities" (p. 536) and "The naturally advantaged are not to gain merely because they are more gifted, but only ... for using their endowments in ways that help the less fortunate as well" (pp. 101–2).

Further yet: for Rawls, what is chosen in the original position is not legislation, nor even (as Buchanan might have it) a constitution, but a set of principles for the conception and formation of a just society. Thus, for example, a set of redistributive taxes and subsidies is not on the menu. Indeed the decision at the original position is among a few definite alternatives (p. 122), not (as in welfare economics) among a continuum of Pareto optima. Further, these principles are moral principles, principles that are to guide a constitutional convention, at which "the veil of ignorance is partly lifted" (p. 197) and at a yet subsequent stage of legislation, at which the veil of ignorance is further, but not entirely, lifted. Moreover, the same judgments are to guide the decisions of private individuals at a fourth stage to comply with the rules (p. 198). Since the terms of the contract are values agreed upon – not a sovereign with powers of enforcement – Rawls is quite concerned with the stability of the contract. This concern seems central especially to chapters 6 through 8. It also distinguishes Rawls' ideas radically not only from welfare economics but also from the social contractarian ideas of Hobbes, which in some sense underlie welfare economics.

Indeed, Rawls seems a bit puzzled as to what Hobbes is about, writing "One may think of the Hobbesian sovereign as a mechanism added to a system of cooperation which would be unstable without it" (p. 497). Rawls' difference from Hobbes seems a key point, so it will be useful to indicate what, in my own opinion, Hobbes' ideas were. For Hobbes, then, the sovereign is not a corrective mechanism but the subject of the social contract itself. So far as individual values are concerned, Hobbes' conception of the social contract is a worst-case analysis. Thus he assumes that individuals are egoists, the worst case for cooperation. To the extent that human beings are motivated as Rawls says they are (in ch. 7) – by their commitment to principles of justice – the case for stability of a Hobbesian social contract is all the stronger. Conversely, though, for a Hobbesian social contract stability does not seem to be the problem. From the viewpoint of non-cooperative game theory (McCain 2014, p. 211) the coercive power of government, so long as it is credible, can stabilize many different systems of laws, so that the problem for social contract theory is the multiplicity of locally stable (Nash equilibrial) contracts. It is here – to choose among the plurality of locally stable equilibria – that the deliberation of agents in the hypothetical original position behind a veil of ignorance is required. Their deliberation is an optimization over a given set of alternatives and is a deliberation that might well be carried on by egoists.

It would go too far to say that Hobbes is not concerned with values. Hobbes says that we are obliged to one another, as fellow subjects of the sovereign, not only to obey the sovereign but also to act peacefully in other ways (Hobbes 1968 [1651], pp. 201–217). These are moral laws, but they derive from the power of the sovereign and are invalid without it. Conversely, their stability is not in question. It is desirable that people try to keep them, but they are no less valid if most people scoff at them – as an egoist might do – since they derive, not from the agreement to act on them, but from the security that results from the agreement to obey the sovereign. This security is the motive for the agreement in the original position, an agreement no less reasonable to egoists than to others because, as Rawls puts it (1971, p. 103), "the well-being of each depends on a scheme of cooperation without which no one could have a satisfactory life."

For Rawls, unlike Hobbes, the principles agreed on at the original position can be stable only if they are usually followed without compulsion. However, even if individuals are motivated by the principles agreed on at the original position, "they may ... lack full confidence in one another. They may suspect that others are not doing their part, and so they may be tempted not to do theirs. The general awareness of these temptations may eventually cause the scheme to break down" (p. 240). All this being so, Rawls – with some seeming reluctance – concedes that some compulsion may be necessary to maintain the stability of the contract (pp. 565–6) but seems to regard this as a special case. This is the problem of stability that costs Rawls a great many words.

If we take the Hobbesian position, then Rawls is mistaken in treating the veil of ignorance as primary and stability as a secondary condition to be considered among the deliberations at the original position. Nevertheless, in the game-theoretic perspective, the stability of one among a set of Nash equilibria is not absolute. Rather, the equilibrium may be metastable. If circumstances render the coercive power of government momentarily incredible (as in France in 1789 and 1848 and in the Arab Spring) an oppressed class will have neither a reasonable obligation nor a motive to support the established order. Civil war or transformation to another Nash equilibrium may occur, or both. If, however, there is no oppressed class – if, that is, society is organized according to Rawls' difference principle – then the social contract may be stable even if the coercive power of government is momentarily incredible. This could be a reason for rational egoists to choose a Rawlsian social contract even if the veil of ignorance is not altogether perfect. Moreover, to the extent that a Rawlsian contract is indeed more stable than other candidates – either for Rawls' reasons or for the reasons sketched here – we might hope that, in the absence of any social contract, a Rawlsian order would tend to evolve. Stable configurations, after all, tend to supplant unstable configurations in an evolutionary process. "The arc of the moral universe is long, but it bends toward justice." This could be a long and bloody history, though. Then the objective of progressive reformers would be to reduce the delay and blood by "intelligent design" of legislation and constitutional change. Thus we arrive at Rawls' difference principle by a route more or less the reverse of Rawls, but a route open to egoists and utilitarians no less than it is open to Rawls' deliberative practical reasoners.

Rawls has been criticized (Cohen 1988; note also Sen 2009, pp. 14, 412 inter alia) for the elements of compulsion and of inequality as incentives in what is, after all, a moral theory. But this is a heritage from the contractarian tradition. The point of a "social contract" is that in enacting the social contract, the citizens are enacting their own will, not that of a stranger. But they may nevertheless be troubled by weakness of will. A rational person, anticipating her own weakness of will, will take precautions against it, even at some cost. An example often used in economics is that people may join Christmas saving clubs that pay no interest, in effect paying the bank to enforce their will. Indeed, ordinary business contracts may have "incentive clauses" (compare McCain 2015, pp. 156–7). Thus incentive provisions in the social contract are not at all inconsistent.

Rawls' ideas were developed over a considerable period before the 1971 book and continued to develop thereafter. In some of the earliest versions (Rawls 1951, 1955, 1957, 1958) neither the original position nor the difference principle are clearly represented and, indeed, it would seem that Rawls' contractarianism evolved gradually. In all this he is consistently concerned with rules for practices, institutions or political systems, and in practice less concerned with personal morality. In 1951 Rawls suggests a very abstract approach to the determination of such ethical rules relying on "sympathetic knowledge" (p. 179) and on conditions of reason that impose impartiality (pp. 181–2). The rules are then in some sense objective. He uses this approach to justify freedom of belief and speech. In 1955, he defends utilitarianism! His suggestion here seems to be an important clarification of rule utilitarianism, which would resolve such longstanding utilitarian issues as punishment and promise keeping. His position in these papers seems to parallel the dichotomy, in game theory, of cooperative and non-cooperative equilibria, but there is no evidence here that he is influenced by game theory. In two papers (Rawls 1957, 1958) – or rather two versions of the same paper, as the first was presented at a conference and the second is an expansion of it – Rawls takes the step forward of characterizing justice as fairness. Here again he rejects utilitarianism. However, the contrast to the difference principle as we find it in *A Theory of Justice* is interesting. In the earlier papers he writes that inequalities will be acceptable only if they "will work out for everyone's advantage" (p. 656) and in the later "for the advantage of every party" (p. 167). Rawls does go on to say that the impartial reasoner should reason as if "he were designing a practice in which his enemy were to assign him his place" (1957, pp. 656, 1958, p. 172). In non-cooperative game theory, this would imply a max-min decision rule. However, there is no mention of a veil of ignorance and Rawls distinguishes his ideas from social contract theories (1958, p. 175).

Moreover, as we have seen, the difference principle in Rawls is not an equalitarian idea in the sense that it might lead to proposals for redistribution. Nevertheless, what economists have tended to take from Rawls is a difference principle on real income per se (Atkinson 2011; Chavas 1994; Green 2014; Mankiw 2013; Hopkins and Kornienko 2010, among many others). And such a difference principle has some important implications, even if they are not what Rawls had in mind.

8.4 Fair distributions of welfare

Executive summary of the section: Foley had proposed a criterion of equality based on ordinal utility, namely that no-one prefer the goods bundle enjoyed by another. For exchange economies there is at least one Pareto optimum that is "fair" in this sense.

Those who proposed that welfare economics ought to reflect some judgment in favor of equality could be embarrassed by the question "equality of what?" The answer that springs most readily to mind, "equality of money income," proves to have many shortcomings. Utilitarian economists had not argued for equality of incomes, but for limited redistribution in order to increase total utility. An equalitarian defender of cardinal utility measures could call for equality of utility, and as we have seen, this sort of reasoning played some part in discussions of welfare economics in the third quarter of the twentieth century. At about the same time, however, an equalitarian economics arose that relied strictly on the ordinalist conceptions of preferences. While it was suggested by earlier writings on mathematical problems of fair division (again, see Dubins and Spanier 1961; Kuhn 1967), the wellspring of this literature was Foley (1967). Foley's comments were informal and brief, but they outlined both a new approach to equity in economics and some of the problems that would be confronted in later work. Foley writes (p. 74),

> If one person consumes more of every good (including leisure) than another, he is better off. If two people have identical preferences and one is in a position preferred by both, they cannot have equal welfare. This suggests a new way to define equality even when preferences are diverse: an allocation is equitable if and only if each person in the society prefers his consumption bundle to the consumption bundle of every other person in the society.

And at p. 75, "In a society which had reached an equitable and efficient allocation every person would see himself as the best off of all those of his own generation when he evaluated their lives in his own preference ordering. This catches some aspects of the common idea of equality." But among other qualifications,

> the comparison can be pushed only so far, and some common sense procedures are necessary when the comparison involves orchestra conductors, painters, chess masters, and so on. The difficulty here is that if a gas station attendant has the desire to be a painter but not the ability, it may be necessary to make the painter's life very unattractive in other ways before the gas station attendant will prefer his own; so unattractive, perhaps, that the painter will envy the attendant while the attendant is still envying him.

The term "envy" is commonly used in this literature to denote a situation in which a person prefers the economic situation of another to her or his own economic situation. But "envy," in normal use, is a "thick" term that has a negative valuation: envy is an emotion that is normally disapproved. (This has caused some discomfort in the literature.) We might disentangle the descriptive content of "envy" and denote it by some circumlocution such as "economic situations that might be expected to give rise to envy." Even that will not quite do. James might envy John because of John's tall stature and good looks, even if James' economic situation is preferable to John's in both John's and James' preference systems. This, too, must be abstracted from. Accordingly, in the balance of this section as in most of the literature on equity in the present sense, the word "envy" will not be used with full linguistic competence but in a special sense, not in reference to an emotion that is disapproved of but only in reference to the condition on preferences. We might set it off by writing, for example, envy*, but that has not been the practice in the literature so this warning must suffice.

The formalization of Foley's remarks began with Schmeidler and Vind (1972). They established that in an exchange economy, there are market equilibria that are both efficient and fair in the sense suggested by Foley. If, for example, the initial endowment comprises an equal share of each commodity, itself a fair allocation, then the exchange that leads to a market equilibrium can only lead to a fair allocation (p. 641). That allocation will also be efficient on the familiar assumptions, and indeed somewhat more generally. This notion of fairness is extended to trading coalitions and the allocation is said to be additively or strongly fair if no coalition could be formed that could carry out feasible trades, repeated an indefinite number of times, that would lead to an allocation preferred by any individual. They establish that strongly fair net trades can only be market equilibria (p. 639). This corresponds to the idea from cooperative game theory that equilibrium allocations are in the core of a trading game.

Feldman and Kirman (1974, p. 997) define a condition of fairness on *trades*, i.e. that no agent would prefer a trade by another to the trade in which she or he is engaged. They then define (p. 997) an index of inequality as a simple count of the number of envy relationships in the economy. (They also define other measures using differences of cardinal utility.) They show that competitive trading from an *arbitrary* fair allocation leads to an allocation that may not be fair (p. 998) and that a fair trade from a fair allocation may lead to an allocation that is not fair (p. 999). In their examples, these consequences follow from unsymmetrical preferences on which the agents differ. There seems to be no reason to exclude such differences. They then argue (p. 999) that fairness (unlike Pareto optimality) is too "unstable" to be a suitable goal for public policy, and propose that their integer measure of inequality be minimized subject to the constraint that no-one be made worse off relative to an arbitrary initial allocation. However, their analysis of this integer programming problem assumes identical preferences, which avoids the very anomalies that motivate their study (p. 999). Their proposal involves equal distribution of a social surplus over the initial position. For their cardinal measures, they reproduce something like the utilitarian position. The ideas of Feldman and Kirman, other than their demonstration that trading from a fair allocation may lead to an unfair one, seem to have had little influence. But their proposal that the equal distribution of a social surplus from trading from an inefficient initial allocation would minimize envy could also be applied where the initial allocation is an equal one. For their case the result would be trivial, since the minimum envy for this trade is zero. For other cases that would arise in the literature, however, it would not be trivial.

The veil of ignorance is not explicitly mentioned in many of the papers on equity as non-envy, but the connection can be made. Non-envious allocations are often linked to Rawls' use of the max-min operator. If the deliberators behind the veil of ignorance know that utility indices have no mathematical properties that would permit imputation of expected utilities, then they might reasonably base their decisions on the max-min operator. Then consider situation 1, in which A envies B, and situation 2, in which A's allocation is improved in the sense that A prefers his allocation in situation 2 to his allocation 1, and B's is reduced, but in such a way that neither envies the other. Suppose situations 1 and 2 are otherwise identical. For a deliberator, the choice is between situation 1 and situation 2, and there are many contingencies, but the only ones that differ are the situations in which the deliberator is realized as A or B. In either case his lesser payoff comes when he is realized as A. If he applies a max-min decision criterion, the deliberator would choose situation 2. Since all deliberators reason in this way, situation 2 is a unanimous choice as between the two. It is the absence of envy that assures us of this. If at situation 2 B were to envy A, then the deliberator's minimum at situation 2 comes when he is realized as B, and max-min yields no decision between 1 and 2. Conversely, if there were no envy in situation 1, we would have no guidance as to which realized agent might receive a transfer. Further, however, it is not necessary that the envy be eliminated. It is sufficient that the disadvantaged party, A, prefers the allocation at situation 2 to the allocation at situation 1. We might say that inequality is "reduced" at situation 2 relative to situation 1, if we may say "reduced" when there is no quantity that is made smaller. Thus we may generalize the case somewhat: Rule I. If at situation 1 A envies B, and if A prefers his allocation at situation 2 to his allocation at situation 1, and B does not envy A at situation 2, then the deliberators' unanimous choice is for situation 2. In simpler terms, we use the envy condition as a signal of inequality. If inequality is present, then a reform that improves the condition of the disadvantaged, without reversing the inequality, will be preferred behind the veil of ignorance.

It is also easy to establish that, in this case, a shift to a situation that is Pareto preferable will be preferred behind the veil of ignorance. If, then, we could construct a complete and transitive ordering of all Pareto-optimal situations in terms of equality, the deliberators might agree on the most equal of Pareto optima as the optimum optimorum – the holy grail of Pigovian and saltwater welfare economics. Even if the optimum optimorum can be determined, it may not be within Graaff's feasibility frontier. That is no theoretical embarrassment – the maximum of the social welfare function probably would not be either, and that was the point of suggesting the feasibility frontier – but it should be known to the deliberators, and give them pause. If the deliberators are less ambitious, instead of attempting to designate the situation to be realized, they might instead consider a rule to be imposed on the public authority to guide its choice among public policies that may be proposed from time to time. Rule I above would be one such rule, and Rule II could be: If situation 2 is Pareto preferred to situation 1, and situation 1 is not preferred to situation 2 under rule I, choose situation 2. This could lead to a piecemeal welfare economics along the lines suggested by Little (2002 [1950]) and Mishan[1] (e.g. 1960).

8.5 Fairness with production

Executive summary of the section: When production is taken account of, there may be "envy cycles" in which each person prefers the goods and work assignment enjoyed by the other, and in such a case existence of an equitable Pareto optimum is not assured.

Pazner and Schmeidler (1974) provide two numerical examples to illustrate that, for more complex economic models, allocations that are both Pareto optimal and equitable may not exist. For both of these, leisure is a source of utility and is used up, and the preference systems are linear.

Varian (1974, p. 64) defines a non-envious allocation as "equitable" and describes it as "fair" only if, in addition, it is Pareto optimal. (Limiting "fair" allocations to those that are efficient seems a terminological novelty, but, as with envy, it will be followed in discussing Varian's contributions.) Varian compares "fairness" in this sense to the social welfare function approach and to Rawls, and asserts that the fairness approach solves problems with both (pp. 55–67). He shows (pp. 67–68) that, for any strongly efficient allocation (that is, any point on a strictly convex utility-possibility frontier), the population can be ranked from worst to best off by the envy relation. This does speak to the question "inequality of what?" He again shows that, for an exchange economy, fair allocations exist, generalizing this result. Then, however, he introduces production into the model. In such a model, envy cycles are possible: there may be nobody whom nobody envies. (For a simple example, see McCain 2017, pp. 37–40.) Thus the ordering by envy is not transitive. Varian then considers two alternative, less demanding criteria. One is coalition fairness (1974, pp. 75–78). For the other (which seems intuitive) he compares two situations as follows: individual i consumes x_i, works q_i hours, and produces z; individual j consumes x_j, works q_j hours, and would have to work $G(z)$ hours to produce z. Then, in Varian's notation, the allocation is equitable* if j does not prefer $(x_i, G(z))$ to (x_j, q_j) for all permutations of i and j. That is, each person compares his own job and the income from it to the income from another job and the hours he would have to work to obtain it. (Notice that $G(z)$ might be infinite.) Varian then considers two initial allocations. First, let everyone have an equal share of the initial endowment of consumption goods and 100 percent of her or his leisure. There is no basis for envy or envy* at this initial allocation, since in every case z is zero. Then, competitive trading to a Pareto optimum yields an equitable* and fair* allocation in this sense. Varian also considers "income-fair" allocations, which he attributes to Pazner and Schmeidler (footnote p. 75). For this approach, the adjusted income is the individual's expenditure on consumer goods plus the value of his leisure time valued at her or his wage (compare Becker 1965). An "income-fair" allocation is one at which all adjusted incomes are equal. Then an income-fair allocation corresponds to competitive trading from an initial endowment at which each person is endowed with an equal share of each good and each person's leisure. In this way it is established that the equalization of adjusted income is fair*. We should recall that the allocation to each person of an equal share of the leisure of others is purely a hypothetical case used to establish the fairness* of equalization of adjusted income. For Varian's other example that is not quite the case. Varian (1975, p. 247) proposes that the fair allocations corresponding to the initial point with each person retaining usufruct of 100 percent of her or his leisure could be realized by a market economy with government-enforced equalization of wealth. In that paper he also gives a more extended criticism of, and comparison of his idea with, Rawls and the social welfare approach.

Pazner and Schmeidler (1978) propose yet another equity concept: egalitarian-equivalent allocations. An allocation x is egalitarian equivalent if there is a hypothetical allocation y with equal division of all commodities that yields each person the same preference level she or he has at x. The hypothetical allocation y needs not be feasible and in general would not be. For exchange economies, Pareto-efficient egalitarian-equivalent allocations exist and are a superset of the

Pareto-efficient fair allocations (p. 678). However, extending this to the case of production, a familiar problem arises. Each person's leisure is, in principle, a distinct good. The natural extension of the egalitarian reference bundle would seem to be one at which each person has equal leisure. Now, strictly speaking, we might demand that each person has an equal allocation of each person's leisure. But Pazner and Schmeidler concede that there needs be no solution in which "labor services are in equal proportions" (pp. 681–2). Instead, they show by a fixed-point argument that there will be a "canonical ray ... i.e. a ray passing through both the egalitarian reference-bundle and the average bundle corresponding to" the egalitarian-equivalent allocation (p. 681). This is a necessary condition for the construction of the solution. Why this reference allocation is considered as egalitarian and the solution as egalitarian without any condition of equal or proportional labor is unclear.

Vohra (1992) presented yet another difficulty. He establishes by example that for an economy with increasing returns, there are cases in which no envy-free Pareto optimum exists (pp. 190–91, 193–197). For these examples, preferences are only quasi-convex, not strictly convex: that is, the indifference curves are piecewise linear. This limits the number of Pareto optima to a finite set. Vohra also proposes a relaxed criterion of fairness, which is that there is a feasible allocation that is envy free that provides the same utilities to agents as the candidate allocation (even though there may be envy at the candidate allocation). While this is similar to egalitarian-equivalent allocations, the reference allocation in this case is feasible but might not require equal division. The existence of this no-envy allocation is proven by a fixed-point argument. However, although Vohra's criterion differs from egalitarian equivalence, it is subject to a similar criticism that it is not clear why the *equivalence* of a Pareto-optimal allocation to one that is envy free has any normative significance.

Clearly, production creates difficulties for fairness concepts based on Foley's equitable distributions. Indeed, even for fair* and egalitarian-equivalent allocations, the resolutions do not quite speak to Foley's example of the painter and the gas station attendant. It seems that Foley's gas station attendant might be happy to work longer hours if he could spend them as a painter, even at his own more meager income. The disutility of labor then depends not only on the hours but also on the job to which the person is assigned, and the question of a fair allocation of jobs arises! Without a formal representation of such an allocation problem, it seems unlikely that we can expect an allocation in such a world that is both fair and efficient.

8.6 Further developments in the theory of fairness

Executive summary of the section: This section discusses a number of relatively egalitarian extensions of the concept of fairness derived from Foley, some with alternative normative justifications.

S.-C. Kolm is the author of a large body of writing on equity and distribution in two languages dating from 1966. His 1996 paper is wide ranging and will serve to represent his contributions. By 1973 he had proposed the criterion of superequitable allocations, which is reviewed in the 1996 paper. A super-equitable allocation is one at which no individual would prefer any *weighted average* of others' allocations to her or his own allocation (Kolm 1996, p. 163). For Kolm, the main drawback of the equity criterion proposed by Foley is that it will not in general be unique and may have many instances (p. 170). Kolm argues that equal-income Pareto optima are superequitable (p. 167). However, this clearly applies only to exchange economies. Extending his basic argument to a case in which the "capacities" of different individuals to produce differ, Kolm would have lump-sum transfers equalize their "disposable income," that is, what was above called "adjusted income" (p. 175). This is offered as an efficient superequitable allocation with production. Kolm shrugs off the problems raised by Varian and Pazner and Schmeidler (pp. 160, 162, 179), attributing them to confusion (p. 174).

Now, Kolm might have a point here. The idea that more productive individuals would be assigned to longer hours arises from a rather simple model of heterogenous productivity – that a more productive person is one who delivers more abstract labor power per hour, and that the product of a particular period of work is proportionate to the labor power supplied (see, e.g. McCain 2015, pp. 196–200). This may be oversimplified. For some jobs, such as assembly line workers and administrative assistants, it is important to be there when the others are; for others, such as night watchmen, to be at work when the others are not. For each of these, the marginal product of time spent is discontinuous, and nothing is gained by keeping a highly productive administrative assistant at work when there is nothing for him or her to do. But, in the absence of an appropriately more complex model of production and labor, we cannot suppose that the results for the exchange economy will be recovered in a model that is even more complex than the received model of production and exchange.

It seems unlikely that equitable allocations exist for economies with production and if they exist may not be efficient. This has led scholars to propose alternative, less demanding criteria. This, however, reproduces the problem with social welfare functions that we might have hoped to solve. There is an alternative that might have been adopted, and Kolm (1996, p. 163) gives a hint toward it. He writes:

> A property of the relation 'more equal' considered here is that, if an allocation is 'more equal' than another, its individual allocations are averages of the individual allocations in the other … Obviously, this relation is transitive, there is no 'more equal' than equal (identical individual allocations), and, for each commodity, the smallest quantity is not smaller and the largest quantity is not larger in the 'more equal' allocation.

An equity ordering, even if transitive, would presumably not be a complete ordering. Thus, it might not support a social choice function (Sen 1970). This is further considered in the appendix to this chapter.

Baumol (1982, 1986) discussed equity in the sense of non-envy with a particular view to applications, especially to rationing. He reports (1986, p. vii) that his first conception of the theory was subjectively original, but that he soon learned that he had been scooped by Varian among others. Addressing exchange economies, Baumol characterizes non-envious allocations and notes that exchange economies typically will possess a large region of "superfair" allocations at which each trader strictly prefers his own allocation to that of the other (pp. 19–33). Relying extensively on Edgeworth box graphics, he defines a "fairness boundary" to characterize the superfair region. Then, allowing for production, he reviews three concepts of fairness from the earlier literature:

1   Non-envy, with leisure as a consumption good. He calls this "consumption fairness" (p. 42).
2   Varian's fair* allocations, which he interprets as compensation according to contribution and denotes as contribution fairness (pp. 43–44). He notes (footnote p. 44) that contribution fairness is only defined in case of separability in production.
3   Income fairness, which requires that each agent have the same budget constraint.

Baumol gives an ordinary-language discussion of these three fairness concepts in connection with Pareto efficiency, attributing the potential efficiency of income-fair allocations to the use of lump-sum transfers to attain a fair allocation. Baumol has a good point. The need for lump-sum redistributions to reconcile equality and efficiency was well understood by the 1950s, along with the problems of feasibility that follow. The advocates of income fairness do not seem to acknowledge any of this. Nevertheless this applies no less to the other two fairness concepts. For consumption fairness there must be an *initial* redistribution to equal distribution of all goods. Fair* or contribution-fair allocations, as Varian notes (esp. 1975), require equalization of wealth income, and if saving and investment decisions are based on self-interest, these redistributions will not be considered lump sum and efficiency problems will result.

Baumol then contributes several extensions of superfairness theory. The first, incremental superfairness (1986, pp. 52–60) is related to the Feldman-Kirman fair net trades analysis. The second, partial superfairness (pp. 62–64) applies the no-envy criterion to a subset of all goods, quantities of the others being given. He concedes that the normative force of this criterion is less clear than that of the others. The third extension is sequential superfairness (pp. 65–70). This criterion takes the region of superfair allocations in an exchange economy and narrows it by treating this region as a separate Edgeworth box and repeating the superfairness analysis with it. Essentially, the surplus from strictly fair allocations is to be distributed in a way that is itself fair or superfair. Thus some superfair allocations can be more superfair than others. An iterative process can be defined that approaches a best allocation in the limit. It is not clear, however, that this algorithm and its limit are unique. Baumol then goes on to discuss applications and some other ideas, including some defense of "illusion" and of individuals' preference for excise taxes over income taxes even though they pay the same amount in both cases (pp. 216–222).

In an essay drawn from his doctoral dissertation, Piketty (1994) makes a case for a version of income fairness. He criticizes both Varian and Rawls. He interprets fairness in Rawlsian terms as "Distributive justice as 'maximal equal liberty'" (p. 393), but rejects Rawls' difference principle on the grounds that the identity of the least advantaged person may not be knowable. Instead, Piketty interprets "maximal equal liberty" as requiring that all individuals choose from the same budget hyperplane (pp. 392, 397). We might say that equal liberty in this sense is the liberty to consume and to enjoy leisure. It seems Rawls' interpretation of liberty is quite different. Piketty says that the equal-liberty condition as he interprets it is equivalent to the non-envy condition "which is at best a formal coincidence" (p. 394). Indeed it goes too far to say that they are equivalent. Piketty's equal liberty implies non-envy (if preferences are as usually assumed) but the converse surely is not so. An omniscient planner might simply assign the non-envious bundles to individuals, allowing them no liberty at all. But Piketty's argument extracts a radically equalitarian norm from the moral imperative of maximal equal liberty. With income-fair non-envious allocations, people consume *as if* they choose from the same possibility set, but for "maximal equal liberty" it would seem that "as if" is not good enough.

Piketty criticizes Varian (p. 394) on the grounds that his "wealth-fairness" "gives up any attempt to correct inequalities in abilities," and cites Rawls in support of the idea that "innate talents are irrelevant from the viewpoint of social ethics." But this is one side of the coin: the other side is Baumol's complaint (1986, p. 47) that income fairness "literally penalizes the person with superior capabilities." Consider a society comprising among others three persons, Jack, Karl and Larry. Larry possesses a "God-given talent for the game of basketball" (quoted from memory from an interview with "Dr. J.," Julius Erving), and this talent has made him very rich. Karl is an accountant with a "middle-class" income. Jack cannot work because of a physical disability and has no income. Does equal justice require that Jack's lack of ability be offset by some support payment? For Piketty and Rawls it clearly would. If so, then why should Larry's God-given talent not also be offset?

The objective of Piketty's essay, apart from criticism and interpretation of the literature, is to demonstrate a sufficient condition that, for income fairness, there exists at least one allocation that is both fair and Pareto optimal. The condition is (Piketty 1994, p. 397) that aversion to work is inversely related to productivity, that is, that more productive tasks are also less unpleasant at the margin. This avoids the possibility of the productive person envying the leisure of the unproductive while the unproductive person envies the income of the productive. Then, envy cycles are excluded, and considering the continuum of Pareto optima attainable by all possible lump-sum transfers, before production and trading take place, there is at least one that is envy free.

Chavas (1994) offers an alternative formulation of what he calls a fair-equivalent (egalitarian-equivalent) allocation in a paper that takes uncertainty and information into account and considers, in particular, application to an agrarian economy. Thus, his formulation of the Pareto optimum (along lines suggested by Scitovsky 1941) allows for different individual decisions in different states of the world (Chavas 1994, p. 1024). He expresses the distributional norm, together with the norm of Paretian efficiency, as a max-min problem (Chavas 1994, equation 10 at p. 1027). This represents a process something like this: First, consider an allocation that assigns to each person an equal quantity of each good and an equal number of hours in each category of labor. This allocation is not unique: depending on the total hours of labor there may be a continuum of such points. We select one that maximizes a weighted sum of utilities, that is, one that is Pareto optimal subject to the constraint of equal allocations. (The weights for this maximization are yet to be determined.) From this point shift to an efficient, unequal assignment of work hours with money transfers such that each person's utility at this second allocation is the same as that at the first, equal-distribution allocation. This will generate a surplus, since the new production program is efficient while the first was not. The surplus is then divided equally as a second money transfer, a social dividend. The money income generated in this way is then spent at a Walrasian equilibrium that determines the prices of consumption goods. Of course the money transfers and the prices are interdependent – all are simultaneously determined by the max-min problem. As Chavas says (1994, p. 1027) "The solution of the optimization problem (10) always generates the efficient and fair-equivalent allocation." Specifically, among the instruments for the max-min problem are the money transfers, maximizing the smallest money transfer. This is Rawlsian in that, beginning from utilities that are determined by an equal allocation, the person who receives the smallest transfer can be thought of as least favored. To make the money transfers determinate, the maximization yields a specific set of distributional weights, which must be the ones used at each stage of the decision process. As with Scitovsky's formulation of Pareto optimality, of which it seems an extension, the result does not depend on the cardinal utility indices, and the substitution of a different set of utility indices would yield a different set of distributional weights and the same optimal allocation.

Chavas regards this as an instance of egalitarian-equivalent allocations. "The proof can be obtained by construction (see Pazner and Schmeidler 1978) ... If such a move is made all the way to the utility frontier, it necessarily generates a fair-equivalent and efficient allocation." However, Chavas seems to be mistaken here. The Pazner-Schmeidler construction yields a point on the utility-possibility frontier with individual utilities identical to those at an infeasible equal division. Chavas' two-step procedure begins by constructing the best *feasible* equal-division point (let us call it y_1) and then moving along the willingness-to-accept and willingness-to-pay curves to an efficient allocation of labor time and of other goods corresponding to Pareto-efficient prices but at which all utilities are the same as they would be at y_1. This hypothetical allocation (let us call it y_2) is egalitarian equivalent in that it yields the same utilities as y_1, but not efficient in that not all goods produced are distributed. The economy is then raised to the utility possibility frontier by equal money payments. The resulting point on the UPF (let us call it y_3) is not equivalent to y_1. If y_2 were non-envious, then the property of non-envy would be preserved as the money transfers were spent, each person purchasing what she most prefers and thus prefers more than that which the others purchase. But the problem is precisely that y_2 is not in general non-envious. Perhaps we could identify y_4 as y_1 augmented by the goods purchased with the cash transfers and the wage for the labor allocation at y_1. This would preserve the envy-free property of the initial allocation since all would be choosing from the same possibility set. But would it be equivalent to y_3? It would be, only if the equivalent variation of the shifts in labor allocations were to be identical to the compensating variations, which are the amounts paid to compensate for the shift. In general they will not be – an old and well-known issue in welfare economics (Scitovsky 1941; Henderson 1941; Hicks 1942).

McCain ((and Lester) 2001, 2017, pp. 40–47, 201–206) adapted Chavas' approach, referring to allocations determined in this way as "equibeneficial." McCain (2017, p. 40) provides an alternative normative justification for allocations derived in this way: the movement from an equal distribution to an efficient allocation generates a surplus, and the surplus is shared equally (at market prices at the optimum). Chavas' max-min problem can be rewritten as a problem of maximizing the social dividend from the movement from equal distribution to a Pareto-optimal allocation (equation 3A.10a, b at pp. 45, 46 in McCain 2017). The Lagrange equations are isomorphic in the two cases. This maximization is the basis for most of McCain's discussion. Both can also be rewritten as maximization of the weighted sum of utilities with appropriate weights along the lines of Scitovsky (1941). The appropriate weights are the partial derivatives of the expenditure functions with respect to utility at the maximum points (McCain 2017, p. 46). These in turn are the inverses of the marginal utilities of money income. Thus, Robbins' Brahman, with his greater ability to transform money into utility, would have a *lesser* weight in an equibeneficial allocation. McCain then goes on to outline an adaptation of the equibeneficial approach to a case of limited political feasibility of redistribution, and derives a formula for weighted cost-benefit analysis (pp. 201–206).

It is worth noting that equibeneficial allocations in general differ from income-fair allocations. The concepts of income that are equalized are different: equibeneficial allocations are based on the equalization of expenditure net of some wage income, specifically that necessary to maintain the agent at the utility he would enjoy at the equal distribution. Adjusted income for income-fair allocations add to this net expenditure the market value of maximum labor time. Thus those whose labor is less valuable at the efficient allocation would consume more in an income-fair than in an equibeneficial one, relative to those whose labor is more valuable. It is not clear which of these is the more equalitarian. For equibeneficial allocations the benefit to the more able is less than it would be for fair* (contribution-fair) allocations, though, since it is essentially based on an all-or-nothing offer rather than a market evaluation of the labor time committed. Further, unlike fair* allocations, but like income-fair allocations, equibeneficial allocations do allow for compensation to those whose utility is reduced by a handicap (p. 204).

8.7 Concluding reflections

Discussions based on the ideas of Rawls and (particularly) Foley have continued into the twenty-first century, though they seem little known in the economics profession at large. What then can we take from this discussion? The veil of ignorance as we find it in the ideas of Harsanyi and Rawls is an important contribution to normative social theory and to welfare economics in particular. However we construct the veil of ignorance, it provides the analysis of a sort of objectivity that does not seem available otherwise. One can, of course, strive for impartiality without thinking in terms of a veil of ignorance, but the judgment that a particular discourse is free of subjective bias is then a subjective judgment that might be biased. The claim that a Rawlsian or Harsanyian theory is impartial can be demonstrated: detail the "veil of ignorance" by setting out the questions to be decided, what the deliberators are permitted to know and what is supposed to constitute their rationality. If, then, a decision follows plausibly or uniquely from that specification, that decision is justified in a way that is independent of subjective judgments against or in favor of such things as economic equality or neutral taxes. Harsanyi provided such a demonstration for additive utilitarianism. For those who had accepted the single "subjective" judgment that public policy ought to increase satisfaction utility, the rest could be demonstrated. However, one might still, with Robbins, dismiss the utilitarian value judgment as a private prejudice. In the light of Harsanyi's demonstration, a successful argument against additive utilitarianism would have to focus on the nature of rationality, the questions to be decided, the data available to decide them and what may constitute objectivity in normative social theory. This is not to say that one cannot reject Harsanyi's theory. Rawls does. But Rawls' disagreements with Harsanyi focus on the nature of rationality for deliberators behind the veil of ignorance and the data we should suppose that they have access to. The existence of more than one "veil of ignorance" model is an embarrassment. Which, then? It might not be strictly necessary to choose, since Harsanyi, Rawls and the equity models address somewhat different questions. The idea that agents deliberating behind a veil of ignorance would arrive at a unanimous position is somewhat undermined by the inability of philosophers and economists to agree in their judgments as to what the deliberators would conclude. What all these views have in common, though, is that behind the veil of ignorance individuals must be treated in some sense equally, so that a case for some degree of equalization of economic outcomes is supported. At the least, this seems to destroy Robbins' position on distributional values in economics.

Little's position, quoted by Samuelson, that ignorance can lead only to ignorance, is of course true and is of course beside the point. Propositions *about* the ignorance of a decision maker can have powerful implications for the decisions that will be made, and indeed for the decisions that are possible. What, then, do deliberators *know* behind the veil of ignorance? Clearly they must know something about "the way of the world." Rawls tells us that they know economic theory, by which he seems to mean they "know" that market equilibria tend to be efficient, markets are incentive compatible and that capitalism does not lead to increasing inequality. Rawls' position apart, they clearly must know something about the production possibilities in the realized world, and something also about organizational possibilities, market mechanisms, presence or absence of externalities and so on. Another thing that the deliberators behind the veil of ignorance must know is just what ignorance the government must cope with – what the decision makers of the public authority can and cannot know and do. It is here that incentive compatibility comes into the picture. Thus Harsanyi's deliberators might instruct legislators (who are not behind a veil of ignorance) to use whatever data they have to choose policies with positive incremental utilities. Rawls was criticized for the assumption that unequal incomes could benefit the poorest via incentives. His objective, after all, was a theory of ethics, and for ethics, should the rule not be that each person makes appropriate effort regardless of incentives? Perhaps incentives are a necessary condition for the stability of the social contract. In any case, it is appropriate for normative economic theory to take into account limits on the knowledge available to government decision makers. These limits are sure to raise the issue of incentive compatibility.

If the deliberators behind the veil of ignorance know what neoclassical economists believe they know – that utilities have no numerical properties that would allow their aggregation by addition with or without weights – then they might agree on a judgment of equity such as Foley proposed, along with Pareto preference as an efficiency criterion. Taking production as well as exchange into account, it may not be possible to reconcile these values with an optimum optimorum. Nevertheless, at the least, equity in this sense provides economists who favor equality with an answer to the question "equality of what?" Why then has it had little influence on economics and economic policy in general? There are at least two reasons within the body of equity theory itself. First, the results for exchange economies were presented as implying that they show that there is no "trade-off" between efficiency and equity. That was never true. The "trade-off" between efficiency and equity arises because arbitrary lump-sum transfers are impossible, and every model of efficient and "equitable" allocations relies on arbitrary lump-sum transfers.

(In some models these transfers precede trading, but in timeless models such as this that is really no help.) Second, the continued search for an optimum optimorum, and the many "weakened" versions of equity theory contrived to produce such an optimum optimorum, only increased the muddle about equity. Even where the weakened versions have independent normative justifications (as Piketty and McCain argue for income-fair and equibeneficial allocations, respectively) the applied economist is not helped out of her muddle by the pullulation of equity concepts. In any case, an applicable welfare economics will unavoidably be a piecemeal welfare economics (as Little argued and Mishan resolutely demonstrated) and for that purpose what is important about all these conceptions of "equity" is not their differences but what they share: that unbiased reasoning "as if behind a veil of ignorance" leads us to call for an equality of station or circumstances that is rarely realized, and that this equality of station can be judged using only ordinal concepts of welfare, but that when judged in that way equality of station is a quite radically economically equalitarian idea.

Note

1 This possibility is considered in more detail in the appendix to this chapter. The use of the Pareto criterion requires some qualification.

Appendix

In the *Critique of Welfare Economics*, Little insists that (on the one hand) there can be no "social welfare function" without Superman to provide it, but also (on the other hand) that no valid welfare judgment can be made without a value-based assessment of the desirability of the resulting change in the distribution of income. Can anyone really walk this tightrope? To be more fair, can we envision a set of plausible value judgments that would allow us to judge among different distributions of welfare but on the other hand not provide a social welfare function? *Distribution* may be the key word. A social welfare function requires an evaluation of the vector of welfares (albeit only on an ordinal scale). We might instead compute the variance of welfares, or their entropy or a Gini index and judge the distribution of welfares to be better if it has a smaller variance or Gini or a larger entropy. But this demands that our measure of well-being has arithmetic properties that allow weighted sums, which all of these measures require. In this appendix the possibility of a piecemeal evaluation of social situations is explored, relying on the interpretation of equity as non-"envy,"[1] an approach that was of course not available at the time Little's book was written.

In Chapter 8, the theory of equity as non-envy was criticized for the tendency of the authors in that literature to focus on the discovery of an optimum optimorum, or, if not that, a demonstration that there is no "big trade-off" between equity and efficiency. In retrospect those objectives do not seem to have been very helpful. At the same time the tradition of "piecemeal" welfare economics, of Samuelson's "'twere better" propositions, was continued by few other than Ezra Mishan. Yet public policy regimes are typically considered only as pairwise comparisons or in small finite sets, so that a welfare economics of reliable "'twere better" comparisons might be, on the whole, not only adequate but more useful than a theory of unique optima optimora. Let us suppose, then, that deliberators behind the veil of ignorance were to establish on the basis of their deliberations a few rules for the comparative evaluations of social states resulting from differing policy regimes.

The comparison will be among social states from a finite set $S=\{S^1, S^2, \ldots, S^n\}$. In each S^i the population of realized agents is an identical finite set $\mathcal{M} = \{\alpha, \beta, \ldots \theta, \ldots\}$. Each situation S^i is characterized by allocations of goods among agents G_θ^i for each agent θ. Given the preference fields and the opportunities for exchange offered by situation i, G_θ^i is θ's most preferred option among the opportunities available to θ in S^i, with all mutually beneficial exchanges complete. Conversely, the list of goods G_θ^i comprises all distinct characteristics of social states among which θ has any preferences whatever, including, for example, freedoms that are valued for themselves and quantities of public goods supplied. For each agent θ a weak preference relation $\mathcal{V}_\theta$ is defined in the usual way, so that $G_\theta^i \mathcal{V}_\theta G_\theta^j$ or $G_\theta^j \mathcal{V}_\theta G_\theta^i$ for any two situations i, j. In case $G_\theta^i \mathcal{V}_\theta G_\theta^j$ and $\sim G_\theta^j \mathcal{V}_\theta G_\theta^i$ then we have $G_\theta^i \mathcal{P}_\theta G_\theta^j$ strict preference. We suppose that the deliberators know these lists of goods, agents, allocations and preference fields, but do not know as which agent they will be realized in the actual world. Remaining in a world shared by Rawls and the non-envy literature, they also know that there are no utility indices over these preference fields that have meaningful arithmetic properties that would admit of addition and multiplication, so that mathematical expectations and other weighted summations could not be used. Therefore they might make decisions by a max min rule in some sense.

A difficulty is to determine who is least favored in a particular situation. We might rank the agents by envy relationships. If β envies α at S^1, then β is less favored than α at S^1, according to β's own preference ranking. The least favored agent would then be the agent who, at S^1, envies everybody and is envied by nobody. But, as we recall from Varian's discussion among others, there may be no such person. This is the case of an envy cycle. On the other side, there might be more than one person whom nobody envies, that is, a set of least favored persons, and they might not agree. Finally – and this seems a new difficulty – it might be the case that the least favored person is indifferent between S^1 and S^2. Should this indifference dictate that the two social states are socially indifferent if (for example) all other agents are better off in one rather than the other? Or should the deliberators reason that the least favored would *make no objection* to the transition from S^1 to S^2, so that the preferences of others should be considered? This latter suggestion seems right, so in what follows it will be assumed that the preferences of the least favored person *who strictly prefers one of the two social states* will be decisive. As we will see, that will solve some other problems, as well. Finally, those who are least favored at S^2 clould be a completely different group than those least favored at S^1. Should we construe "least favored" as least favored ex ante or least favored ex post? This question will be deferred for the time being.

Now, suppose that for any agent $\theta \in \mathcal{M}$, $G_\theta^2 \mathcal{V}_\theta G_\theta^1$ and for some agent α, $G_\alpha^2 \mathcal{P}_\alpha G_\alpha^1$. That is, situation 2 is Pareto-preferable to situation 1. Let $\mathcal{Y} = \{\theta \in \mathcal{M} | G_\alpha^2 \mathcal{P}_\theta G_\alpha^1\}$ This set has at least one member. Deliberators behind a veil of ignorance might reason as follows. "I might be instantiated either as a member of $\mathcal{Y}$ or of $\mathcal{M}\backslash\mathcal{Y}$. If as a member of $\mathcal{M}\backslash\mathcal{Y}$, I will be no worse off at S^2, so I have no objection to the change. If I am instantiated as a member of $\mathcal{Y}$ and in particular as the least favored member of $\mathcal{Y}$, then my positive preference is for S^2, and that is decisive." Thus we indicate that S^2 is Pareto-preferred to S^1 by writing $S^2 \mathcal{g} S^1$. This gives us

Principle 1. (Pareto principle). If S^2 is Pareto-preferable to S^1, then S^2 is socially preferred to S^1.

Most welfare economists will find this reassuring. The relation $\mathcal{g}$ is quasi-transitive and so supports a choice function (Sen, 1970). Notice that it does not matter how the least favored agent in $\mathcal{Y}$ is determined, but some further thought about that may be useful. If there is $\alpha \in \mathcal{Y}$ such that $\theta \in \mathcal{Y}\backslash\{\alpha\} \Rightarrow G_\theta^2 \mathcal{P}_\theta G_\alpha^1$, then α is the least favored agent in $\mathcal{Y}$ *according to the preferences of every agent*, and so the preferences of α are decisive. But that might not be the case if there were an envy cycle among agents in $\mathcal{Y}$. In such a case, the deliberators behind a veil of ignorance might reason that, if instantiated as any member of the envy cycle, they would be less advantaged than other members of $\mathcal{Y}$, but as the members of the envy cycle will be unanimous in their preference of S^2 to S^1, no ambiguity in the social decision arises. The key point is that for a Pareto shift, *every* agent who has a strict preference between the two social situations prefers the Pareto-superior one. Thus, it is the attention to the least advantaged of *those who have a strict preference between the situations* that gives us the Pareto principle, following from the judgment that, even if there are those who are still worse off whose position is not improved, their indifference between the social states is not decisive; and this in turn seems to follow from the veil of ignorance in this application (so long as we do not consider ex post envy.)

But we may also derive a distributional ranking. At situation S^i let

$$\mathcal{n}_i = \{\alpha \in \mathcal{M} \mid \forall \theta \in \mathcal{M}, \theta \neq \alpha \Rightarrow G_\theta^i \mathcal{V}_\theta G_\alpha^i \text{ and } G_\theta^i \mathcal{V}_\alpha G_\alpha^i\}$$

Remarks: the set $\mathcal{n}_i$ includes those who are envied by nobody ($G_\theta^i \mathcal{V}_\theta G_\alpha^i$) and who do not prefer their own situation to that of anybody else (as $G_\theta^i \mathcal{V}_\alpha G_\alpha^i \Rightarrow \sim G_\alpha^i \mathcal{P}_\alpha G_\theta^i$. Thus, elements of $\mathcal{n}_i$ are least advantaged by the preferences of everyone, including their own preferences. The set $\mathcal{n}_i$ may be null, as Varian's discussion points out.

We will find an additional relationship useful: weak envy. Let us say that α weakly envies β if $G_\beta \, \boldsymbol{\mathcal{V}}_\alpha \, G_\alpha$ so that either $G_\beta \, \boldsymbol{\mathcal{P}}_\alpha \, G_\alpha$ or, for any $G^*_\alpha \ni G_\alpha \, \boldsymbol{\mathcal{P}}_\alpha G^*_\alpha$, $G_\beta \, \boldsymbol{\mathcal{P}}_\alpha \, G^*_\alpha$. That is, if α were made just slightly worse off according to her own preferences, then α would envy β.

Now suppose we are given situations S^1 and S^2 such that

1a. $\exists \alpha \in \boldsymbol{\mathcal{N}}_1 \ni G^2_\alpha \boldsymbol{\mathcal{P}}_\alpha G^1_\alpha$

Remark: Some of the "least favored" are made better off at S^2. Notice that, if $\boldsymbol{\mathcal{N}}_1$ is null, then this condition cannot be fulfilled, so that in any case S^1 cannot be ranked against other states on the basis of the effect on its "least favored," as the "least favored" cannot be identified.

1b. $\forall \alpha \in \boldsymbol{\mathcal{N}}_1, \; G^2_\alpha \boldsymbol{\mathcal{V}}_\alpha G^1_\alpha$

Remark: None of the "least favored" is made worse off according to their own preferences. Put otherwise, the change is a Pareto-improvement among the least-favored.

1c. $\gamma \in \boldsymbol{\mathcal{M}}$ and $G^1_\gamma \boldsymbol{\mathcal{P}}_\gamma G^1_\alpha \Rightarrow G^2_\gamma \boldsymbol{\mathcal{P}}_\gamma G^2_\alpha$.

Remark: No new relations of weak envy are created.

1d. $G^1_\gamma \boldsymbol{\mathcal{V}}_\alpha G^1_\alpha \Rightarrow G^2_\gamma \boldsymbol{\mathcal{V}}_\alpha G^2_\alpha$.

Remark: Any existing relations of weak envy are preserved, although strict envy relations may be transformed to weak envy (i.e. $G^1_\gamma \, \boldsymbol{\mathcal{P}}_\alpha G^1_\alpha$ but $G^2_\gamma \, \boldsymbol{\mathcal{V}}_\alpha G^2_\alpha$). This limitation is a condition of transitivity.

This yields Principle 2. A redistribution (1) from a class of envied agents to those envious of them, while not themselves envied, and (2) which makes no members of that class worse off, and (3) which preserves relations of weak envy is a social improvement.

We denote this relationship by $S^2 \boldsymbol{\mathcal{K}} S^1$. The relationship $\boldsymbol{\mathcal{K}}$ is transitive. The proof follows.

Lemma 1: $\boldsymbol{\mathcal{N}}_1 \subset \boldsymbol{\mathcal{N}}_2$.

Proof: $\alpha \in \boldsymbol{\mathcal{N}}_1 \Rightarrow \forall \theta \in \boldsymbol{\mathcal{N}}_1, G^1_\theta \boldsymbol{\mathcal{V}}_\theta G^1_\alpha$ and by c, $G^2_\theta \, \boldsymbol{\mathcal{V}}_\theta \, G^2_\alpha$. Further, $G^1_\theta \, \boldsymbol{\mathcal{V}}_\alpha \, G^1_\alpha$ and by d, $G^2_\theta \, \boldsymbol{\mathcal{V}}_\alpha \, G^2_\alpha$

Theorem 1: The relationship $\boldsymbol{\mathcal{K}}$ is transitive.
Proof: Suppose $S^3 \boldsymbol{\mathcal{K}} S^2$ and $S^2 \boldsymbol{\mathcal{K}} S^1$.
1) By $S^2 \boldsymbol{\mathcal{K}} S^1$, $\alpha \in \boldsymbol{\mathcal{N}}_1 \Rightarrow \alpha \in \boldsymbol{\mathcal{N}}_2$, $G^2_\alpha \, \boldsymbol{\mathcal{P}}_\alpha G^1_\alpha$ by condition a for $S^2 \boldsymbol{\mathcal{K}} S^1$, $G^3_\alpha \, \boldsymbol{\mathcal{V}}_\alpha G^2_\alpha$ by condition b for $S^3 \boldsymbol{\mathcal{K}} S^2$, and by the transitive property of the preference relation we have $G^3_\alpha \, \boldsymbol{\mathcal{P}}_\alpha G^1_\alpha$. This is condition a for $S^3 \boldsymbol{\mathcal{K}} S^1$.

2) By $S^2 \mathcal{K} S^1$, $\alpha \in \mathcal{N}_1 \Rightarrow G_\alpha^2 \mathcal{V}_\alpha G_\alpha^1$; further $\alpha \in \mathcal{N}_1 \Rightarrow \alpha \in \mathcal{N}_2 \Rightarrow G_\alpha^3 \mathcal{V}_\alpha G_\alpha^2$; and transitivity yields $G_\alpha^3 \mathcal{V}_\alpha G_\alpha^1$, condition b. for $S^3 \mathcal{K} S^1$.

3) Conditions c and d for $S^3 \mathcal{K} S^1$ follow from the transitivity of implication. QED.

Remark: The price paid for transitivity here may seem high. On the other hand, so long as there are any noncyclical envy relationships in existence, a proposal that would improve the situation of those "least favored" in terms of their own preferences and those of others can be evaluated as an improvement, even if it makes the rich much richer. This seems to provide the justification for proposals that would raise the bottom of the income distribution without being concerned about the top (see e.g. Mankiw 2013, Baker et al. 2017) Further, consider a simple example as follows:

Example: consider situations 1, 2, 3, $\mathcal{M} = \{\alpha, \beta\}$. Suppose that

I.i $G_\alpha^1 \mathcal{V}_\alpha G_\alpha^2 \mathcal{P}_\alpha G_\alpha^3$.

I.ii $G_\beta^3 \mathcal{P}_\beta G_\beta^2 \mathcal{P}_\beta G_\beta^1$.

I.iii $G_\alpha^1 \mathcal{P}_\beta G_\beta^1$.

I.iv $G_\beta^3 \mathcal{P}_\alpha G_\alpha^3$.

I.v $G_\alpha^2 \mathcal{V}_\alpha G_\beta^2$, $G_\beta^2 \mathcal{V}_\beta G_\alpha^2$.

We then have $G_\beta^2 \mathcal{K} G_\alpha^1$, $G_\beta^2 \mathcal{K} G_\alpha^3$, and a shift from either G_α^1 or G_α^3 to G_α^2 creates an envy-free Pareto optimum in this small example.

Behind the veil of ignorance, the deliberator might reason "If I am instantiated as any member of the set $\mathcal{N}_1$, then the argument for Pareto-preference can be applied: either I favor situation S_2 or I have no objection to the shift from S_1 to S_2. If I am instantiated as a member of $\mathcal{M} \backslash \mathcal{N}_1$, then I may prefer S_1 to S_2, but as there are others worse off than I am by any preference ranking, my preferences would not then be decisive.

We then have two rankings over social states, $\mathcal{G}$ and $\mathcal{K}$. The relations $\mathcal{G}$ and $\mathcal{K}$ are closely related, as $\mathcal{K}$ requires Pareto-ranking among a subset of the population. It follows that the two rankings cannot contradict one another. The proof is much like the proof of the antisymmetric property of the relation $\mathcal{G}$.

Lemma 2: $S^1 \mathcal{K} S^2 \Rightarrow {\sim} S^2 \mathcal{G} S^1$. Proof: $S^1 \mathcal{K} S^2 \Rightarrow \exists \alpha \in \mathcal{N}_2 \subset \mathcal{M} \ni G_\alpha^1 \mathcal{P}_\alpha G_\alpha^2$. This contradicts the Pareto condition that $\forall \alpha \in \mathcal{M}$, $G_\alpha^2 \mathcal{V}_\alpha G_\alpha^1$.

Lemma 3. $S^1 \mathcal{G} S^2 \Rightarrow {\sim} S^2 \mathcal{K} S^1$ Proof: From the Pareto ranking, $\forall \alpha \in \mathcal{M}$, $G_\alpha^1 \mathcal{V}_\alpha G_\alpha^2$. Thus, it cannot be the case that for any $\beta \in \mathcal{N}_1$, $G_\beta^2 \mathcal{P}_\beta G_\beta^1$, contradicting condition a. for $S^2 \mathcal{K} S^1$.

Thus, it might be proposed to compose the two rankings, as $S^1 \mathcal{R} S^2$ if either $S^1 \mathcal{G} S^2$ or $S^1 \mathcal{K} S^2$. However, this compound ranking would not be transitive. Example: consider situations 1, 2, 3, $\mathcal{M} = \{\alpha, \beta, \gamma\}$. Suppose that

II.i $G_\alpha^1 \mathcal{P}_\alpha G_\alpha^2 \mathcal{V}_\alpha G_\alpha^3$.

II.ii $G_\alpha^1 \mathcal{P}_\beta G_\beta^1$.

II.iii $G_\beta^3 \boldsymbol{P}_\beta G_\beta^2 \boldsymbol{P}_\beta G_\beta^1.$

II.iv $G_\alpha^2 \boldsymbol{V}_\alpha G_\beta^2.$

II.v $G_\beta^3 \boldsymbol{P}_\alpha G_\alpha^3.$

II.vi $G_\gamma^1 = G_\gamma^2 = G_\gamma^3$

Here the transition from situation 1 to 2 is an improvement, since the agent who is envious (by ii) is made better off (by iii) but the relationship of weak envy is not eliminated (by iv). Finally, no other person is affected (by vi). Further the transition from situation 2 to 3 is an improvement, as 3 is Pareto-preferable, making β better off (by iii) and no-one worse off (by i and vi). However, the transition from situation 1 to 3 is not an improvement under the Paretian principle 1 (since α is worse off at situation 3 than 1 by i) and is not an improvement under principle 2 since α envies β at situation 3 (by v). Deliberating behind the veil of ignorance the deliberator might reason, "If instantiated as agent β, I prefer situation 3 to 1, but if instantiated as agent α, I prefer 1 to 3, so I cannot say which is less favored and can make no judgment as between the two."

It may then be appropriate to weaken the Pareto condition somewhat. Let us consider a little more carefully how the "least favored" are determined. Suppose that

2a. $\forall \theta \in \boldsymbol{M},\ G_\theta^2 \boldsymbol{V}_\theta\ G_\theta^1$

2b. $\exists \gamma \in \boldsymbol{M} \ni G_\gamma^2 \boldsymbol{P}_\gamma\ G_\gamma^1$

2c. $G_\gamma^1 \boldsymbol{V}_\gamma G_\alpha^1 \Rightarrow G_\gamma^2 \boldsymbol{V}_\gamma G_\alpha^2$

2c. says that no new relations of strict envy are created, so these conditions describe a Pareto-improvement that creates no new relations of strict envy. Express this by writing $S^2 \boldsymbol{\mathcal{7}} S^1$. Thus we have

Principle 3. Amended Pareto principle: If S^2 is a Pareto-improvement relative to S^1, and no relations of strict envy exist at S^2 that do not exist at S^1, then S^2 is socially preferred to S^1.

Behind the veil of ignorance, a deliberator might reconsider some cases of Pareto improvement. We have not yet taken account of ex post envy rankings. Supposing that 2.a. and 2.b. are fulfilled but $\exists \alpha, \beta \ni G_\beta^1 \boldsymbol{V}_\beta\ G_\alpha^1$ but $G_\alpha^2 \boldsymbol{P}_\beta\ G_\beta^2$ The deliberator might reason that "Supposing I am instantiated as α, even if I am among the least favored ex ante, I am not among the least favored ex post – thus, supposing $G_\alpha^2 \boldsymbol{P}_\alpha\ G_\beta^2$, there is at least one ordering by which I am not among the least preferred, namely β's ex post preferences, and so my preference for S^2 is not decisive." But condition 2.c. excludes the supposition that $G_\alpha^2 \boldsymbol{P}_\beta\ G_\beta^2$

Further,

Lemma 4. The relation $\mathcal{J}$ is transitive. Proof. First, $S^3\mathcal{J}S^2\mathcal{J}S^1 \Rightarrow S^3 g S^2 g S^1$ and the transitivity of g gives us condition 2.a. and 2.b. for $S^3\mathcal{J}S^1$. Second, the transitivity of implication yields the third condition.

Lemma 5. $S^2\mathcal{J}S^1 \Rightarrow \sim S^1\mathcal{K}S^2$

Proof: Since $S^2\mathcal{J}S^1 \Rightarrow S^2 g S^1$, this follows from lemma 3 above.

Lemma 6. $S^2\mathcal{K}S^1 \Rightarrow \sim S^1\mathcal{J}S^2$

The proof is the same as for Lemma 2.

Now, again consider a compound rule:

Principle 4: compound principle. If either $S^2\mathcal{J}S^1$ or $S^2\mathcal{K}S^1$, then S^2 is socially preferred to S^1. Then write $S^2\mathcal{E}S^1$.

Theorem: The relation $\mathcal{E}$ is transitive.

Proof: There are four cases.

III.i $S^3\mathcal{J}S^2\mathcal{J}S^1$

III.ii $S^3\mathcal{K}S^2\mathcal{K}S^1$

III.iii $S^3\mathcal{K}S^2\mathcal{J}S^1$

III.iv $S^3\mathcal{J}S^2\mathcal{K}S^1$

For the first two cases, $S^3\mathcal{E}S^1$ follows from the transitivity of $\mathcal{J}$ and $\mathcal{K}$ respectively. For case iii. $S^3\mathcal{K}S^1$. We have 1.a. for $S^3\mathcal{K}S^1$ from 1.a. for $S^3\mathcal{K}S^2$ and 2.a. for $S^2\mathcal{J}S^1$, with the transitivity properties of the preference relation. We have 1.b. for $S^3\mathcal{K}S^1$ from 1.b. for $S^3\mathcal{K}S^2$ and again 2.a. for $S^2\mathcal{J}S^1$, with the transitivity properties of the preference relation. We have 1.c. for S^3KS^1 from 1.c. for $S^3\mathcal{K}S^2$ and for $S^2\mathcal{J}S^1$, again with the transitivity properties of the preference relation. We have 1.d. for $S^3\mathcal{K}S^1$ from 1.d. for $S^3\mathcal{K}S^2$, 2.c. for $S^2\mathcal{J}S^1$, and the transitivity of implication. For case iv, again, $S^3\mathcal{K}S^1$. The argument is essentially the same. Thus, in cases ii-iv, $S^3\mathcal{K}S^1$, while in case i, $S^3\mathcal{J}S^1$, and accordingly, in any case the compound condition $S^3\mathcal{E}S^1$ is realized.

Here, again, the price of transitivity may seem high. The deliberators behind the veil of ignorance might, however, recognize that a nontransitive relation would not be suitable. Indeed we might understand their objective as the discovery of a *transitive* rule for ranking social situations. Still, it is not clear that $\mathcal{E}$ is unique and thus a certain result of their deliberations. Further, the ordering is not complete. This can be established by an example:

$\mathcal{S}=\{S^1, S^2\}$

$\mathcal{N}=\{\alpha,\beta\}$.

IV.i. $G^1_\alpha \mathcal{P}_\alpha G^2_\alpha$

IV.ii. $G^2_\beta \mathcal{P}_\beta G^1_\beta$

IV.iii. $G^1_\alpha \mathcal{V}_\alpha G^1_\beta$

IV.iv. $G_\beta^2 \mathcal{V}_\beta G_\alpha^2$

IV.v. $G_\alpha^1 \mathcal{P}_\beta G_\beta^1$

IV.vi. $G_\beta^2 \mathcal{P}_\alpha G_\alpha^2$

Here, i. and ii establish that both states are Pareto optima. By v, a shift from 2 to 1 violates 1.d. and 2.c. so $\sim(S^2 \mathcal{K} S^1)$ and $\sim(S^2 \mathcal{F} S^1)$. By vi, similarly, a shift from 1 to 2 similarly violates both rules. Thus, the two states are unrankable.

Recall Little's proposed compound rule from the *Critique of Welfare Economics*. The rule is that a shift of social situations that improves the distribution of income and that passes the Scitovsky test is a social improvement. That rule could be criticized on two grounds: first, that Little offered no clear criterion for a "better" income distribution and second that the Skitovsky test presupposes that costless lump sum redistributions can be made. Perhaps some criterion based on equity as non-envy, such as $\mathcal{K}$, could fill the void for Little's distributional criterion. Suppose, for example, we have S^1, S^2, and S^3 with $S^2 \mathcal{K} S^1$ and $S^3 \mathcal{P} S^2$ and further $S^3 \mathcal{K} S^1$. Then the distribution is improved at S^2, but in ways that are inefficient so that a further change to S^3 makes some better off, none worse off, and retains the distributional improvement at S^2. Then the shift from S^1 to S^2 should not be adopted and S^3 should be adopted instead. For example, S^1 might incorporate free trade with a proportional income tax, S^2 a protectionist regime with a proportionate income tax, and S^3 free trade with an earned income tax credit and a slightly higher marginal rate, if (factual assumption) the redistributive tax system creates less waste than protectionism. Then protection should not be adopted and redistribution via the earned income tax credit should be adopted instead. Of course, if the factual assumption were reversed, the case would be settled for protectionism.

But we can do a bit better than this. In case $S^2 \mathcal{K} S^1$ and $S^3 \mathcal{P} S^2$, we might have $S^1 \mathcal{K} S^3$, a cycle, because the shift from S^2 to S^3 creates some new envy relations that can be reduced or eliminated by a return to S^1. If, however, we have $S^2 \mathcal{K} S^1$ and $S^3 \mathcal{F} S^2$, then from part iii of theorem 2, we have $S^3 \mathcal{K} S^1$, and no cycle can occur. Thus, the use of the relationship $\mathcal{F}$ seems to accomplish part of what Little intended with the Scitovsky criterion. But perhaps not all. Little noted that a shift to a Pareto optimum would always satisfy the Scitovszky criterion. Suppose that for all $S^i \in \mathcal{M}$, $S^3 \mathcal{P} S^i$. Then, again, $S^3 \mathcal{P} S^2$ in particular, but the possibility of a cycle such that $S^1 \mathcal{K} S^3$ is not excluded. The fact that the shift to S^3 is a shift to a Pareto optimum does not assure us that $S^3 \mathcal{F} S^2$, so, in some cases, the criterion suggested here will exclude a shift to a new social situation even though the new social situation is a Pareto optimum. In that it would differ from Little's.

So far the social ranking function has been one of "strict" preference. We might instead define a weak social ranking by $S^1 \mathcal{G} S^2$ iff $\sim S^1 \mathcal{E} S^2$. In terms of deliberation behind the veil of ignorance, $S^1 G S^2$ could be read as "There is no reason to choose S^2 over S^1." But it is not clear that this would be helpful, since $S^1 \mathcal{G} S^2$ and $S^2 \mathcal{G} S^1$ does not mean that the advantages of S^1 and S^2 are in any way equal, but only that the deliberators behind the veil of ignorance can make no distinction between them. This will recall Little's critique of formal preference theory in the individual case: in the absence of an intuitive indifference relation, observation of choices cannot assure us that any alternatives are indifferent choices. It is more clearly a problem here, since the objective was precisely to form a ranking of social states in the absence of any intuitive basis for the ranking. Here the compound criterion $\mathcal{E}$ can be contrasted to a utilitarian criterion. If we have a measure of the aggregate utility of $S^1 \in \square$, $\mathcal{U}(S^1)$, then the observation that $\mathcal{U}(S^1) \geq \mathcal{U}(S^2)$ and $\mathcal{U}(S^2) \geq \mathcal{U}(S^1)$ does imply that that $\mathcal{U}(S^1) = \mathcal{U}(S^2)$, the aggregate utility is the same in both cases. Conversely, any complete weak preference relation over social situations can be expressed by a family of index utility functions equivalent under a monotonic transformation, just as an individual preference field can be, and any member of that family will imply interpersonally comparable utility functions, at least in the sense that one person's loss of welfare is offset against gains by another. But however we may criticize utilitarianism for allowing such an offset, the relationship $\mathcal{K}$ also does it. In substituting a non-envy criterion for a utility criterion, we recognize that there are many criteria for the comparison of social situations (that is, many individual preference fields and envy relationships) but that recognition means that an incomplete ordering may be unavoidable.

Note

1 In this appendix, the thick term "envy" will be used with less than complete linguistic competence, as in the chapter, to refer only to a condition on preferences and not at all to refer to the emotion commonly referred to as "envy," and accordingly the quotation marks will be eliminated in what follows.

References

Atkinson, Anthony B. (2011) The Restoration of Welfare Economics, *American Economic Review* v. 101, no. 3 (May) pp. 157–161.

Baker, James A., Martin Feldstein, Ted Halstead, N. Gregory Mankiw, Henry M. Paulson, Jr., George P. Schultz, Thomas Stephenson and Rob Walton (2017) *The Conservative Case for Climate Dividends* (Washington, D.C.: Climate Leadership Council).

Baumol, William J. (1982) Applied Fairness Theory and Rationing Policy, *American Economic Review* v. 72, no. 4 (Sep) pp. 639–651.

Baumol, William (1986) *Superfairness: Applications and Theory* (Cambridge, Mass.: MIT Press).

Becker, Gary (1965) A Theory of the Economics of Time, *Economic Journal* v. 75, no. 3 (Sep) pp. 493–517.

Breit, William and William P. Culbertson (1970) Distributional Equality and Aggregate Utility: Comment, *American Economic Review* v. 60, no. 3 (Jun) pp. 435–441.

Buchanan, James and Gordon Tullock (1962) *The Calculus of Consent: Logical Foundations of Constitutional Democracy* (Ann Arbor, MI: University of Michigan Press).

Chavas, J. P. (1994) Equity Considerations in Economic and Policy Analysis, *American Journal of Agricultural Economics* v. 76, no. 5 (Dec) pp. 1022–1033.

Cohen, G. A. (1988) *History Labor and Freedom: Themes from Marx* (Oxford: Clarendon Press).

Dubins, L. E. and E. H. Spanier (1961) How to Cut a Cake Fairly, *American Mathematical Monthly* v. 68 (Jan) pp. 1–17.

Feldman, Allan and Alan Kirman (1974) Fairness and Envy, *American Economic Review* v. 64, no. 6 (Dec) pp. 995–1005.

Fleming, Marcus (1952) A Cardinal Concept of Welfare, *Quarterly Journal of Economics* (Aug) pp. 366–384.

Foley, Duncan K. (1967) Resource Allocation in the Public Sector, *Yale Economic Essays* v. 7 (Spring) pp. 73–76.

Friedman, Milton and L. J. Savage (1948) The Utility Analysis of Choices Involving Risk, *Journal of Political Economy* v. 56, no. 4 (Aug) pp. 279–304.

Friedman, Milton and L. J. Savage (1952) The Expected-Utility Hypothesis and the Measurability of Utility, *Journal of Political Economy* v. 60, no. 6 (Dec) pp. 463–474.

Green, David A. (2014) What Is a Minimum Wage For? Empirical Results and Theories of Justice, *Canadian Public Policy/Analyse de Politiques*, v. 40, no. 4 (Dec) pp. 293–314.

Harsanyi, John (1953) Cardinal Utility in Welfare Economics and in the Theory of Risk-Taking, *Journal of Political Economy* v. 61, no. 5 (Oct) pp. 434–435.

Harsanyi, John (1955) Cardinal Welfare, Individualistic Ethics, and Interpersonal Comparisons of Utility, *Journal of Political Economy* v. 63 (Aug) pp. 309–321.

Henderson, A. (1941) Consumer's Surplus and the Compensating Variation, *Review of Economic Studies* v. 8, no. 2 (Feb) pp. 117–121.

Hicks, J. R. (1942) Consumers' Surplus and Index-Numbers, *Review of Economic Studies* v. 9, no. 2 (Summer) pp. 126–137.

Hildreth, Clifford (1953) Alternative Conditions for Social Orderings, *Econometrica* v. 21, no. 1 (Jan) pp. 81–94.

Hobbes, Thomas (1968 [1651]) *Leviathan* (Harmondsworth: Penguin Pelican).

Hopkins, Ed and Tatiana Kornienko (2010) Which Inequality? The Inequality of Endowments versus the Inequality of Rewards, *American Economic Journal: Microeconomics* v. 2, no. 3 (Aug) pp. 106–137.

Kolm, S. C. (1996) The Theory of Justice, *Social Choice and Welfare* v. 13, no. 2, pp. 151–182.

Kuhn, H. W. (1967) On Games of Fair Division, *Essays in Mathematical Economics in Honor of Oskar Morgenstern*, edited by M. Shubik (Princeton, N.J.: Princeton University Press) pp. 29–37.

Lange, Oskar (1934) The Determinateness of the Utility Function, *Review of Economic Studies* v. 1, no. 3 (Jun) pp. 218–225.

Lerner, Abba P. (1944) *Economics of Control* (New York: Macmillan).

Lerner, Abba P. (1970) Distributional Equality and Aggregate Utility: Reply, *American Economic Review* v. 60, no. 3 (Jun) pp. 442–443.

Little, I. M. D. (1952) Social Choice and Individual Values, *Journal of Political Economy* v. 60, no. 5 (Oct) pp. 422–432.

Little, I. M. D. (2002 [1950]) *A Critique of Welfare Economics*, 2nd Edition (Oxford: Clarendon).

Mankiw, N. Gregory (2013) Defending the One Percent, *Journal of Economic Perspectives* v. 27, no. 3 (Summer) pp. 21–34.

Marshak, Jacob (1954) Probability in the Social Sciences, *Mathematical Thinking in the Social Sciences*, edited by P. F. Lazarsfeld (Glencoe, Ill.: Free Press).

McCain, Roger A. (1972) Distributional Equality and Aggregate Utility: Further Comment, *American Economic Review* v. 62, no. 3 (Jun) pp. 497–500.

McCain, Roger A. and Bijou Lester (2001) An Equity-Based Redefinition of Underemployment and Unemployment and Some Measurements, *Review of Social Economy* (June).

McCain, Roger A. (2014) *Reframing Economics: Economic Action as Imperfect Cooperation* (Cheltenham: Edward Elgar).

McCain, Roger A. (2015) *Game Theory and Public Policy*, 2nd Edition (Cheltenham: Edward Elgar).

McCain, Roger A. (2017) *Approaching Equality: What Can Be Done about Wealth Inequality* (Cheltenham: Edward Elgar).

McManus, Maurice, Gary M. Walton and Richard B. Coffman (1972) Distributional Equality and Aggregate Utility: Further Comment, *American Economic Review* v. 62, no. 3 (Jun) pp. 489–496.

Mishan, E. J. (1960) A Survey of Welfare Economics, 1939–1959, *Economic Journal* v. 70, no. 278 (Jun) pp. 197–265.

Pazner, E. A. and D. Schmeidler (1974) A Difficulty in the Concept of Fairness, *Review of Economic Studies* v. 41 (July) pp. 441–443.

Pazner, E. A. and D. Schmeidler (1978) Egalitarian Equivalent Allocations: A New Concept of Economic Equity, *Quarterly Journal of Economics* v. 92 (Nov) pp. 671–687.

Pestieau, Pierre, Uri Possen and Steven Slutsky (2002) Randomization, Revelation, and Redistribution in a Lerner World, *Economic Theory* v. 20, no. 3 (Oct) pp. 539–553.

Piketty, Thomas (1994) Existence of Fair Allocations in Economies with Production, *Journal of Public Economics* v. 55, pp. 391–405.

Rawls, John (1951) Outline of a Decision Procedure for Ethics, *Philosophical Review* v. 60, no. 2 (Apr) pp. 177–197.

Rawls, John (1955) Two Concepts of Rules, *Philosophical Review* v. 64, no. 1 (Jan) pp. 3–32.

Rawls, John (1957) Justice as Fairness, *Journal of Philosophy* v. 54, no. 22 (Oct) pp. 653–662.

Rawls, John (1958) Justice as Fairness, *Philosophical Review* v. 67, no. 2 (Apr) pp. 164–194.

Rawls, John (1971) *A Theory of Justice* (Cambridge, Mass.: Belknap Press).

Samuelson, Paul A. (1964) A. P. Lerner at Sixty, *Review of Economic Studies* v. 31, no. 3 (Jun) pp. 169–178.

Schmeidler, David and Karl Vind (1972) Fair Net Trades, *Econometrica* v. 40, no. 4 (Jul) pp. 637–642.

Scitovsky, Tiborde (1941) A Note on Welfare Propositions in Economics, *Review of Economic Studies* v. 9, pp. 77–88.

Sen, Amartya (1970) *Collective Choice and Social Welfare* (London: Holden-Day).

Sen, Amartya (1973) On Ignorance and Equal Distribution, *American Economic Review* v. 63, no. 5 (Dec) pp. 1022–1024.

Sen, Amartya (2009) *The Idea of Justice* (Cambridge, Mass.: Belknap Press).

Theil, Henri (1967) *Economics and Information Theory* (Amsterdam: North-Holland).

Varian, H. R. (1974) Equity, Envy and Efficiency, *Journal of Economic Theory* v. 9, pp. 63–91.

Varian, H. R. (1975) Distributive Justice, Welfare Economics, and the Theory of Fairness, *Philosophy and Public Affairs* v. 4, pp. 223–247.

Vohra, Rajiv (1992) Equity and Efficiency in Non-Convex Economies, *Social Choice and Welfare* v. 9, no. 3 pp. 185–202.

Walton, Douglas (1989) *Informal Logic: A Handbook for Critical Argumentation* (Cambridge: Cambridge University Press).

9 Diverging paths

In the later twentieth century, economic research has been more and more channeled into what many call "silos," that is, professional subspecializations that communicate little with one another and are often unaware of developments outside their subspecialization. Krugman (1995, p. 2) has called this professionalization, but some of these subspecializations are less professional than others on the indicia that Krugman suggests. And some have been less successful than others. This chapter, accordingly, traces several diverging (but in some cases intersecting) paths of discourse. Thereafter, it considers a recent contribution to the economics of public policy that does not rely on welfare economics: Mankiw's *Defending the One Percent* (2013).

9.1 Coase and his school and externalities

Executive summary of the section: Ronald Coase criticized arguments from externality as incomplete in that they ignored transaction costs. The large literature that resulted (including some written by the author of this book) proceeds from arguments that are formally fallacious.

Ronald Coase (1910–2013) lived a life that was long, extraordinary and without doubt blessed. The paper which was most important[1] in bringing him the Nobel Memorial Prize (1991) was written while he was an undergraduate studying for a bachelor of commerce degree and published a few years later (Coase 1937) to little immediate notice. Coase did not receive the PhD degree until the age of 41,[2] which must be exceptional among Nobel laureates. The only aspect of his work that is of concern to us here is his attack on the Pigovian concept of externalities in "The Problem of Social Cost" (1960). Coase's position is that if one economic actor imposes some externality on another, then the two will come to some bargain to limit or compensate the externality, and in the absence of transaction costs this bargain will be efficient. Further, a shift of property rights that would reverse the externality would lead to the same allocation of resources, again in the absence of

transaction costs and neglecting any income effects. These propositions constitute "the Coase theorem." But Coase observed that transaction costs are
always present and cannot be ignored, and argued that the law could and
commonly did award property rights in such a way as to reduce transaction
costs. Coase concedes (p. 18) that, given transaction costs, Pigou might be
right in some cases:

> there is no reason why, on occasion ... governmental administrative reg-
> ulation should not lead to an improvement in economic efficiency. This
> would seem particularly likely when, as is normally the case with the
> smoke nuisance, a large number of people are involved and in which
> therefore the costs of handling the problem through the market or the
> firm may be high ... [But] There is, of course, a further alternative, which
> is to do nothing about the problem at all. And given that the costs
> involved in solving the problem by regulations issued by the govern-
> mental administrative machine will often be heavy (particularly if the
> costs are interpreted to include consequences which follow from the
> Government engaging in this kind of activity) it will no doubt be com-
> monly the case that the gain which would come from regulating the
> actions which give rise to the harmful effects will be less than the costs
> involved in Government regulation ... [Therefore] All solutions have costs
> and there is no reason to suppose that government regulation is called for
> simply because the problem is not well handled by the market or the firm.

This is hardly a ringing contradiction of Pigou! But it was taken that way.[3]
Coase adopts the interpretation of "social cost" or externalities due to Ellis
and Fellner (1943), ignoring the extension of the concepts of externality by
Bator (1957, 1958). None of these authors is cited. It seems that Coase's
paper might have been written 20 years earlier, and his method is older still,
comprising, as it does, plausible reasoning with small-scale examples. Had
Coase gotten it right nevertheless, none of that would matter; but Aivazian
and Callen (1981) demonstrated that the "Coase Theorem" is false. Now,
Aivazian and Callen used the methods of cooperative game theory, and the
counterargument might be made that their model was not what Coase had in
mind, but if not then it is unclear just what Coase did have in mind. In any
case, considered as an argument against Pigou, Coase's argument is fallacious. It has the form "Pigou has not taken transaction costs into account,
therefore (in general) Pigou is mistaken; that is, "If A then B, not A, therefore
not B," the fallacy of denying the antecedent. (Alternatively it could be construed as the argument from fallacy, "Pigou's argument is fallacious, therefore
his conclusion is false." This also is a formal fallacy.) Now, in the spirit of
reasonable dialog, a formal fallacy may nevertheless have some persuasive
force: we see that, for a world of positive transaction costs, Pigou's argument
is incomplete. This places a burden of proof on those who support Pigovian
taxes to complete the argument. But the response was already in the literature

in Bator's writing. Further, the same criticism can be made against Coase: Coase has neglected the argument that a Pigovian tax could in principle support efficient incentives, whereas compensation to the victims does not, so that the Pigovian tax could improve over even a feasible scheme of bribery subject to modest costs of transaction. Coase also ignores the possibility that taking account of transaction costs might lead to novel arguments in favor of government intervention (e.g. McCain 1994). All in all, while Coase deserves credit for his early insight about the importance of the costs of transaction, his discussion of "social cost" deserves no more attention than the Royal Swedish Academy of Science gave it.

Nevertheless, it gave rise to a large literature. A good and representative instance is Cheung's (1973) "The Fable of the Bees." This takes Meade's example of bees and pollination and notes that in fact, beekeepers and orchardists do sometimes contract to place beehives in or near the orchards for purposes of pollination. Here, again, we see the fallacy of denying the antecedent: since we observe transactions that Meade's (1952) illustrative example assumes away, Meade's conclusion must be wrong. This is a bit worse, since Meade's discussion is not even an argument, but an illustrative example that needs be true only in some, even hypothetical, cases to do its work. Coase himself, in a collaboration with Demsetz (1974), attacked Mill's example of the lighthouse. Their examples in which lighthouses were provided by "the private sector" are taken from medieval Europe, when the distinction of public and private sectors was not so clear in that an association of businessmen could in effect be the government of a city.

Then why has this literature been influential? On the one hand, it is difficult to avoid the notion that political convenience had something to do with it: at a time when externalities (and in particular negative environmental externalities) were increasingly a matter of popular concern outside economics, it provided a "protective belt" (Musgrave and Pigden 2016) for economists who wanted to defend a laissez-faire political economy. On the other hand, discussion of the influence of transaction costs on the allocation of resources can be divorced from this defensive role, and reference to "the Coase theorem" is sometimes a signal of that sort of inquiry. However, for a history of welfare economics, no more needs be said about it.

9.2 Distributional weights in cost–benefit analysis

Executive summary of the section: To the extent that cost–benefit analysis relies on the Kaldor test, it shares the deficiencies of that test. One response was a proposal to weight costs and benefits according to their distributional impact.

Cost–benefit analysis can be a branch of applied welfare economics, although in the very large literature under this label there are analyses that bear little if any relation to welfare economics. However, a common method often deployed by applied economists, relying on estimates of consumer surpluses and such, is an application of the Kaldor-Hicks test of potential Pareto improvement. As such it shares the shortcomings of that method: it implicitly assumes that the marginal utility of income is the same for all who benefit from or bear the costs of the project that is evaluated by the cost–benefit analysis. The idea that these measures of costs and benefits ought to be modified to allow for distributional aspects of projects evaluated must have been in the minds of many economists in the twentieth century, but Weisbrod (1968) is widely credited with making the idea explicit in a paper that contrasted the use of distributional weights in cost–benefit analysis favorably with the simpler procedure of treating the efficiency (in standard cost–benefit terms) and the distributional impact as separate bases for the evaluation of projects. Weisbrod (p. 192) proposes to derive weights by income and other categories of beneficiaries from the actions of governments, in a sort of adaptation of the principle of revealed preference. He illustrates this approach by an application to four water-resource projects (pp. 198–203). Negative weights are derived for some groups (p. 201). In comments on the paper, Haveman (1968, p. 210) questions the normative significance of weights derived in this way. This aspect of Weisbrod's proposal was also criticized by, inter alia, Musgrave (1969) and Mishan (1982).

A major obstacle to applications of this approach is (as Weisbrod conceded) lack of data. This is probably the principal reason why there have been fairly few published applications. An example is the study of proposals for sites for a third London airport (none of which ever seems to have been carried forward) by Nwaneri (1970). This study follows Eckstein (1961) in deriving weights from marginal income tax rates, saying "we take the current tax structure as optimal." He does find that the results of the studies would be changed if distributional weights were used. By contrast, Timothy Hau (1986) derives weights from a social welfare function. Thus he associates himself with "the a priori school ... as distinct from Weisbrod's imputational school." This distinction seems to be due to Brent (1984).[4]

But both schools faced criticism and opposition from one of the most influential figures in economic cost–benefit analysis: Arnold Harberger (1978, 1984). He calculates (1978) a number of examples and concludes that the impacts of distributional weights on the results of cost–benefit analysis are implausibly large. In general, the weights used are for representative – that is average – members of particular groups among beneficiaries or those who bear the cost. Apart from that he does not (unlike e.g. Nwaneri) allow for differences of income among beneficiaries or those harmed. (For the kinds of examples he considers this would be very difficult.) An exception is his derivation of an optimal income tax schedule from distributionally weighted taxpayer sacrifices. With diminishing marginal utility of income, he determines, the optimal tax structure would be regressive. This is indeed implausible. In Harberger (1984) he argues that distributional concerns in cost–benefit analysis are better treated as consumption externalities, arising because some people prefer states of the world in which others increase their consumption of goods that meet basic needs.

Harberger's attack was in turn criticized by Squire (1980) and Layard (1980). Squire notes that with constant weights, i.e. constant marginal utilities of money, the optimal tax schedule would be even more regressive. Thus, in fact, weighting does lead to less regressivity. Layard takes the same point further, pointing out that tax rates consistent with distributional weights that decline with rising income can be differently computed with opposite results. Essentially, Harberger had made an arbitrary choice of a constant of integration. Layard also contradicts Harberger's assumptions about the determinants of distributional weights. Supposing that the tax system is optimal, these weights can be related to the administrative costs of pure redistribution via the tax system. Harberger had argued that these costs, though non-zero, would be small, which would imply only a small difference in distributive weights. Layard provides examples that support a contrary position. In his response, Harberger adopts a new position on distributional weights, saying that they should be used but that net benefits should not be reported that exceed the net benefits of the least wasteful alternative project that might attain the same objective. (This seems consistent with Little's criterion, but Harberger makes no such claim.) Harberger then essentially concedes that both critics' examples are valid, but asserts that they do not affect his conclusion.

Throughout this discussion, the imputational approach is used by all sides, with marginal tax rates as indicators of the government's "value" of distribution. The critique of Weisbrod by Haveman, Musgrave and Mishan seems to make a key point. If the purpose of welfare economics is to criticize the decisions of government, then the use of the government's own decisions to determine the results of the application of welfare economics to public policy would seem to be too limiting. It would allow us at most to criticize the *consistency* of those decisions, but not at all to criticize any *distributional bias* that they might display. By contrast, the estimation of consumer surpluses and such derives the criterion from the decisions of people in the marketplace, not those of the government, and thus can criticize governments for biases that lead to inefficient government decisions (including status quo bias). Indeed, why should we suppose that government per se sets *any* value on either efficiency or an equitable distribution of resources? Government is not a unitary decision maker but a power structure through which distinct classes and strategically placed groups assert their power (McCain 2014, pp. 216–221). This is transparently true of "democratic" governments but no less true of dictatorships, only the assertion of group power in the second case is more likely to be both violent and covert. The value of applied welfare economics is that it enables the members of these various groups to criticize the government from a position that does reflect such values, insofar as criticism is permitted.

While the controversy between Harberger and his critics was hardly resolved, little more was heard of the imputational approach to weighted cost–benefit analysis (compare, e.g., Johansson-Stenman 2005). In any case, all sides conceded that cost–benefit analyses, however computed, would only represent one of a plurality of ways of evaluating public projects. If we aspire to a discussion of public policy that would constitute a reasonable dialog, a favorable cost–benefit analysis of a project would be an argument for it that could be undercut either by an evaluation on a different basis (such as equity or national defense) or by a differently computed cost–benefit analysis, so long as the data and assumptions underlying all arguments are transparent.

9.3 A cardinalist counterattack

Executive summary of the section: In a large number of papers and a book, in the late twentieth century, Ng proposed an updated welfare economics founded on additive utilitarianism.

In the latter decades of the twentieth century Yew-Kwang Ng made a number of contributions to welfare economics, including a text (Ng 1980) that deserves its place on my shelves alongside Little's and Graaff's book-length treatments of welfare economics. As outlined in the book, Ng's work is a campaign to assimilate the contributions of the New Welfare Economics and what this book has called saltwater welfare economics into a renewed cardinalist welfare economics. But Ng was an army of one, and however powerful its weapons or arguments, an army of one is unlikely to prevail.

Ng observes (p. 6) that welfare economics can be interpreted as positive economics if one takes the definition of social welfare simply as descriptive, but would then have no independent normative force; if instead it proceeds from the analyst's fundamental value judgments then it has, for that person, normative standing. Ng affirms his utilitarian value judgment (p. 11) and argues that utility is measurable after all (pp. 13–15), and, demonstrating his utilitarian values, dedicates his book to "the welfare of all sentients." He argues that preference differs from individual welfare in terms that would be echoed in the later literature on behavioral welfare economics (pp. 7–9; compare Bernheim 2016; Infante et al. 2016). He defends tests of welfare change such as the Kaldor test, and particularly Little's compound test as he interprets it, as useful in a world of limited information, despite the possibility (as he sees it) of a social welfare function.

In a distinctive contribution, Ng relates his additive utilitarian social welfare function to a weak majority rule criterion (pp. 128–131). He adopted Armstrong's view (1939, 1951) that indifference is non-transitive, discussed here in chapter 4, section d. Armstrong (we recall) had argued that utility is quantitative but imperfectly perceived, so that, given alternatives x and y, an individual will be indifferent between them if $|u(x)-u(y)|<\varepsilon$. Then ε, the threshold of perception, can be thought of as a unit of utility which is comparable from one individual to another. Ng traces this idea back to Borda and Edgeworth (p. 129) and to some psychological literature. Following a hint in Armstrong (1951, p. 264), Ng (1980, p. 129) proposes his weak majority preference principle: if x is preferred to y by a majority of the population *and the rest are indifferent* between x and y, then x is socially preferred to y. This is consistent with additive utilitarianism: one half or more gain at least ε by the switch from y to x, while one half or fewer lose something less than ε. Ng shows (1975) that in fact it implies an additive utilitarianism, and this is his substitute for Arrow's (1951) impossible social welfare function. This is not, as I interpret Ng, the justification for his utilitarianism, so much as an alternative way of expressing it that Ng believes is more difficult to reject than additive utilitarianism per se. But Ng's utility is something a bit different than the utility that Robbins and Harrod debated. Robbins' Brahmin might derive much more satisfaction from his consumption than the untouchable because he is more sensitive to the absolute quantum of pleasure that consumption can give, without being any more sensitive to utility *differences*. Ng would not recognize such a difference. Ng concedes (1975, p. 131) that a Benthamite social welfare function could be consistent with a quite unequal distribution of income and of welfare. But he rejects (p. 150) the idea that Armstrong would not quite reject (1951, p. 269): that welfare should in some cases be equalized relative to the additive maximum. This he characterizes as utility illusion.

Ng goes on to incorporate in his framework the important contributions to welfare economics at mid-century: externalities in modern terms, public goods, feasible utility frontiers and the theory of the second best. Ng's theory of the third best was discussed in Chapter 7. Ng's contributions give us an attempt to recover not just the additive utilitarianism of Pigou's welfare economics, but its coherence. In terms of those objectives, it seems successful. But given the cultural triumph of ordinalism among economists, it demanded too much: a reversal of that cultural hegemony. That had to wait for the growing evidence in behavioral economics that ordinalism was simply wrong. By then Ng (2003) would be among the advocates for the use of survey data on self-reported life satisfaction in economics, and further discussion of his work will take place in that context.

9.4 Capabilities

Executive summary of the section: In his more recent work Sen proposes that capabilities, not attainments or utility, should be the basis for the evaluation of public policy.

As we have seen, Amartya Sen had by the early 1970s made crucially important contributions to welfare economics, including among others both a resolution of the issues raised by Arrow's impossibility theorem and the insight that "cardinal" utilities might enter into welfare calculations not simply by addition but with weights, possibly non-linear, that would allow for any degree of equalitarian values beyond those implied by maximizing the sum of utilities. Thereafter, however, his ideas turned in a new direction, with a rejection of "welfarism" as an approach to normative social science. The "impossibility of a Paretian liberal" seems to have been the pole around which Sen's ideas turned. A central concept for Sen's writing on normative social science since that time is "capabilities," and the "capabilities" approach in economic development and normative social science has become the center of a large and important literature, largely outside economics (see Sen 1982, 1985, and 2009, ch. 11, especially notes 9, p. 233 and 10 references in the text at p. 235).

A person's capabilities, as briefly as possible, are the things she can do if she chooses to. This is closely connected to what is often called positive freedom or "freedom to." Suppose, for example, that women (as a gender or women of a particular class) are prohibited from attending school. This limits the woman's capability in an obvious way – she is unable to attend school – and since education is a basis of still other capabilities (such as those of reading a recipe or an employment contract) it limits her capabilities also in other indirect ways. Suppose, then, that the prohibition on schooling women is eliminated, but there are no schools for her to attend. By the removal of the prohibition on schooling for women, her liberty has been increased. Her "freedom from" coercion has been increased. But her "freedom to" attend school has not been increased, and her capabilities continue to be restricted very much as before. A policy focused on capabilities would not only remove public obstacles to the education of women, but would allocate resources to assure that schools are available to extend the capability of girls to attend school.

This discussion will rely on Sen's account in *The Idea of Justice* (2009). While this is convenient, as the book is recent and gives an overview of many of Sen's contributions over the years, the book has a broader objective, as the title suggests, and this objective does not correspond particularly well with welfare economics (quite aside from Sen's rejection of "welfarism"). His theme emerges in the first pages: there is no one basis for the distinction of justice and injustice (pp. 1–2). Rather "plural grounding" is required. That is, injustice (of slavery or of the oppression of women, for example) can be established on various bases, and especially when these arguments agree, the case is made that injustice should be eliminated even though no agreement is reached over the limits of justice and injustice in general. Accordingly, Sen rejects "transcendental institutionalism," which he identifies inter alia with social contract theories such as Rawls', calling instead for comparison of concrete social alternatives, which he finds in different forms in the ideas of Adam Smith, Bentham, Mill and Mary Wollstonecraft (pp. 7–8).

The capability approach would value the increase of capabilities in the population, aside from the achievements (pp. 235–238) or satisfaction of wants of the population. This is subject to a criticism that will occur to any economist and to most non-economists. Let me illustrate it with a real example. In the United States and some other countries there are public policies to guarantee small business loans. The rationale is that because of the detailed economics of markets for loan capital, potential businesspeople may be unable to get access to capital that would enable them to form a successful new business, or successfully expand an existing business. The public loan guarantees may then enable some to start or expand successful businesses who would not otherwise be able to, thus expanding their capabilities. But many people, probably most people, do not choose to establish businesses. Are they therefore better off for acquiring a capability they never care to use? A critic of Sen's view would say that they are not.

We should pause to consider the indirect consequences of the policy for a person who does not form a business. It might be argued that because the loan guarantees lead to a more productive and competitive economy I benefit from them as a consumer, even though I do not choose to start a business myself. The consumer's benefit from a more productive and competitive economy is precisely what a "welfarist" evaluation of the loan guarantee program would focus on, and that welfare economics has relied on from the writing of Pigou forward. This is the kind of argument the capability approach is meant to go beyond, and the argument is that even though one may have no wish to start a business, and apart from any benefits that the policy might bring to her in other aspects of her life, she is better off simply because of the increase in her capability to form a business.

In the language of economists, we might think of an individual possibility frontier defined not only on conventional goods and services but also over other dimensions of the good life. We could then (tentatively!) think of an increase in capabilities as a local outward shift in that possibility frontier. What we could say is that such a shift could not make the person worse off, but would not make the person better off unless it would lead to a change in the person's decision among her possibilities. This is related to the independence of irrelevant alternatives, which tells us that if the shift of the possibility frontier is localized away from the chosen point, it will not modify the choice made, and it follows – as economists usually understand benefits or well-being – that it cannot be of benefit to the person as a result. Sen tells us that economists are mistaken to understand benefits or well-being in that way, and this is, among other things, a radical rejection of the independence of irrelevant alternatives.

The connection of the capabilities approach to "freedom to" presents some further difficulties. At p. 383 Sen acknowledges these, quoting Honora O'Niell, "Unfortunately much writing and rhetoric on rights heedlessly proclaims universal rights to goods and services … without showing what connects each presumed right-holder to some specified obligation-bearer(s), which leaves the content of these supposed rights wholly obscure." To the extent that capabilities depend on such "rights to goods and service" their content seems similarly obscure. Again and again Sen distinguishes capabilities from attainments by examples in which people are forced to do what they wish to do anyway. Thus, their capabilities are impaired even though their attainments are not. These examples have logical force, but they distort the major role of compulsion in society, which is to require people to do what they would not choose to do, and thus to some extent miss the point of freedom.

Sen tells us (e.g. 2009, pp. 66, 234, 254, 260–262, 299) that the capabilities approach is put forward as a substitute for primary goods in Rawls' analysis. If that were the whole story, it would seem to be a step forward. Behind the veil of ignorance, a deliberator would see an increase in the capacities of a realized agent, ceteris paribus, as an improvement. In the case of public guarantees of small business loans, a deliberator would not know whether, in the society formed, he would want to form a business or not. That being so, the agent behind a veil of ignorance would rationally place some value on the capability to do so per se. Conversely, behind the veil of ignorance, there could be no evaluation based on attainments, since attainments depend on some things that could not be known behind the veil of ignorance, such as preferences, consequent decisions and idiosyncratic characteristics. Further, this would justify Rawls' seemingly arbitrary priority of equal liberty, since an increase in equal liberty would expand the capabilities of many agents and reduce the capabilities of none.[5] Since capabilities are multidimensional, there may be some ambiguity – a policy change might extend capability on some dimensions and contract it on others – but this is no less an issue with Rawls' unspecified list of primary goods, apart from equal liberty.

But Sen rejects other aspects of Rawls' contractarian approach. In place of Rawls' deliberator behind the veil of ignorance, Sen would have a Smithian "impartial spectator" (e.g. pp. 44, 70, ch. 6) who may be from "far as well as near" (p. 125). Further, Sen insists on the "plural grounding" of social judgments. Thus, the fact that a change is in the interest of a representative agent must be weighed against other considerations, which may be deontological, such as the obligation that comes with a capability to use that capability in certain ways (pp. 205–207), or may be other regarding, or both. At the same time, Sen's examples generally assume that the person whose capabilities are limited or expanded is aware of their own preferences or situation (see, e.g., pp. 229, 370–372). And Sen is quite critical of the veil of ignorance itself (e.g. pp. 66–74, pp. 126–152). But what does this leave us with? If capabilities are a useful substitution within a contractarian position, do they remain helpful if we substitute quite a different approach?

Consider first Sen's (Smith's) impartial spectator. Sen tells us that the impartial spectator is a source of information not available to the deliberators behind the veil of ignorance (pp. 108–109). Further, this will avoid parochialism. By contrast, the deliberators behind the veil of ignorance may be influenced by "entrenched tradition and custom" (p. 45). Following Smith (2000 [1759]), Sen uses the defense of infanticide in ancient Greece as an example of the tyranny of custom (2009, p. 404). But why do we need to suppose that the deliberators behind the veil of ignorance would be parochial? The deliberation behind the veil of ignorance is hypothetical, and the ignorance of individual interest, together with knowledge of such things as economic theory, is a way of framing a kind of objectivity of the conclusions. We have seen that the conclusions vary with the knowledge that the deliberators are assumed to have. In Harsanyi's analysis, for example, they know the list of all admissible utility functions. Knowing that and very little else, they conclude for utilitarianism. Why may we not suppose that these hypothetical deliberators are aware of all the tribal customs known to cultural anthropology, but do not know to which tribe they belong?

There is a real problem here that needs to be set to one side. Since, in Hobbes' tradition, social contractarianism is a justification of sovereign power, it seems to say nothing about the relations among subjects of different sovereigns. But this is not to say that the deliberators know themselves to be members of a particular sovereignty and bound by its customs and traditions. Quite the contrary.

On the other side, why do we suppose that the Smithian impartial spectator would take into account the interests or values of the agents in the observed society? Presumably the impartial spectator would be motivated by Smithian sympathy. Even so, this might lead the impartial spectator to paternalism, establishing for the observed society goals that are not justified by "how people feel." Sen admits this as an (inconclusive) argument for utilitarianism against the capabilities approach (Sen 2009, p. 274). On the other hand, the deliberators behind the veil of ignorance take the interests and values of agents in the realized society into account because they are their own values. In enacting the social contract, we recall, they are enacting their own will.

Further, why do we suppose that a spectator from "far away" would be impartial? A spectator from "far away," however innocent of the "entrenched tradition and custom" of the observed society, might nevertheless not be impartial. If the spectator were to come from a wealthy, leisured and cultured class in his own society, he might well feel more "sympathy" with the leisured and cultured members of the society observed, however different their culture. Colonialism supplies ample instances of this.

In place of the veil of ignorance, Sen would have public reason (e.g. pp. 121–122 and note part IV) with "open impartiality" (ch. 6) determine the direction of public policy. This would incorporate information from actual people from their own perspectives. For example, the voices of women, enlightened by their own experience and reason, would be no less heard than those of males. The voices of people of different countries would be equally heard. Sen recognizes (pp. 106–7, esp.) that this dialog may not be conclusive, but regards as arguments as objective if they are sustained in the face of public reasoning. These standards again recall Walton's reasonable dialog. To determine public policy, Sen relies on processes of social choice in the light of his own discovery (1969, 1970) that an intransitive ordering might nevertheless supply a social choice function.

There seem to be two problems with Sen's use of his result on social choice functions. The example of non-transitive ordering used in his (1970) essay on social choice is the Paretian ordering. The Paretian ordering essentially relies on the agreement of the preference orderings of different individuals. But Sen is speaking of conflicting orderings based on different *principles*. That is to say, Sen envisions an ordering that is not just intransitive but *equivocal*. Sen asserts (pp. 398–399) that this makes no difference, and at a formal level, he may be right. But there is a difference of substance: it is one thing to say "neither situation 1 nor situation 2 is better than the other because either John or James is worse off at either of them" and quite another to say "neither situation 1 nor situation 2 is better than the other because John and James cannot decide what principles to apply to rank them." And there may be formal difficulties. Sen's notion of incorporating various values by an extended Pareto principle seems to presuppose that the values can be expressed as rankings. This is not quite clear. Consider the deontological view that capacities bring with them obligations to use the capacities in favor of others, which Sen supports by the authority of the Buddha (p. 205). This expresses a powerful moral intuition with which many will agree, but does it supply even an incomplete ordering over social states?

In the large, Sen's disagreement with Rawls seems to come to Sen's rejection of the idea that ignorance can improve discourse. He would have discourse on social issues draw on the widest possible range of information, judging that in actual discussions ignorance is more likely to conceal and preserve abuses than to improve anything. But, really, Sen is talking past Rawls, and they are addressing different questions. Sen charges the spectator to be impartial; Rawls tells us how to judge impartiality. (And Smith, in his use of the impartial spectator, seems closer to Rawls than to Sen.) Sen's public reason is real and imperfect, Rawls' deliberations hypothetical and in some sense perfect. To reason *as if* behind a veil of ignorance, or *as if* one were an impartial spectator, imposes on our reason a kind of discipline that seems appropriate for normative social science, and one suspects that the deliberators behind a veil of ignorance would prefer institutions in which public policy would be responsive to Sen's public reason.

9.5 A welfare-economic critique of Mankiw's "Defending the One Percent"

Executive summary of the section: Mankiw, like Sen, rejects welfarism but proposes to substitute a norm of "just desert." This section argues that Mankiw's discussion is far from satisfactory as a substitute for welfare economics.

Is it, then, possible to do normative economics without using the learning of welfare economists in the twentieth century at all? That seems to be Mankiw's aim in his (2013) "Defending the One Percent." It cannot be fairly said that Mankiw does not think carefully about the value judgments he makes, although he confesses frankly to being an amateur at philosophy (p. 22). It can fairly be said, however, that so far as the learning of twentieth-century welfare economics is concerned, Mankiw's defense would have been right up to date in 1899 – when John Bates Clark published *The Distribution of Wealth*, espousing substantially the same ideas Mankiw sets forth. Mankiw seems unaware of Clark's writing.[6] Mankiw rejects utilitarianism and proposes to put in its place what he calls a "just deserts" criterion (Mankiw 2013, p. 32; 2010, p. 293); that is, a norm of compensation according to contribution. He then identifies the contribution with the value of the marginal product at a market equilibrium. This is precisely Clark's position.

Recall the discussion of Pareto optimality as a criterion of social choice among welfare economists in the 1940s. As Lange and others observed, this criterion would be insufficient because the market equilibrium is contingent on the distribution of income. But this criticism applies well beyond the scope of Pareto optimality. It suggests that *any* attempt to justify a distribution and allocation of goods and services by reference to the properties of a market equilibrium must fail. Mankiw's argument (and Clark's) attribute to market equilibria a property of justice, quite independently of any judgment of efficiency. But this property of justice, no less than the efficiency of a hypothetical market equilibrium, is contingent on the particular market equilibrium which in turn depends on the distribution of income. Thus the argument is in effect that the existing distribution of income is just because it is the existing distribution of income. This is a vacuous circularity. For those who are in a hurry, little more needs be said. For those who are less easily persuaded, the remainder of this section will point out a number of other confusions in Mankiw's writing on distribution. In many cases as in this case, the critique will draw on the history of welfare economics (and of economic thought more broadly).

Mankiw's position is unequivocally that distribution according to contribution is just (2010, p. 295, 2013, p. 32.) As he notes (2013, p. 33), this is far from a new idea. But there are several questions that can be addressed to an advocate of distribution according to contribution.

1   Contribution to what? A utilitarian could answer that, and Pigou does: contribution to aggregate utility. But that answer is not available to Mankiw.
2   How are we to measure the individual contributions, given the interdependence of many activities in a market society? Mankiw chooses the value of marginal productivity, and it is true that this construct allows in a certain way for interdependency. But, from a normative perspective, does it allow for interdependency in the right way? We recall that Sidgwick (1883, p. 505; refer to the appendix to Chapter 2) rejected marginal utility as a standard of justice for just that reason. Why are Mankiw and Clark right and Sidgwick wrong about that?
3   Is payment according to compensation viable? If not, is there some second-best position, or must the enterprise be abandoned as bankrupt?

Now consider the position of Marx and the Ricardian socialists on just pay. The Ricardian socialist position was "Labor creates all value; therefore, all value should go to labor." This is a straightforward norm of compensation according to contribution. In answer to the first question, contribution is the contribution to the aggregate value produced in society or, equivalently, to the aggregate fund of labor power of society. The reference to value seems to answer the second question, and the third will be left open for now. Marx's position is a bit more nuanced and is usually misunderstood (see McCain 2017, pp. 151–152). The position Marx advocated for the workers' party and state was "to each according to his work." But Marx understood that a portion of the produce of society would have to be set aside for investment, which would be carried out by the workers' state on behalf of the workers as a class. Thus in a sense all value would go to the workers and the viability of the workers' state would nevertheless be assured.

For another view on distribution according to contribution, consider Varian's (1974, p. 75) equitable* allocations (Chapter 8). Varian's "wealth-fair" allocations can be interpreted as a case of distribution according to contribution. He remarks (p. 73) that his criterion "only allows you to complain about another agent's consumption if you are willing to match his contribution to the social product." In this case, though, not total income but labor income at market equilibrium is the individual's contribution: to implement it requires the state to equalize wealth (1975, p. 246). The answer to the first question is that the individual's contribution is measured by the market value of the product of his labor, the value marginal product of labor. (Since Varian demonstrates that there is on the usual assumptions a unique market equilibrium satisfying his conditions this is not vacuous.) Since labor income will only be part of total income, and the surplus is distributed equally, there is no issue as to the viability of Varian's version of market socialism (or, as he prefers, "people's capitalism"). But we should recall Baumol's objection (1986) that Varian's contribution fairness is determinate only if production is separable.

Even if we are committed to distribution according to contribution, then, why are the Ricardian socialists, Marx and Varian, wrong and Mankiw right in their interpretations of contribution?

For Mankiw, however, the question of viability does arise, since he expects that the whole of social income is to be distributed by marginal productivity. Suppose, then, that production is carried on subject to increasing returns to scale, on the average. Then the marginal productivity payments add up to more than the total product, so that payment according to marginal productivity is non-viable. (Refer to the appendix to Chapter 3 for more detail.) This has been known since von Wieser's *Natural Value* (1889) and the failure of his attempts nevertheless to define the contribution of each individual illustrates that this obstacle is most likely insurmountable. This problem arises because of strong complementarity, which von Wieser assumed to be the case, and must be very likely in the cases of technological innovation that Mankiw particularly stresses.

Mankiw (2010, pp. 293–295) refers to Nozick's *Anarchy, State, and Utopia* (1974) and writes, "This perspective is, I believe, what Robert Nozick [and others] have in mind." A careful reading of Nozick would correct this belief.[7]

Nozick rejects all end-state criteria, and payment according to one's value marginal productivity, however just, is an end-state criterion. Indeed, any market equilibrium criterion for outcomes would be rejected by Nozick. This dilemma becomes deeper as Mankiw considers the possibility of market failure. Mankiw would admit taxes (assessed on a benefit principle) for the production of public goods (2010, p. 296). The people who produce these services deserve a compensation commensurate with *their* contribution, he tells us; thus taxes are unavoidable but are just so far as they are assessed on the beneficiaries. The reasoning seems to be that these are transactions that the beneficiaries *would* make voluntarily if only they could. But this is an appeal to a potential Pareto improvement. As we have seen, potential Pareto improvement is a very weak tool for welfare economics, but more to the point, it is clear that Nozick would reject it: potentially or hypothetically voluntary exchange is not enough. Nozick requires actual mutually voluntary exchange. Along the same lines, Mankiw allows for externalities. As Mankiw notes, he has long been a supporter of Pigovian taxes as a remedy for negative externalities. Indeed, he has been (Mankiw 2009) and has more recently been one of the sponsors of a proposal for a carbon tax with the proceeds remitted as a social dividend (Baker et al. 2017). His rationale for Pigovian taxes is that to the extent that income is based on a negative externality, it is an exception to the "just deserts" and is to that extent unjust. He also seems to believe that those who produce positive externalities are no less entitled to the value of their contribution, leading to Pigovian subsidies. Even some transfer payments to the poor may be admitted, to the extent that the transfers constitute a public good, and here Thurow 1971 is cited. But this, again, is an appeal to a potential Pareto improvement.

It seems that Mankiw cannot do without potential Pareto improvement as a part of his "just deserts" theory. If a group of beneficiaries *could* compensate the producers of a public good or a positive externality, then the "just deserts" of those who produce the public good are to be computed as if the compensation had taken place, and the "just deserts" of the beneficiaries are the value marginal product of their activities only net of the compensation. Put otherwise, it is not the equilibrium of an actual market that determines "just deserts" but of a hypothetical market corrected for market failures. This is not so far from Pigou, and that may seem promising: Pigou without utilitarianism! But not so fast! Suppose that a public good is produced and the beneficiaries could indeed compensate those who produce it and still remain net beneficiaries. Then the difference between the benefits ex ante compensation and ex post compensation comprise a surplus. The surplus could be distributed in infinitely many ways, depending on the wages of public-goods producers and the net tax on the beneficiaries, and these outcomes differ in terms of the distribution of income. Thus we are back at the vacuous circularity mentioned before, but the case is actually a little worse. Does anyone justly deserve the surplus? The beneficiaries of the public good have not created it, so it hardly seems reasonable to think that they deserve any of the surplus at all. If anyone deserves the surplus, it would be the public employees who produced it. Given the importance of the public goods Mankiw mentions (national defense, police and the courts system) to private-sector production, the surplus would seem to comprise most of gross domestic product. Now, I very much doubt that Mankiw would advocate raising public employee pay and taxes until the consumption standards of the private sector correspond to what they would be in the absence of police, courts and national defense, "and the life of man solitary, poore, nasty, brutish, and short." But the just compensation of the public employees would presumably be based on the *marginal* contribution of a public employee to the quantum of public good produced, and if the marginal productivity of labor in producing the public good diminishes, then the just compensation to public employees would be less than the total value of the public good to the beneficiaries. This is also a surplus, and while it may not be obvious, it is the same surplus as before, since the just market wage of the public employees is the compensation necessary to leave them no worse off. It seems we must conclude that no-one, public employees nor beneficiaries of the public goods, can justly be given the surplus.

Thus, the sum of "just" compensation according to contribution may be either more or less than the product available. But, to be sure, a surplus is less problematic than a shortage, since the surplus presumably could be distributed as a social dividend, as Mankiw and his collaborators suggest in Baker et al. (2017).

Now to Mankiw's case against utilitarianism. Mankiw repeats without comment the traditional claim that utility is immeasurable (2013, p. 28), though he concedes that the problem may be soluble in principle, he says that "as of now, there is no scientific way to establish whether the marginal dollar consumed by one person produces more or less utility than a marginal dollar consumed by a neighbor." Evidently Mankiw was unaware in 2013 of the literature in behavioral economics then published, and that will be reviewed in Chapter 10. That apart, Mankiw relies on a number of cases that seem troubling or that conflict with "moral intuition." He reasonably dismisses mind experiments about pushing people in front of trolleys as too outlandish to deserve his attention.[8] His point that utilitarian ethics would recommend a radical international redistribution of income is quite correct (2010, pp. 291–2, 2013, p. 28) and clearly very much against the selfish interests of citizens of the United States, this author included; but that interest, decisive as it is in practice, is hardly a moral claim. Thus we arrive at what he clearly thinks of as a decisive argument: that a consistent utilitarian would recommend a tax graduated by height (Mankiw 2010, 2013; Mankiw and Weinzierl, 2010). Now, in one sense, this gets to the heart of the issue. If a person comes to the marketplace with resources that others do not have, and that he himself did not create, and because of those resources is more productive than others, is he justly entitled to returns to those resources he did not create? As a number of basketball coaches seem to have said, "You can't teach them to be seven feet tall." And if seven-foot-tall athletes are justly entitled to the salaries they obtain on account of their genetic heritage, why should a person who inherited billions of dollars not be justly entitled to the returns on those billions? But it fails as an argument against utilitarianism. As Mankiw and Weinzierl concede (2010, p. 173) that "most Pareto-efficient allocations include height-dependent taxes." This would include, for example, a social welfare function that identifies individual utility with real income and weights each person's real income at one; that is, that maximizes Pigou's "national dividend" without regard to distribution. Further, they concede that a height tax could be a Pareto improvement over present practice, though they calculate that such a tax would be very small. But they consider the tax as hypothecated only to redistribution among size classes. If instead the neutral height tax were to some extent substituted for existing non-neutral taxes, there would be a gain in the form of a reduction in the excess burden of the taxes offset. This is the actual case for neutral taxes in general and Mankiw and Weinzierl do not take it into account. Further, that being so, it seems that a case could be made that "just deserts" could favor a height tax. By allowing for a reduction of taxes on productive activity, a height tax – despite violating "just deserts" at the margin – could result in an allocation of resources more closely aligned with productivity and so with "just deserts" on the whole. And on the other hand, a utilitarian argument can be made against it. Taking a Millian rule-utilitarian perspective, one might argue (and I would argue) that public measures that impose different public obligations and grant different privileges to people on the basis of personal characteristics such as height and skin color have such a bad historical record that it would be a sound constitutional rule to exclude them as a category. This is, of course, a "slippery slope" argument, but as one who has fallen more than once on slippery slopes, I would give such an argument serious attention.

Mankiw also dismisses a social contract rationalization along Rawls' lines (2013, p. 32). His counterargument here is that deliberators behind a veil of ignorance would opt for mandatory kidney donation, since that would insure them against the inability to get a needed kidney transplant.[9] Mankiw seems to have missed Rawls' lexicographic ranking of liberty as the first of the primary goods, not to be sacrificed for the others. Surely proprietorship of one's own body is an iron condition of liberty, and so mandatory donations would be excluded. (A Millian utilitarian would probably reason similarly.) But the irony here is that a Rawlsian social contract framework would probably offer Mankiw the best route to support the "just deserts" approach that he proposes. Recall that Rawls' reasoning is *not* equalitarian and allows for any degree of inequality provided that the worst-off are made better off as a result. Thus, if it could be shown that a system of rewards according to contributions would so increase the national dividend that even the worst off would benefit, the deliberators behind the Rawlsian veil of ignorance would perforce endorse it. Thus the practical argument is transformed, in a Rawlsian frame, into a moral argument. This is not to say that Mankiw's argument would be persuasive in this form, but it would transfer the discussion from one about moral standards to one about facts, as Mankiw wishes to do.

Mankiw appeals to moral intuitions for support (2010, p. 291, 2013, pp. 28–29), but his position is not intuitionist; that is, he makes no claim that moral intuitions are self-evident and universal. It seems to be enough if they are popular. He does not reflect that moral intuitions may conflict, as vividly illustrated by Sen's example of the three children and the flute (2009, pp. 12–15). And when moral intuitions do conflict, what then? We can ignore them and attempt to rely on reason, as Bentham and Rawls do. Alternatively, we can choose among them the one we like best. That seems to be Mankiw's strategy. But in this case we will always be tempted to choose the one that best supports our own claims to be justly entitled to what we have (along with others in parallel situations). Even if we resist that temptation, and choose the intuition that seems to us right even if it undermines our claim to be entitled to what we have, we must in fairness concede the right of others to make a different, equally arbitrary choice. In that sense, the choice can only be a selfish one, even if it is not self-interested. It seems that intuition does not answer any questions of normative thought, except so far as it is suggestive of promising avenues for reason.

9.6 Chapter conclusion

By the last quarter of the twentieth century, the powers and limits of ordinalist microeconomics to clarify questions of welfare economics were established. The case for free markets as Pareto optimal was in tatters, both because the market conditions that could realize the Pareto equivalencies seemed unlikely to be realized and because of doubts that the Pareto equivalencies could be defended as criteria for normative social science. Cost–benefit analyses based on the Kaldor test could be rejected as neglecting the importance of distribution. "Welfarism" could seem too narrow and to neglect the importance of freedom for human flourishing. To some, perhaps to many, it seemed time for new approaches – including, as one possibility, a return to and extension of Pigou's utilitarian welfare economics. Despite giving rise to some vigorous literatures, none of these has influenced the consensus of economic thinking on welfare and policy in the current century. Another "new approach" proposed by Mankiw would be a return to the ideas of John Bates Clark, but that proposal raises questions that might require another century of work if it were to replace welfare economics as a basis for the evaluation of public policy.

Notes

1   The press release of the Royal Swedish Academy of Sciences dated October 15, 1991, www.nobelprize.org/nobel_prizes/economic-sciences/laureates/1991/press.html, accessed December 28, 2017, discusses "The Problem of Social Cost" without making reference to externalities or social cost! Rather, they treat it as an elaboration of his earlier writing on the influence of transaction costs on organization. This section of the book is concerned with just what the Royal Swedish Academy of Sciences left out.

2 According to his curriculum vitae at the Ronald Coase Institute, www.coase.org/coa secv.htm, accessed December 28, 2017, Coase's PhD from the University of London was dated 1951.

3 I recall, as a graduate student in the mid-1960s, hearing my teachers qualify their assessments of economic ideas by saying, "But then, you have to take transaction costs into account." However, Coase was not yet on the reading list, and I had no idea what it might mean to take transaction costs into account. I later found my own way into the Coasian literature and made some modest contributions to it (McCain 1986, 1988, 1992, 1994) somewhat in the spirit of the passage quoted. Note also McCain 2014, pp. 102–104.

4 The author would be grouped with the a priori school, having proposed in McCain (2017), appendix to chapter 10, a derivation of weights from a second-best model derived from the fairness theory discussed in the previous chapter.

5 To be clear, the liberty to dispose of property as one chooses is not an instance of equal liberty, since property is never equally distributed. We may recall "the majestic quality of the law which prohibits the wealthy as well as the poor from sleeping under the bridges, from begging in the streets, and from stealing bread." Instances of equal liberty would include freedom of speech and the freedom to pray as one chooses. This is not to say that the liberty to dispose of property is of no value, but that its value is instrumental.

6 A JSTOR search for pieces authored by Mankiw in which Clark is mentioned returned no hits.

7 Compare Varian (1975). For a brief critique of Nozick's position, see McCain (2017, p. 27).

8 Since there is no issue there, further comment on trolley examples is digressive and so reserved to a footnote. The examples posit a person on a bridge over a trolley track with the trolley careening toward a group of children. The person on the bridge is accompanied by a fat man and has a lever that could drop the fat man in front of the trolley, stopping the trolley and saving the children, but killing the fat man. Many who respond to such examples are reluctant to take responsibility for killing the fat man, even though several children will perish if they do not. Mankiw seems right in saying that the example is implausible, and the point of the experiments is that people often seem to respond differently depending on how the question is framed. But in war, real people must sometimes make the decision to sacrifice fewer lives to save more. Further, trading fewer lives for more may be an issue in public policy in respect of health care, safety and emergency services, for example. How then would a committed Benthamite act utilitarian respond to a trolley problem? While I am not sure – being more of a Millian rule utilitarian myself – here is what I suspect: "If the person on the bridge will not take the responsibility to drop the fat man and save the children, the person on the bridge is not making a moral decision but a decision that caters to his private prejudice, a selfish if not exactly self-interested decision. Nobody said that moral actions are easy."

9 This poses an interesting question that may not have been investigated. Markets for body parts are widely prohibited, and Mankiw's reasoning seems to take it for granted that they are. If there were markets for body parts Mankiw's example would fail. Why then are they prohibited? Would this prohibition be chosen behind a veil of ignorance, and if so, what are the implications for Mankiw's example?

References

Aivazian, Varouj A. and Jeffrey L. Callen (1981) The Coase Theorem and the Empty Core, *Journal of Law and Economics* v. 24, no. 1 (Apr) pp. 175–181.

Armstrong, W. E. (1939) The Determinateness of the Utility Function, *Economic Journal* v. 49, no. 195 (Sep) pp. 453–467.

Armstrong, W. E. (1951) Utility and the Theory of Welfare, *Oxford Economic Papers, New Series* v. 3, no. 3 (Oct) pp. 259–271.

Arrow, Kenneth J. (1951) *Social Choice and Individual Values* (New York: Wiley).

Baker, James A., Martin Feldstein, Ted Halstead, N. Gregory Mankiw, Henry M. Paulson, Jr., George P. Schultz, Thomas Stephenson and Rob Walton (2017) *The Conservative Case for Climate Dividends* (Washington, D.C.: Climate Leadership Council).

Bator, Francis M. (1957) The Simple Analytics of Welfare Maximization, *American Economic Review* v. 47, no. 1 (Mar) pp. 22–59.

Bator, Francis M. (1958) The Anatomy of Market Failure, *Quarterly Journal of Economics* v. 72, no. 3 (Aug) pp. 351–379.

Bernheim, B. Douglas (2016) The Good, the Bad, and the Ugly: A Unified Approach to Behavioral Welfare Economics, *Journal of Benefit-Cost Analysis* v. 7, no. 1 pp. 12–68.

Baumol, William (1986) *Superfairness: Applications and Theory* (Cambridge, Mass.: MIT Press).

Brent, Robert J. (1984) Use of Distributional Weights in Cost–Benefit Analysis: A Survey of Schools, *Public Finance Quarterly* v. 12, pp. 213–230.

Cheung, S. N. S. (1973) The Fable of the Bees: An Economic Investigation, *Journal of Law and Economics* v. 16, no. 1 (Apr) pp. 11–33.

Clark, John Bates (1899) *The Distribution of Wealth* (New York: Macmillan).

Coase, Ronald (1937) The Nature of the Firm, *Economica N.S.* v. 4, pp. 386–405.

Coase, Ronald (1960) The Problem of Social Cost, *Journal of Law and Economics* v. 3, no. 1 pp. 1–44.

Coase, Ronald and H. Demsetz (1974) The Lighthouse in Economics, *Journal of Law and Economics* v. 17, no. 2 (Oct) pp. 357–376.

Eckstein, O. (1961) A Survey of the Theory of Public Expenditure Criteria, *Public Finances: Needs, Sources and Utilization: A Conference of the Universities National Bureau Committee for Economic Research* (Princeton, N.J.: Princeton University Press).

Ellis, Howard S. and William Fellner (1943) External Economies and Diseconomies, *American Economic Review* v. 33, no. 3 (Sep) pp. 493–511.

Harberger, Arnold C. (1978) On the Use of Distributional Weights in Social Cost-Benefit Analysis, *Journal of Political Economy* v. 86, no. 2.2 (Apr) pp. 87–120.

Harberger, Arnold C. (1984) Basic Needs versus Distributional Weights in Social Cost-Benefit Analysis, *Economic Development and Cultural Change* v. 32, no. 3 (Apr) pp. 455–474.

Hau, Timothy D. (1986) Distributional Cost-Benefit Analysis in Discrete Choice, *Journal of Transport Economics and Policy* v. 20, no. 3 (Sep) pp. 313–338.

Haveman, Robert (1968), Comments on "Income Redistrbution Effects and Benefit-Cost Analysis," *Problems in Public Expenditure Analysis*, edited by Samuel B. Chase, Jr. (Washington, D.C.: Brookings Institution).

Infante, Gerado, Guilhem Lecouteux and Robert Sugden (2016) Preference Purification and the Inner Rational Agent: A Critique of the Conventional Wisdom of Behavioural Welfare Economics, *Journal of Economic Methodology* v. 23, no. 1 pp. 1–25.

Johansson-Stenman, Olof (2005) Distributional Weights in Cost-Benefit Analysis: Should We Forget about Them? *Land Economics* v. 81, no. 3 (Aug) pp. 337–352.

Krugman, Paul (1995) *Development, Geography, and Economic Theory* (Cambridge, Mass.: MIT Press).

Layard, Richard (1980) On the Use of Distributional Weights in Social Cost-Benefit Analysis, *Journal of Political Economy* v. 88, no. 5 (Oct) pp. 1041–1047.

Mankiw, N. Gregory (2009) Smart Taxes: An Open Invitation to Join the Pigou Club, *Eastern Economic Journal* v. 35, pp. 14–23.

Mankiw, N. Gregory (2010) Spreading the Wealth Around: Reflections Inspired by Joe the Plumber, *Eastern Economic Journal* v. 36, pp. 285–298.

Mankiw, N. Gregory (2013) Defending the One Percent, *Journal of Economic Perspectives* v. 27, no. 3 (Summer) pp. 21–34.

Mankiw, N. Gregory and Matthew Weinzierl (2010) The Optimal Taxation of Height: A Case Study of Utilitarian Income Redistribution, *American Economic Journal: Economic Policy* v. 2, no. 1 (Feb) pp. 155–176.

McCain, Roger A. (1986) Transaction Costs and a Theory of Public Policy, *Review of Social Economy* v. 45, no. 3 (Dec).

McCain, Roger A. (1988) Information as Property and as a Public Good, *Library Quarterly* v. 58, no. 3 pp. 265–282.

McCain, Roger A. (1992) Transaction Costs, Labor Management, and Codetermination, *Advances in the Economic Analysis of Participatory and Labor-Managed Firms*, edited by D. Jones and J. Svejnar (Greenwich, Conn.: JAI Press) pp. 173–204.

McCain, Roger A. (1994) The Case for Minimal Protection of Intellectual Property Rights: Game Theoretic and Cost of Transaction Perspectives (Presented, International Conference on the Economics of Intellectual Property Rights, Venice, Italy).

McCain, Roger A. (2014) *Reframing Economics: Economic Action as Imperfect Cooperation* (Cheltenham: Edward Elgar).

McCain, Roger A. (2017) *Approaching Equality: What Can Be Done about Wealth Inequality* (Cheltenham: Edward Elgar).

Meade, J. E. (1952) External Economies and Diseconomies in a Competitive Situation, *Economic Journal* v. 62, no. 245 pp. 54–67.

Mishan, E. J. (1982) The New Controversy about the Rationale of Economic Evaluation, *Journal of Economic Issues*, v. 16, No. 1 (March), pp. 29–47.

Musgrave, Richard A. (1969) Cost-Benefit Analysis and the Theory of Public Finance, *Journal of Economic Literature* v. 7, no. 3 (Sep) pp. 797–806.

Musgrave, Alan and Charles Pigden (2016), Imre Lakatos, *Stanford Encyclopedia of Philosophy*, available at: https://plato.stanford.edu/archives/win2016/entries/lakatos/, as of December 29, 2017.

Ng, Yew-Kwang (1975) "Bentham or Bergson? Finite Sensibility, Utility Functions and Social Welfare Functions", *Review of Economic Studies* v. 42, no. 4 (Oct) pp. 545–569.

Ng, Yew-Kwang (1980) *Welfare Economics: Introduction and Development of Basic Concepts* (New York: Wiley Halsted Press).

Ng, Yew-Kwang (2003) From Preference to Happiness: Towards a More Complete Welfare Economics, *Social Choice and Welfare* v. 20, no. 2 pp. 307–350.

Nozick, Robert (1974) *Anarchy, State and Utopia* (New York: Basic Books).

Nwaneri, V. C. (1970) Equity in Cost-Benefit Analysis: A Case Study of the Third London Airport, *Journal of Transport Economics and Policy* v. 4, no. 3 (Sep) pp. 235–254.

Sen, Amartya (1969) Quasi-Transitivity, Rational Choice and Collective Decisions, *Review of Economic Studies* v. 36, no. 3 (July) pp. 381–393.

Sen, Amartya (1970) *Collective Choice and Social Welfare* (London: Holden-Day).

Sen, Amartya (1982) Rights and Agency, *Philosophy and Public Affairs* v. 11, no. 1 (Winter) pp. 3–39.

Sen, Amartya (1985) *Commodities and Capabilities* (Amsterdam: North-Holland).

Sen, Amartya (2009) *The Idea of Justice* (Cambridge, Mass.: Belknap Press).

Sidgwick, Henry (1883) *The Principles of Political Economy* (London: Macmillan).

Smith, Adam (2000 [1759]) *The Theory of Moral Sentiments* (Amherst, N.Y.: Prometheus Books).

Squire, Lyn (1980) On the Use of Distributional Weights in Social Cost-Benefit Analysis, *Journal of Political Economy* v. 88, no. 5 (Oct) pp. 1048–1049.

Thurow, Lester C. (1971) The Income Distribution as a Pure Public Good, *Quarterly Journal of Economics* v. 85, no. 2 (May) pp. 327–336.

Varian, H. R. (1974) Equity, Envy and Efficiency, *Journal of Economic Theory* v. 9, pp. 63–91.

Varian, H. R. (1975) Distributive Justice, Welfare Economics, and the Theory of Fairness, *Philosophy and Public Affairs* v. 4, pp. 223–247.

von Wieser, Friedrich (1889) *Natural Value* (London: Macmillan and Co., translated into English by Christian A. Malloch, edited with an introduction by William Smart).

Weisbrod, Burton A. (1968) Income Redistribution Effects and Benefit-Cost Analysis, *Problems in Public Expenditure Analysis*, edited by Samuel B. Chase, Jr. (Washington, D.C.: Brookings Institution).

10 Happiness and behavioral welfare economics

In the later twentieth and twenty-first centuries, economics has been increasingly influenced by research and research methods from the other social sciences: survey research, particularly on satisfaction with life, and experimental methods along with some theoretical ideas from behavioral psychology. Each of these developments has challenged welfare economics. For the most part, these challenges remain open. At the same time, the response to these challenges has given some new life to the discussion of welfare economics.

10.1 Happiness

Executive summary of the section: Questionnaire studies have produced a good deal of information on self-reported satisfaction with life or happiness. A few prominent economists interpret happiness in this sense as welfare and would put it at the center of welfare economics.

Economists have not been leaders in the use of questionnaire studies to judge the states of mind of the creatures they study. In the latter half of the twentieth century and in this century, however, social scientists have conducted many questionnaire studies in which the participants are asked to rate their satisfaction with life, and often with particular aspects of life, on a relative scale.

Richard Easterlin (2003, pp. 11176–11177) explained this approach as follows:

I take the terms happiness, utility, well-being, life satisfaction, and welfare to be interchangeable and measured by the answer to a question such as that asked since 1972 in the United States General Social Survey (GSS): "Taken all together, how would you say things are these days – would you say that you are very happy, pretty happy, or not too happy?" A substantial methodological literature has developed on the reliability, validity, and comparability of the answers to such questions. The consensus is that the responses, although not without their problems, are meaningful and reasonably comparable among groups of individuals ... Needless to say, I am speaking of average effects; there is considerable dispersion about the mean.

It was a paper by Easterlin (1974) that brought these studies to the attention of the economics profession. This paper documented the "Easterlin paradox": despite the substantial increase in gross domestic product per capita in the United States in the postwar period, "happiness" had shown no such tendency to increase. It is true, as Di Tella and MacCulloch (2006, p. 26) write, that "happiness responses are positively correlated with individual income at any point in time: the rich report greater happiness than the poor within the United States in a given year." But this greater happiness seems to be a function of *relative* income. Those who are richer than their neighbors, or richer than they had expected to be, are happier. Di Tella and MacCulloch continue, "A similar pattern has been observed in a large number of countries, including France, the United Kingdom, Germany and Japan, and for different periods of time."

The data from questionnaires can be used to relate reported happiness to other life circumstances, such as disability and marital status. Married people tend to be happier than unmarried, those who are unemployed are unhappier than those who are employed, even if they have the same income (Clark and Oswald, 1994) and, in the words of Blanchflower and Oswald (2004, p. 400), "sexual activity enters strongly positively in an equation where reported happiness is the dependent variable. The more sex, the happier the person." Unsurprisingly, people who are disabled are less happy than others, but the reported happiness of a person who becomes disabled recovers somewhat, toward but never quite to the reported happiness of people who are fully abled. This phenomenon, adaptation, is common in the reports of life satisfaction – for example, a sudden increase in income will result in a considerable increase in happiness, but over time, adaptation will result in a regression of happiness toward, but not quite to, its original level.

It is now pretty well accepted that there is some relation between real income and reported happiness, after other influences and adaptation are allowed for. In 2001, Easterlin writes "As far as I am aware, in every representative national survey ever done a significant positive bivariate relationship between happiness and income has been found." Stevenson and Wolfers write (2008, p. 2) "Across the world's population, variation in income explains a sizable proportion of the variation in subjective well-being. There appears to be a very strong relationship between subjective well-being and income, which holds for both rich and poor countries." Not surprisingly, this is subject to the principle of diminishing marginal utility: happiness rises most rapidly with increasing income when income is low. Easterlin observes (2001, p. 468) that the reduced impact of income on happiness at higher income levels "does not occur when happiness is regressed on log income, rather than absolute income. Put differently – if the same proportional rather than absolute increase in income is assumed to yield the same increase in happiness, then income change at upper income levels causes the same increase in happiness as at lower." Stevenson and Wolfers also find that life satisfaction varies linearly with the logarithm of income (2008; see e.g. figures 7–9, appendix B).

A few economists have taken the view that welfare economics ought to treat self-reported happiness as the maximand, among them Ng, Layard and Frey and his collaborators. In 1980, Layard proposes that Easterlin's (1974) observations can be explained by a rat-race hypothesis along the lines of Duesenberry's (1949) theory of consumption and saving. This implies (he notes) that an income tax at a positive rate may be efficient. In effect, a person who earns a relatively high income creates an externality, by reducing the relative income and so the happiness of others, and the income tax is a Pigovian corrective tax (p. 739). Adaptation to expected income and expected status is discussed, with suggestions of loss aversion (pp. 745–747). Without comment, Layard uses an additive social welfare function (p. 745).

Ng (1996) discusses happiness and surveys in terms that show some influence from Kahneman (1993, which will be discussed below) and proposes a survey of happiness designed to elicit "just perceivable increments" of utility (an idea discussed in Chapter 9). In Ng (1997) he expands the view that reported happiness is cardinal utility for the purposes of economics, and Ng (2003) again draws on Kahneman's concept of experienced utility, which Ng treats as equivalent to reported satisfaction. Ng puts a good deal of stress on the tendency of happiness to be greater with income or consumption that increases gradually than with stable, but flat, income or consumption. Thus, he argues, once basic needs are met increasing current consumption reduces future happiness, relative to given future consumption (p. 324). But this, he argues, is irrationally ignored by most people in making their consumption decisions. Thus, Ng relates his ideas to behavioral welfare economics (considered below) and makes a welfare-economic argument against growth policies.

Van Praag and Ferrer-i-Carbonell (2004) used questionnaire data on self-assessed satisfaction with life in general and in a number of distinct domains – job, housing, leisure use, etc. – together with econometric methods to aggregate satisfaction. They extended this to consideration of a number of policy issues including, for example, a cost–benefit assessment of airport noise.

Layard (2005) is a call for a welfare economics that interprets self-reported happiness as utility and as the maximand for a reasoned public policy. It can be fairly described as a neo-Benthamite manifesto. Bentham is remembered as "one of the greatest thinkers of the enlightenment" (p. 5). "I believe that Bentham's idea was right and that we should fearlessly adopt it and apply it in our lives" (p. 112). Layard begins by summarizing some of the findings of happiness and related studies (ch. 2). He dismisses Mill's quibble with Bentham over pushpin and poetry, taking Bentham's side (p. 22). He then revisits the Easterlin paradox and relative income (chs 32–36) and argues that the modest increase in happiness consequent on rising real incomes has been offset by declining happiness due to negative cultural and economic changes, including deteriorating work-life balance and increasing inequality (pp. 50–52), broken families, decreased trust, reduced social life and shifting spiritual values. Television is seen as a major villain in the piece (ch. 6). The alternative is a more cooperative society (ch. 7).

At one point he does seem to deviate from Benthamism, precisely in defending Bentham against criticism from those who reject utilitarianism as a form of consequentialism. "If I decide to do something, everything that follows is a consequence, including the action itself" (p. 119). Now, Pigou seems to be a better Benthamite than Layard in holding that utility comprises only subjective states of mind. But Layard is not simply wrong, here. Self-reported happiness is not a subjective state of mind but a speech act. To use the language of qualia, self-reported happiness does not comprise qualia, unlike Bentham's pleasures and pains. At best, we might suppose that self-reported happiness is an assessment of one's utility qualia overall. But the example Layard gives points up the difficulty with that interpretation. "For example, suppose I am an employer who is worrying about whether to sack someone. The act of sacking someone has a special quality – a massive exercise of power of one person over another. I would rather avoid it … I do consider the means as well as the end" (pp. 119–120).

Now, we might interpret this by saying that, when she sacks an employee, the employer experiences an undesirable quale, the opposite of a "warm glow," and that quale is what the employer would rather avoid. This would be consistent with the work of Benz and Frey (2008). They find that self-employed business proprietors express more satisfaction with their lives and with their work than others, on the average, and Benz and Frey interpret this as evidence of the importance of "procedural utility" (p. 363). Procedural utility is utility from the activities that produce income, as distinct from the utility derived from consuming the products that income can buy. In one questionnaire, they find evidence that this satisfaction is determined by the characteristics of the work done, including the use of one's own initiative (pp. 377–9). This seems consistent with the idea that the reported satisfaction is correlated with the desirability and number of qualia arising from aspects of the work, e.g. from acting on one's own initiative.

But that is not what Layard says. He says that the *act* has a special quality, and that the act, the means, is what the employer would rather avoid. We suppose that the employer has evaluated firing as regrettable, by perfectly cold reasoning without considering her own feelings. This conviction might lead the employer to report herself as less happy – but that would mean that her report is not a reliable assessment of the employer's utility qualia. Now, Layard is *right* to say that self-reported happiness could reflect the assessment of means as well as the qualia that result from them. This is not an assessment of utility as Bentham would understand it. On the other hand, Layard deviates consciously from Bentham, in an equalitarian direction, by suggesting that the incremental happiness of a miserable person should be weighted more heavily, in a social welfare comparison, than that of a person already happy (p. 132). All in all, this is neo-Benthamism, not Benthamism, just as neoclassical economics is not classical economics.

The criticism Layard means to defend Bentham from is valid in a purely formal sense. Suppose that it were an empirical fact, and known to be an empirical fact, that people are on the average happier in a "rationally organized" totalitarian dictatorship in which deviation from the rational organization were punished by hideous torture, than in other social systems. The disutility of the torture of the deviant minority would be supposed to be more than offset by the increased happiness of the majority, especially if the threat of torture were an effective deterrent that would need to be used very seldom. Utilitarians could then reasonably be accused of supporting heinous torture. But if this supposed empirical fact were true and known to be true, I suspect that most utilitarians would abandon or modify their utilitarianism. Does that mean that utilitarians are inconsistent or, to borrow a phrase from Mankiw (2013), that they use utilitarian reasoning "as a drunkard uses a lamp post – for support rather than illumination"? No: it means that utilitarian ideas rest partly on certain judgments of empirical fact, as well as on plausible reasoning along the lines of "it is absurd to call a decision good when it does nobody any good." These empirical judgments were brought out particularly by John Stuart Mill, the "second founder of utilitarianism", and are plausible and are supported by some of the literature on self-reported happiness, such as the study of Benz and Frey. Layard, however, does not seem to understand that that is what Mill is about in his differences with Bentham.

Following his neo-Benthamite program at chapter 8, Layard points out some useful ideas from economics, along with their limits (2005, ch. 9). He follows with policy recommendations, some quite heterodox – among them meditation[1] (p. 187).

Bruno Frey (2010) summarizes results from a decade or more of research applying happiness surveys to economic and political concerns, with a number of collaborators, including his work with Benz cited above. Frey also treats reported satisfaction of life as "experienced utility" and remarks (p. ix) "the ways of measuring experienced utility are continually being improved." His position is utilitarian, he says, but not consequentialist, as (p. 16) "Procedural utility should also be considered." But this is a confusion – procedural utility is a subjective state of mind that is a consequence of carrying forward a particular procedure, whether the procedure is managing a business or eating dinner. Frey also cites extensively work in behavioral economics (some of which will be considered below) to argue that "decision utility" may not correspond to "experienced utility." Frey goes on to apply the concepts of self-reported satisfaction to a number of issues in welfare economics, some traditional, and some less so.

10.2 Sen contra Layard

Executive summary of the section: Sen rejected Layard's espousal of happiness as the criterion for normative social science, raising questions for the happiness approach in general.

In the course of his defense of capabilities as one of the dimensions of justice, Sen (2009, ch. 13) criticizes utilitarianism as an alternative and takes the ideas of his "long-standing friend" (p. 273) Richard Layard as representative of utilitarianism, though he confesses that "I wish I could move my friend ... from all Bentham to a little Mill" (p. 275 fn). Sen's criticism of Layard rests strongly on the phenomenon of adaptation – when, for example, people who are deprived become accustomed to their deprivation and treat it as normal, reporting happiness close to – if not quite at – the level that would be reported by a person not comparably deprived. This is clearest in the case of disabling injury, which is observed to lead to a sharp decline in reported happiness followed by a recovery to something only slightly less than the earlier level before the injury. Sen mentions this case, as well as oppressed minorities, subordinated women, sweated workers and impoverished sharecroppers (pp. 275, 282–283). Adaptation is also central to Layard's critique of the substitution of income for happiness as a measure of well-being, with which Sen agrees fully (p. 273). Nevertheless he sees utilitarianism as "deeply unfair to those who are persistently deprived" (p. 282).

But this book has argued that the utilitarianism of Pigou (and Bentham, Mill and Sidgwick) is not at all the neo-Benthamism of Layard but that Pigou's "utility" comprises a category of what more recent philosophic inquiry calls "qualia." On that interpretation of utility, how may we interpret adaptation? The case of disabling injuries may be clearest. We see that, when a person goes on living with the pain of injury, he reports happiness nearer the original level. The subject becomes habituated to pain. Does that mean that the pain is felt as less, or that the person becomes accustomed to pain of the same intensity and so treats it as normal in reporting his satisfactions with life? To answer this question would require research in neuro-science that I am not aware of, if it exists. But on the face of it, it does not matter. First consider the second case: pain of the same intensity comes to be thought of as normal, and so has less influence on reported happiness. This simply means that reported happiness is an unreliable indicator of utility and needs some correction as such. In this case Sen's criticism is a valid criticism of Layard's neo-Benthamism but not of a more traditional utilitarianism. Second, suppose that because of neurological changes, the intensity of felt pain is lass over time. In that case the reported happiness is a reliable correlate of relative evaluation of the qualia experienced, and Sen's criticism is valid neither with respect to Layard's views nor traditional Benthamism.

As Sen observes, paraphrasing Wittgenstein, pain is the feeling of pain, nothing else, and the same equation applies to all utility-qualia. Utility, then, is not a measure, dimension, aspect or correlate of welfare, but the substance of welfare, and reports of welfare are correlates at best, Layard to the contrary and Sen's views notwithstanding.

10.3 Taking stock

Executive summary of the section: Preference and "happiness" surveys each reflect an individual's comparison of aggregate experienced qualia. Preferences, if knowable, have the advantage of bringing the "measuring rod of money" into play.

What, then, is the significance of these new developments to welfare economics? As Chapter 7 suggested, the significance is very much the same for happiness measures as for observations of preference. Thinking of individual welfare or utility as a category of qualia, we must first concede that qualia may have no arithmetic properties, as Kennedy suggested; but the qualia we are concerned with are the causal consequences of certain physical events, specifically the consumption, possession or use of particular goods and services that are themselves results of social production or the conduct of procedures that may produce them. These causes may have arithmetic properties: thus, the Marshall-Pigou "measuring rod of money." Indeed some qualia may have arithmetic properties. The sensation of the color red, like Bentham's pleasure and pain, might be characterized as having dimensions of intensity and duration. But that is not very helpful. Further, with Mill's recognition that pleasures may have different qualities, some of which may be known only in retrospect, Bentham's simple arithmetic becomes more complex. If the qualia resulting from economic activity differ qualitatively, then Pigou's requirement that the psychic return to satisfactions be brought under the categories of more and less might not be satisfied.

It is here that revealed preference might come to our help, if it were empirically valid. When people choose, with full knowledge, between qualitatively different satisfactions, we may infer that they have chosen the qualia they prefer, and which in that sense are the "greater." If we then suppose that there is a one-to-one correspondence between vectors of quantities demanded and productive services supplied, on the one hand, and the sets of qualia that result from them, on the other hand, then the theory of revealed preference as developed by neoclassical economics might capture Pigou's categories of greater and less. But behavioral science makes it clear that this simple, direct interpretation will not do. True preferences – or some reasonable substitute, such as experienced utility – will be required.

Once again, preference is a subjective experience: can we think of it as a quale? Is there something *it is like* to prefer one thing to another? If I say, "I prefer a hike this morning to spending the morning reading newspapers," that is a speech act. The speech act more specifically is a comparison of sets of qualia. Suppose again that I say "I assess my overall quality of life at seven on a scale of ten," perhaps by filling in a blank on a questionnaire. This, again, is a speech act. The speech act refers to a much larger and more complex comparison of sets of subjective mental states. Qualia of satisfaction of wants and needs would seem to be included, along with the qualia of enjoying a beautiful sunset, and also included in this comparison are other things that are not qualia, such as opinions. One aspect of my quality of life may be my belief that my children are well, though this belief could be mistaken. In addition to this complexity, the scale of the assessment is inherently idiosyncratic. Aside from differences in temperament, the answers may reflect differences in points of reference. Nevertheless, if a person is often enjoying qualia of want-satisfaction that he prefers rather than those he does not, the person is likely to choose a higher assessment than he would choose in the opposite case. Thus, taking a large sample, we might expect a correlation between the responses and the average valuation of qualia of economic want satisfaction for the individuals sampled. If we then find that the responses to the surveys increase in decreasing proportion with the purchasing power of income, we are justified in concluding that the marginal utility of income decreases. The real income-adjusted average happiness response provides an indicator of the utility of income as price indices provide an indicator of preferences, and the two indicators are more closely related than most economists would suppose, and are probably about equally reliable.

10.4 Behavioral welfare economics

Executive summary of the section: The growth of behavioral economics has particularly challenged the theory of revealed preference, which is a crucial basis of ordinalist welfare economics. Behavioral welfare economics has emerged as a result, without, so far, any consensus as to the resolution of the challenge.

In the period since Atkinson declared that welfare economics had disappeared, one of the most important changes in economics as a whole has been the emergence of behavioral economics, as witness the award of the Nobel Memorial Prize for 2017 to Thaler. Behavioral economics may now be thought of as mainstream. Behavioral economics encompasses a wide range of theories and experimental and other empirical studies, but a common theme is that individual choices often deviate from any rational or maximizing pattern. This presents challenges for welfare economics, since welfare economic theories have commonly relied on the assumption that observed choices in the marketplace are such as to maximize a coherent preference system. Experimental and other evidence that people do not make choices in this way threatens to invalidate most propositions of traditional welfare economics (see e.g. McQuillen and Sugden 2012). At the same time, behavioral economics supports some policy interventions that would not be envisioned by traditional welfare economics: "nudging" decisions by modifying the decision frame (Camerer et al. 2003; Thaler and Sunstein 2008). The need to adapt welfare economics to incorporate a behavioral positive economics has created new controversies and, consequently, something of a rebirth of welfare economic research. On the other hand, behavioral economics has itself little coherence, tending instead to accumulate a literature of unrelated "behavioral anomalies" (Elster 2009).

One of the first explicit responses to this challenge came from a Nobel-honored scholar responsible for much of the evidence on "anomalies" of choice, Daniel Kahneman, with collaborators (1997). The title of their article, "Back to Bentham," has probably been misinterpreted (McQuillen and Sugden 2012, pp. 556–557) as suggesting that "happiness" measures from surveys should guide normative social science somewhat as Layard has proposed. Rather, the overall message of the Kahneman et al. discussion seems to be expressed at p. 388: "some peculiarities of preferences are unlikely to be understood … without first understanding experienced and remembered utility." Accordingly their research is devoted to those things. They deny that utility is unmeasureable; rather (p. 388), "experienced utility has much in common with subjective temperature." They provide evidence that 1) remembered utility tends to be biased relative to experienced utility, and 2) decisions tend to be guided by those biased memories, and so themselves may be biased away from maximization of expected utility. Note that many surveys of self-reported "happiness" provide evidence of remembered utility, not experienced utility. Kahneman et al. reject the notion of time-discounted utility (pp. 377, 393) so perhaps "back to Pigou" would be an equally apt title. In short, this is a work of positive economic psychology, not of welfare economics. Nevertheless, they say (p. 389) "Economists … may prefer another interpretation, in which experienced utility is the objective function that a benevolent social planner would wish to maximize."

That is not, however, a dominant position in the literature of behavioral economics. Certainly reliance on self-reported "happiness" is one possible response to the anomalies, but as we have seen, "happiness" economists have not been motivated so much by anomalies of choice as motivated positively by the growing evidence on self-reported well-being (e.g. Ng 2003; Layard 2005). It is also possible to take the view that, due to the anomalies, welfare economics is simply a blind alley of research (Gul and Pesendorfer 2007; Infante et al. 2016). These two ideas apart, most of the discussion of the anomalies in behavioral welfare economics has fallen into one or the other of two schools of thought. On the one hand, some hypothesize specific boundedly rational choice processes that imply biases away from maximizing choice; then the biases are inverted to recover "true" unbiased preferences (see e.g.

Koszegi and Rabin 2007; Salant and Rubinstein 2008; Rubinstein and Salant 2012; Manzini and Mariotti 2014). On the other hand, some have proposed to base a criterion of welfare on observed choices insofar as the choices are consistent, either without (e.g. Bernheim 2009, 2016) or with interpretation of the choices as revealing particular instances of "true" preferences (e.g. Fleurbaey and Schokkaert 2013). This leads to a welfare ordering that is incomplete, so that the project of this school of thought is to derive a welfare criterion from an incomplete ordering. While Bernheim and his collaborators focus narrowly on Paretian comparisons, Fleurbaey and Schokkaert derive a distributional criterion from the incomplete ordering over consumption vectors, along the lines of the non-envy concept of equity.

In some of the earlier papers in the first of these two schools of thought, "true" preferences were discussed in the context of choice anomalies, and were often informal or incidental to the development of the choice model itself. This is generally the case in, e.g., Camerer et al. (2003) and Thaler and Sunstein (2008). An early exception that is often mentioned and criticized is Bleichrodt et al. (2001); but this is an attempt to advise physicians as to how they might choose treatments for patients unable to speak for themselves. Gul and Pesendorfer (2001) discuss temptation, where the chooser may lack the strength of will at the moment of choice to choose the item that would most increase her welfare. As a result, the person may prefer a choice set that does not create temptation. Because of temptation, the choice made depends on the choice set presented, i.e. whether the choice set creates temptation or not. This dependency of choice on the choice set, and the possibility that the person might have a preference over choice sets, plays an important part in the subsequent literature. In this case the "true preference" over specific alternatives is the preference that would be expressed if the chooser could commit herself in advance of the moment of choice, by selecting a non-tempting choice set (p. 1405). A parallel is drawn to time inconsistency (Strotz 1955). In the case of time inconsistency, however, the dominated choices are subgame perfect or Bellman optimal and so are often represented as rational.

Koszegi and Rabin (2007) argue that welfare-relevant preferences cannot be derived from choice behavior alone (p. 478) and note, following Gul and Pesendorfer (2001), that individuals may have preferences over choice sets. They suggest that these may be even more complex than Gul and Pesendorfer suggest, so that commitment may not reveal "true" preference over specific alternatives. They extend the ideas of Gul and Pesendorfer to a discussion of the "gambler's fallacy," showing how replicated choices may reveal mistakes as well as "true" preferences. Salant and Rubinstein (2008), focusing on choice functions rather than welfare economics, further generalize the Gul and Pesendorfer approach by associating choice ranking with frames. They make choices among particular alternatives a function of a pair, (A,x), where A is a "frame" and x is the set of alternatives available. The meme (A,x) has become a label for models related to the Rubinstein and Salant approach. In that there are about as many ways to derive "true" preferences as there are behavioral choice models, this could become a very long catalog. Instead see the catalog at Stango et al. (2017).

Bernheim and his collaborators (chiefly Rangel) have been the vanguard of the second school of thought. Bernheim rejects preference as a criterion of welfare (Bernheim 2009). Instead of "true preferences" the proposed welfare ordering is "unambiguous choice," that is, z is taken as better than y only if y is never taken when z is on offer (p. 297) regardless of the frame or situation of choice. But (p. 310) some instances of choice where anomalies are known to be common may be ignored. Bernheim (pp. 290–291) cites Little for support for the idea that choices, not preference, should be the criterion of welfare. But Little's view was supported in part by his comment that "a man may support a wife who makes his life unbearable, and without getting any pleasure from the fact that he may be doing his duty" (Little 2002 [1950], pp. 21–22). This sense of duty needs create no choice anomaly, and seems quite different from Bernheim's reasoning in rejecting preference as a welfare criterion. Further, as Bernheim notes (p. 304) in the case of time inconsistency, unambiguous choice may lead to decisions that are strictly dominated in terms of a known preference relation. All this suggests that the connection of unambiguous choice to welfare is less clear than Bernheim argues. Mandler (2013) criticizes Bernheim on the grounds that his Paretian criterion would have little power to discriminate among allocations, as the Pareto set with unambiguous choices would encompass most allocations.

Bernheim (2016) reiterates the reliance on unambiguous choice (pp. 15, 44) despite reporting (p. 13) that his opinions have shifted. If anything they seem to have shifted still further against preference as a welfare criterion. He stresses that welfare is a subjective phenomenon (p. 17) and entertains the possibility that a person's "ultimate goal is to achieve certain mental states ('internal goods')." (Might we say, "qualia"?) He notes Mill's suggestion that some utilities might differ in quality. (However, he ignores Mill's judgment that these qualitative differences could be ranked and that the ranking could be learned by experience.) Further, when preferences are expressed they are constructed de novo from more basic subjective states of mind (p. 20) and there is no reason to expect them to be consistent. These points are offered to support Bernheim's argument that preferences are not a reasonable criterion of welfare, so that revealed preference theory is at once mistaken and irrelevant. Bernheim then proposes a "unified framework" for welfare economics, comprising the unambiguous choice criterion together with selective use of data from experiments, neuro-economics and surveys.

The position of Bernheim and his school has stimulated responses that reinforce arguments for a "true preference" approach. Rubinstein and Salant (2012), drawing on their earlier work modeling preferences, argue that it is possible as a rule to reconstruct "true preferences" by modeling choice behavior with a "distortion function" derived from the choice model (pp. 375, 385). They note that when choices are interpreted in a model, a model that allows for mistakes may lead to "true preferences" that contradict Bernheim and Rangel's "unambiguous choice" criterion (p. 378). They focus particularly on "satisficing" choice models (pp. 379–383), models with "small" errors (pp. 383–385) and "framing" effects (pp. 385–386). They define a frame as "additional information regarding the circumstances in which the individual displays the preference ordering." In the case of "small" errors, cyclical preferences are not consistent with the model, while some instances of decisions dependent on frames (specifically where choices are influenced by advertising) a cardinal utility function may be recovered from evidence on intensity of preference.

Manzini and Mariotti (2014) in their response to Bernhiem (2009, see esp. Manzini and Mariotti 2014, pp. 345, 351, 357) defend the use of a model of choice to recover something like "true" preferences or a utility ranking (p. 349). They are opposed to "as if" models of choice. Their position is that a verified model of non-rational choice should be used to extract "true" preferences. They discuss some of the difficulties in this, enumerating three classes of failures (pp. 352–355) with some possible solutions. They put particular emphasis on models of stochastic choice (pp. 350, 357). Their contribution will be further considered below.

In addition to these schools of thought, there remains the pessimistic position that welfare economics is impossible in the light of the anomalies and the rethinking they have stimulated. For example, Gul and Pesendorfer (2007), seemingly shifting from their earlier work, argue that Paretian economics is actually positive economics, in the nature of a stability test (p. 472). As such, Paretian models are not normative economics and cognitive biases are irrelevant to them. They then argue that normative judgments simply "are moral and philosophic questions not 'economic' questions" (p. 474). Thus, it seems, behavioral economics is irrelevant both for Paretian and normative economics. The interpretations and assertions about the economics literature in this paper may fairly be described as distinctive.

Infante et al. (2016) take a similar skeptical view, at least of behavioral welfare economics. To attempt to discover "true preferences," they say, is to posit an "inner rational agent" within the shell of the irrational agent. In this they follow Hausman (2012), but unlike Hausman they reject this "preference purification" as illegitimate. At the same time they reject Bernheim's "unambiguous choice" on the same grounds. They argue inter alia that even the hypothetical perfect calculator might not have consistent preferences. They suggest (p. 16) that the same chosen particular alternative in a different frame really is a different object, so far as preferences are concerned. Their treatment of the Allais paradox (p. 18) is persuasive on this score. They consistently rely on the idea (fact) that preferences are *subjective*.

Infante et al. have a point. It is hardly plausible that real human beings have stable context-independent preferences for individual decisions, since we do not make the same choices on every occasion, even from the same choice set. Shrimp for dinner sounds good, but shrimp for dinner every night could become unbearable. Vacations derive some of their charm from the contrast to the day-to-day routine. I'm sure there are some who would play golf every day if they could, but must spend some days earning a living. This is quite a conventional case of the allocation of time, but it makes the choice to play golf on a particular day context dependent. In the cases of shrimp and vacations, the subjective experiences that influence the choices, what in this book have been called qualia, may themselves be context dependent (as both Bernheim 2016 and Infante et al. 2016 suggest), so that even if preferences among qualia are consistent, observed decisions need not be. If there is a consistent preference system over individual choices, it can only be instantaneous and therefore unobservable. Welfare economics does not need a system of preferences over individual choices: market data record average or usual choices over an extended period – habitual behavior. It is quite possible that these usual patterns of choice could be consistent even when day-to-day choices are not. We might have shrimp for dinner once a month, meatballs once a week and prime rib twice a year, and these patterns could be predictable and consistent with transitive preferences. However, the experimental data of behavioral economics is mostly about individual choices. Certainly this information is important for welfare economics, for example where the individual choice is a choice of a pension fund: but perhaps we put too much emphasis on the consistency of individual choices in experiments.

But this may not impeach the models of anomalies in behavioral economics. In those models there is a more or less clear (in some cases only plausible) standard of what the person would choose if she were fully informed, attentive and reflective. In the absence of an "inner rational agent" these results suffer from a lack of coherence; but lack of coherence does not imply falsehood. To reject these analyses on philosophic principles because they can be interpreted as positing a non-existent homunculus within the brain would be to propose a rather novel methodological principle. On the other hand, an instantaneous, unobservable consistent preference system over at least some (market) decisions would be sufficient for neoclassical welfare economics. Behavioral anomalies do bear against the hypothesis that preferences are instantaneously consistent, especially where their experimental frames overlap or replicate the restricted domain of market decisions. What Infante et al. do impeach is the revealed preference approach itself.

The difficulty lies elsewhere. Behavioral welfare economics along the lines of Rubinstein and Salant (2012) and Manzini and Mariotti (2014) seem to rely on the idea that, at least for a given choice situation, people will all make their decisions by the same process. Bernheim (2009, 2016) avoids reliance on any one model, but nevertheless his procedure for excluding some decisions from the welfare-relevant domain seems to rely on some similar judgment. But human beings are complex and unpredictable: is it not plausible that two or more individuals might use quite different (both boundedly rational) decision processes to address the same decision situation? Or indeed that the same person might use different procedures at different times, for example, when the situation is novel and after it becomes habitual, or depending whether the person is rushed or tired? Now, Manzini and Mariotti refer in particular to their own model of stochastic choice (p. 357), noting that for such a model, data on the distribution of choices could assist in the recovery of something like true preference. But models of stochastic choice based on full rationality are well established in the literature, as witness the Nobel Memorial Prize award to Daniel McFadden (see McFadden 1973). In these models, individual utility functions are distributed in some random way over individuals, so that individuals make different choices with probabilities that can be derived from the distribution. In these full rationality models, the choice is the one that maximizes the individual's utility. For a model such as that of Manzini and Mariotti, a decision that yields greater utility is chosen with greater probability. Suppose that we were to consider a group of people who have different utility functions and who use heuristics of a number of different kinds to make decisions. The decision made by a particular person will reflect the relative "utility" of the different choices along with any bias in that individual's choice process. The elements of bias may vary from one person to another, and to the extent that the choice process of an individual is unpredictable (or generates a random bias element as the Manzini and Mariotti process does) the bias element may approximate a random variate. What this suggests is that the Manzini and Mariotti model, or some model like it, might be appropriate as a master model that approximates the choices of a representative member of the group. This *would* be an as-if model, though, contrary to Manzini and Mariotti's stated purpose. Nor may we assume that the bias element would be a normal variate. In a case of minimum information it would be normal, but for some consumption situations, such as the consumption of addictive substances, strong empirical evidence may exist for a predictable bias away from rationality. Thus, the master model would have to allow for such bias. Resources for a research project along these lines may be found in the large study by Stango et al. (2017). This is an attempt to reduce behavioral economics to a parsimonious (if not coherent!) consensus. They say (p. 6) that "consumer-level behavioral tendencies are both common and heterogenous." Nevertheless, they develop some promising tools to analyze those tendencies as a whole.

10.5 Behavioral welfare economics and the veil of ignorance

Executive summary of the section: Taking the Rawlsian "veil of ignorance" as a standard of impartial reason in normative social science, we ask whether it might resolve some of the controversy in behavioral welfare economics.

The Rawlsian "veil of ignorance" is a standard for unbiased reason in normative social theory. Thus, we might ask, what are the implications for behavioral normative economics of a veil of ignorance analysis, and vice versa? Since Rawls and Harsanyi offer different "veil of ignorance" analyses, it may be useful for present purposes to point out some specific differences between their discussions, and that of Lerner as well. The differences take the form of different answers to questions that together define a "veil of ignorance" analysis as a category.

Question 1. What question are the deliberators behind the veil of ignorance to address?

For Harsanyi, the question is to specify a social welfare function, that is, a consistent social preference function over alternative allocations of consumer goods to individuals. For Rawls it is a set of ethical principles to guide participants in a constitutional convention, legislators (as the veil of ignorance is raised stage by stage) and individuals participating in the society created by the constitutional convention and the legislature. For Lerner the question is whether redistribution of income toward equality can be expected to increase aggregate utility on the average.

Question 2. What may the deliberators know despite their ignorance?

Rawls notably says that, behind the veil of ignorance, the deliberators do not know their concept of the good; but they do know a list of primary goods, such as liberty and wealth, that enable an individual in the realized society to effectively pursue her life plan, whatever it may be. Rawls also says that the deliberators know something of economic theory, including the "fact" that market outcomes do not generate increasing inequality of wealth. (This "fact" was widely believed by economists when he wrote the first edition.) For Harsanyi the deliberators know that individuals possess consistent preference systems over vectors of consumer goods and over uncertain prospects of such vectors. For Lerner, the principle of diminishing marginal utility of money is known to the deliberators, but the relative capabilities of different individuals for satisfaction are unknown.

Question 3. How are the deliberators to construe their interests as agents in the realized society?

The answer to this question must be consistent with that for Question 2. For Rawls, access to the primary goods is in the interests of the agents in the realized society. For Harsanyi and Lerner, the interest of agents in the realized society is to attain a higher ranking in their preference systems. (We may say "to maximize utility" without self-contradiction, but numerical utility in both cases plays its role only within the veil of ignorance.)

Question 4. In what sense, if any, are the deliberators rational in their deliberations?

For Harsanyi, the deliberators base their decisions on Bayesian rationality as construed by Marshak (1954) in the light of von Neumann and Morgenstern's utility theory. Lerner's theory can also be interpreted as Bayesian, although he is less explicit on this. Rawls, by contrast, uses a max-min criterion. Now, in game theory, max min is "rational" only in zero-sum games (Nash 1950), but the max-min criterion also generalizes cut-and-choose cake-cutting models of fairness (Dubins and Spanier 1961; Kuhn 1967). Since Rawls is concerned with "justice as fairness," and indeed the veil of ignorance convention is directed to decisions that are fair in the sense that they are unbiased, a concept of rationality that incorporates an ideal of fairness may be more appropriate than the Bayes-Marshak rationality. On the other hand, the max-min criterion has some well-known problems, in that it may recommend a policy that makes the worst off only a little better off, and many others, who are not worst off but nevertheless miserable, much more miserable.

Now let us address the four questions in the case of a "veil of ignorance" approach to behavioral welfare economics.

Question 1. What question are the deliberators behind the veil of ignorance to address?

It seems that the answer (for the purposes of welfare economics) will be nearer to Harsanyi than to Rawls, though perhaps we need not go so far as to demand a social welfare function. As Sen has pointed out, welfare economics in the social welfare function tradition has tended to be a search for a "transcendental institutionalist" answer. Instead, as Sen suggests, we might ask instead for applicable guidelines that a legislator or citizen might use to rank small finite sets of economic policy alternatives as better or worse in the light of their consequences for human well-being.

Question 2. What may the deliberators know despite their ignorance?

Evidently they will know that agents in the realized society will make economic choices via behavioral processes that may deviate from classical rationality, and we must assume that they know whatever we suppose we know about economic theory in general. However, there are at least two ways that "behavioral processes" can be construed. On the one hand, we may assume that agents have "true preferences," but that their actual choices may deviate from them; on the other hand we may suppose that preferences are constructed in response to the specific choice context and may not be either context independent or consistent (Bernheim 2009, 2016). Whichever of those views we adopt, we assume that the deliberators behind the veil of ignorance know what we suppose we know. Thus, there may be at least two "veil of ignorance" models for behavioral economics, contingent on different hypotheses of behavioral choice processes. This should not deter us from proceeding: after all, our policy recommendations are always contingent on the hypotheses we entertain about positive economics – what else is positive economics for? Moreover, it is at least possible that the two versions of behavioral welfare economics might converge on similar policy recommendations, at least in many cases.

Question 3. How are the deliberators to construe their interests as agents in the realized society?

Despite what was just said, there must be two possible answers to this question corresponding to the two possible answers to the former question. If the deliberators know that the agents have "true preferences," then it is natural to construe the true preferences as expressing the interests of the agents in the realized society. (This is not self-evident, but the interpretation of "interest" will always be somewhat arbitrary. In any case the merits of this interpretation are well known in the neoclassical economics literature.) If we adopt the assumption that there are no consistent underlying "true preferences," the case is less clear.

Question 4. In what sense, if any, are the deliberators rational in their deliberations?

For behavioral welfare economics, there are two aspects of this question. First, should we suppose that the deliberators are themselves boundedly rational? Here, I submit, the answer is a definite no. The purpose of the veil of ignorance convention is twofold: to support answers that are unbiased and that are rational to the greatest possible degree. It remains to consider whether the deliberators should adopt a standard like that of Harsanyi, that is, Bayesian or, at least, positively responsive to the interests of every realized agent, or one that, as Rawls', incorporates fairness in the rationality concept itself. These may not be strict alternatives: given numerical utilities, as Sen (1973) points out, any strictly convex function of individual utilities expresses some bias toward equal distributions of welfare, and the max min is the limiting case of this. Relative to Harsanyi's analysis, such a convex function would express some risk aversion (not by the agents in the realized society, which Harsanyi pointedly ignores, but by the deliberators behind the veil of ignorance). On the other hand, we must consider also the possibility that agents in the realized society have no "true preferences," that is, no underlying preference over choice alternatives that is consistent and transitive. Thus, it would be necessary for the deliberators behind the veil of ignorance to construct some rational basis for inferring propositions about welfare from propositions of observed choice. One way to do this might be for the deliberators behind the veil of ignorance to construct "true preferences" on the basis of whatever generalizations empirical behavioral economics offer them, somewhat as Harsanyi has them construct numerical utility functions. When a theorist conjectures "true preferences" that differ from observed choices in a particular choice experiment, the theorist can reasonably be accused of expressing a personal opinion. However, the veil of ignorance convention could resolve that problem as it is intended to resolve the problem of making distributional decisions based on personal opinion. Another possibility is that well-being might be identified with "happiness" as indicated by responses to a questionnaire on self-reported satisfaction with life. Such responses, even if not definitive, could be useful to the deliberators behind the veil of ignorance to construct a "true preference" for contrast with behavioral choices. For the purposes of welfare economics, some bridge from observed choices to well-being seems quite necessary, and whatever that bridge might be, it would seem to entail "true preferences" in the sense of ranking alternatives in terms of increasing well-being. It seems that the deliberators behind the veil of ignorance would instruct legislators and critics of public policy to make use of whatever evidence economic and neuro-science may give them to judge true preferences or true utility as the substance and measure of individual welfare.

10.6 Concluding reflections

It has often been said that economics is the most mature of the social sciences. In a simple chronological sense that seems to be true. It does not mean, however, that economists have nothing to learn from the other social sciences. In particular, the surveys of satisfaction with life and certain aspects of life provide data relevant to welfare economics. The position of scholars like Ng and Layard, that happiness in this sense should be the maximand for welfare economics seems to go too far, though, for two reasons. First, they are averages, with a great deal of indiosyncratic variation around the average. Institutions that accommodate individual idiosyncracy can have benefits that are not directly visible in surveys of happiness. This is the great genius of market institutions and the subject of a great deal of economic theory. Second, the survey reports are reports of remembered utility, and as Kahneman (et al. 1997) has argued, remembered utility may be biased relative to experienced utility. On the other hand, the fact that reported happiness seems to vary linearly with the logarithm of real income seems to bear strongly on the old question of the diminishing marginal utility of income, and the surveys provide important quantitative information on the importance of what Pigou called non-economic welfare, such as the happiness derived from marriage and family life, exercise of initiative and stable employment.

The evidence of behavioral "anomalies" of choice challenges welfare economics and, particularly, it challenges the hypothesis of revealed preference. But welfare economics is concerned with the implications of choices made predictably in a market or other social system, not with choices made in a laboratory context. This is not to dismiss the laboratory studies. The difficulty is that experiments designed to elicit instances of biased choice do elicit them, but in ways that may differ from one experiment to another. If we then consider data on market activity, the data presumably will aggregate various biases, but to what extent? How will they all balance out? There is no reason to think that they cancel one another, and perhaps they reinforce the overall bias. But this is the question we need to answer: what is the relation between market decisions and rational decisions? It seems that the answer will differ from one application to another. Unavoidably, "internalities" take their place alongside externalities in the economics of public policy. The parallel shows how, in practical applications, behavioral welfare economics is likely to influence public policy. Thinking of public policy discussions as something like Sen's public reason or Walton's reasonable dialog, valuation of policies on the basis of market data (as in cost–benefit analysis or comparisons of real income aggregates) will make a defeasible prima facie case for one policy or another. But this argument might be challenged by arguments from externality, "internality" or non-economic welfare, and sometimes the challenge will be decisive.

Note

1 I do not mean to suggest that meditation is not good advice – it probably is – but only that it is a little surprising in a work on economic policy. Clearly, though, Layard means to go beyond economic policy.

References

Benz, Matthias and Bruno S. Frey (2008) Being Independent Is a Great Thing: Subjective Evaluations of Self-Employment and Hierarchy, *Economica, New Series* v. 75, no. 298 (May) pp. 362–383.

Bernheim, B. Douglas (2009) Behavioral Welfare Economics, *Journal of the European Economic Association* v. 7, no. 23 (Apr–May).

Bernheim, B. Douglas (2016) The Good, the Bad, and the Ugly: A Unified Approach to Behavioral Welfare Economics, *Journal of Benefit Cost Analysis* v. 7, no. 1 pp. 12–68.

Blanchflower, David G. and Andrew J. Oswald (2004) Money, Sex and Happiness: An Empirical Study, *Scandinavian Journal of Economics* v. 106, no. 3 (Sep) pp. 393–415.

Bleichrodt, H., J.-L. Pinto-Prades and P. Wakker (2001) Making Descriptive Use of Prospect Theory to Improve the Prescriptive Use of Expected Utility, *Management Science* v. 47, pp. 1498–1514.

Camerer, Colin, Samuel Issacharoff, George Loewenstein, Ted O'Donoghue and Matthew Rabin (2003) Regulation for Conservatives: Behavioral Economics and the Case for "Asymmetric Paternalism," *University of Pennsylvania Law Review* v. 151, no. 3 (Jan) pp. 1211–12254.

Clark, Andrew E. and Andrew J. Oswald (1994) Unhappiness and Unemployment, *Economic Journal* v. 104, no. 424 (May) pp. 648–659.

Di Tella, Rafael and Robert MacCulloch (2006) Some Uses of Happiness Data in Economics, *Journal of Economic Perspectives* v. 20, no. 1 (Winter) pp. 25–46.

Dubins, L. E. and E. H. Spanier (1961) How to Cut a Cake Fairly, *American Mathematical Monthly* v. 68 (Jan) pp. 1–17.

Dusenberry, James S. (1949) *Income, Saving, and the Theory of Consumer Behavior* (Cambridge, Mass.: Harvard University Press).

Easterlin, R. A. (1974) Does Economic Growth Improve the Human Lot?, *Nations and Households in Economic Growth: Essays in Honour of Moses Abramovitz* (New York: Academic Press).

Easterlin, Richard A. (2001) Income and Happiness: Towards a Unified Theory, *Economic Journal* v. 111, no. 473 pp. 465–484.

Easterlin, Richard A. (2003) Explaining Happiness, *Proceedings of the National Academy of Sciences of the United States of America* v. 100, no. 19 (Sep) pp. 11176–11183.

Elster, Jon (2009) Excessive Ambitions, *Capitalism and Society* v. 4, no. 2 (Article 1).

Fleurbaey, Marc and Erik Schokkaert (2013) Behavioral Welfare Economics and Redistribution, *American Economic Journal: Microeconomics* v. 5, no. 1 (Aug) pp. 180–205.

Frey, Bruno S. (2010) *Happiness: A Revolution in Economics* (Cambridge, Mass.: MIT Press).

Gul, Faruk and Wolfgang Pesendorfer (2001) Temptation and Self-Control, *Econometrica* v. 69, no. 6 (Nov) pp. 1403–1435.

Gul, Faruk and Wolfgang Pesendorfer (2007) Welfare without Happiness, *American Economic Review* v. 97, no. 2 (May) pp. 471–476.

Hausman, Daniel (2012) *Preference, Value, Choice, and Welfare* (Cambridge: Cambridge University Press).

Infante, Gerado, Guilhem Lecouteux and Robert Sugden (2016) Preference Purification and the Inner Rational Agent: A Critique of the Conventional Wisdom of Behavioural Welfare Economics, *Journal of Economic Methodology* v. 23, no. 1 pp. 1–25.

Kahneman, Daniel, Peter P. Wakker and Rakesh Sarin (1997) Back to Bentham? Explorations of Experienced Utility, *Quarterly Journal of Economics* v. 112, no. 2 (May) pp. 375–405.

Koszegi, Botond and Matthew Rabin (2007) Mistakes in Choice-Based Welfare Analysis, *American Economic Review* v. 97, no. 2 (May) pp. 477–481.

Kuhn, H. W. (1967) On Games of Fair Division, *Essays in Mathematical Economics in Honor of Oskar Morgenstern*, edited by M. Shubik (Princeton, N.J.: Princeton University Press) pp. 29–37.

Layard, R. (1980) Human Satisfactions and Public Policy, *Economic Journal* v. 90, no. 360 (Dec) pp. 737–750.

Layard, R. (2005) *Happiness: Lessons from a New Science* (New York: Penguin).

Little, I. M. D. (2002 [1950]) *A Critique of Welfare Economics*, 2nd Edition (Oxford: Clarendon).

Mandler, Michael (2013) Indecisiveness in Behavioral Welfare Economics, *Journal of Economic Behavior and Organization* v. 97, pp. 219–235.

Mankiw, N. Gregory (2013) Defending the One Percent, *Journal of Economic Perspectives* v. 27, no. 3 (Summer) pp. 21–34.

Manzini, Paola and Marco Mariotti (2014) Welfare Economics and Bounded Rationality: The Case for Model-Based Approaches, *Journal of Economic Methodology* v. 21, no. 4 pp. 3443–3360.

Marshak, Jacob (1954) Probability in the Social Sciences, *Mathematical Thinking in the Social Sciences*, edited by P. F. Lazarsfeld (Glencoe, Ill.: Free Press).

McFadden, Daniel (1973) Conditional Logit Analysis of Qualitative Choice Behavior, *Frontiers in Econometrics*, edited by P. Zarembka (New York: Academic Press).

McQuillin, Ben and Robert Sugden (2012) Reconciling Normative and Behavioural Economics: The Problems to Be Solved, *Social Choice and Welfare*, v. 38, no. 4 (April) pp. 553–567.

Nash, John (1950) Equilibrium Points in n-Person Games, *Proceedings of the National Academy of Science* v. 36, pp. 48–49.

Ng, Yew-Kwang (1996) Happiness Surveys: Some Comparability Issues and an Exploratory Survey Based on Just Perceivable Increments, *Social Indicators Research* v. 38, no. 1 (May) pp. 1–27.

Ng, Yew-Kwang (1997) A Case for Happiness, Cardinalism, and Interpersonal Comparability, *Economic Journal* v. 107, no. 445 (Nov) pp. 1848–1858.

Ng, Yew-Kwang (2003) From Preference to Happiness: Towards a More Complete Welfare economics, *Social Choice and Welfare* v. 20, no. 2 pp. 307–350.

Rubinstein, Ariel and Yuval Salant (2012) Eliciting Welfare Preferences from Behavioural Data Sets, *Review of Economic Studies* v. 79, no. 1 (Jan) pp. 375–387.

Salant, Yuval and Ariel Rubinstein (2008) Choice with Frames, *Review of Economic Studies* v. 75, no. 2 (Oct) pp. 1287–1298.

Sen, Amartya (1973) On Ignorance and Equal Distribution, *American Economic Review* v. 63, no. 5 (Dec) pp. 1022–1024.

Sen, Amartya (2009) *The Idea of Justice* (Cambridge, Mass.: Belknap Press).

Stango, Victor, Joanne Yoong and Jonathan Zinman (2017) The Quest for Parsimony in Behavioral Economics: New Methods and Evidence on Three Fronts (National Bureau of Economic Research, Working Paper 23057).

Stevenson, Betsey and Justin Wolfers (2008) Economic Growth and Subjective Well-Being: Reassessing the Easterlin Paradox (National Bureau of Economic Research, Working Paper 14282).

Strotz, Robert Henry (1955) Myopia and Inconsistency in Dynamic Utility Maximization, *Review of Economic Studies* v. 23, no. 3 pp. 163–180.

Thaler, Richard and Cass R. Sunstein (2008) *Nudge* (New York: Penguin).

van Praag, B. M. S. and A. Ferrer-i-Carbonell (2004) *Happiness Quantified* (Oxford: Oxford University Press).

11 Whither?

Executive summary of the chapter: This chapter summarizes, drawing on the previous discussion to suggest some elements of a restored welfare economics.

The previous ten chapters of this book have been primarily backward looking, drawing on the literature of welfare economics and closely related fields, and selectively on other literatures with a view to interpretation and understanding of the welfare economic literature. One might leave it at that, and perhaps one should. On the other hand, Sir Anthony Atkinson (2011), ten years after pointing out the disappearance of welfare economics, sounded a call for its restoration, not as a return to the "status quo ante," but as a recognition of economics as a moral science with a moral responsibility to address values more broadly. Atkinson describes three "avoidance strategies" by which economists evade distributional issues. One is to assume them away, using "representative agent" models. The other two are variants on Robbins' strategy: appeals to a (non-existent or vacuous) consensus among economists on the values to be applied, or leaving non-economic values to non-economists as a matter of specialization. Atkinson does not say that all are fallacious (in Walton's 2011, sense: "That pattern is for the proponent to press ahead too aggressively to jump to a conclusion uncritically by overlooking the defeasibility of the argument scheme in question"). Nor does he point out that, so far as they appeal to a "utilitarian" consensus among economists while ignoring the redistributive implications of utilitarianism, they are self-contradictory.

As this book has previously argued, economics is thick, which is to say that the language of economics is unavoidably valuative. One cannot use the language of economics without making reference to (if not necessarily affirming) certain value judgments. Any economic analysis of a policy will express some (however limited) value judgments, amounting to an economic evaluation of the policy. This might seem to support a position close to those of Hicks and Kaldor (about 1940) and consistent with one of the "avoidance strategies": this economic evaluation is the economist's job, and the "non-economic values" can be left to others. But first, as critics of Hicks and Kaldor pointed out, the economic evaluation is contingent on the distribution of income, and so is not in fact determined until the distribution of income is determined. And therefore the distribution of wealth must also be determined, since the distribution of wealth is a determinant of the distribution of income. On the other side, it is unlikely that specialists in other areas would have more to say about impacts on distribution than economists. Thus, evaluation of the distribution of income is an aspect of the economic evaluation, whatever philosophic or other issues it may raise. Second, even for more strictly non-economic values, such as the happiness consequent on marriage, interactions of economic and non-economic values can be complex. Happiness from marriage may depend on employment that is stable but that allows for "family time." Here, again, economists will be able to make important contributions to the discussion of those interdependencies that would not come from scholars in other fields. After all, "interdependency" is another way of saying "trade-off," and few other fields focus as directly on trade-offs as economists do. Third, the market data have less privilege than the New Welfare Economics supposed, and than the discussion of "thickness" may have suggested. An "I want" statement expresses a value both innately and incorrigibly and an "I want this more than the x dollars I will have to pay" expresses that value in dollar terms. But there is a leap from "I want" to "I offer" or "I will accept." As Armstrong (1939), Ng (1980) and Kahneman et al. (1997) have pointed out, the "I offer" will be based on estimated or remembered utility – on the qualia that are *expected* to follow – and these expectations and memories might be mistaken. Where we have evidence that these expectations are predictably likely to be mistaken, that evidence must be taken into account. Thus market data cannot stand alone but must be evaluated in the light of other data: the same data relied on by other social sciences. Fourth, if the discussion of the implications of non-economic and distributional conditions for economic policy is not carried on among economists, it may not take place at all.

On one point there seems to be a broad consensus of economists, from Pigou through most neoclassical economists of the twenty-first century (though excluding, inter alia, Sen, Layard and Mankiw, for quite different reasons). It is this: welfare comprises subjective states of mind. This is explicit in Pigou and the other utilitarians (perhaps excepting Layard). In the case of ordinalists, preference is a subjective state of mind, or an aspect of states of mind. Even Little, for whom comparison of social states should rest on choice rather than preference, nevertheless identified welfare with subjective happiness. A further consensus is that welfare consequently cannot be observed directly but can only be inferred. For the ordinalists, the only evidence that bears on the case is the observed choices of market participants. But the difficulty with this evidence (as we learned in the period around 1940) is that these choices are contingent on the distribution of income, so that judgments based on such evidence can be unequivocal only for policy transitions that do not modify the distribution of income. There being no such policy transitions, the ordinalist economics of mid-century could answer no questions of welfare economics, however successful in analyzing market equilibria. As we have seen, the identification of welfare with preference led to other confusions as well, such as the impossibility of a "Paretian liberal."

This book has argued that economists might draw on the philosophic literature on qualia to obtain a better understanding of welfare qua subjective states of mind. This suggests a question that Kennedy (1954) alone among welfare economists addressed: can utility be added? The union of two utility qualia is not one quale, but a set of two distinct qualia. This suggests that the problem of aggregating utility, either interpersonally or intrapersonally, is deeper and more difficult than has generally been recognized. Further, as Mill had noted, utilities that are similar with respect to intensity and duration may differ in quality. Here, it seems, we must rely on preferences to bring welfare "under the category of greater and less" even if we cannot rely on them exclusively. But we can speak only of a person's preferences among her own qualia, since she has no direct knowledge of the qualia experienced by others.

Put otherwise, the construction (and disaggregation) of measures of "real income" or "the national dividend" are a proper task for economics, and preferences are a key tool for this. Here, of course, behavioral anomalies present a difficulty. Consider, for example, an addictive drug with legitimate uses, such as a barbiturate painkiller. For an individual, consider two arrays of dated quantities of consumption goods x_i and y_i, and suppose that for x_i the quantities of barbiturates is greater. Suppose, however, that the individual would prefer y_i to x_i if he were fully informed and capable of resisting temptation, but in fact chooses x_i. Suppose further that $\sum p_i x_i > \sum p_i y_i$. Thus the conventional computed real income would be greater in the case of x_i. It seems that it would be appropriate in such a case to reduce the weight on barbiturates below their price for the computation of real income.

The case would be different for an externality such as air pollution from automobile use. We can envision a sequence of consumption quantities x_i with v_i an index of pollution implied by the conditions corresponding to x_i; and another sequence y_i with w_i the corresponding indices of pollution. We may suppose that the individual would prefer y_i, w_i to x_i, v_i and would choose the first of these if he could, but he cannot because pollution is determined by a large-group equilibrium. We may further suppose that $\sum p_i x_i > \sum p_i y_i$. But the individual's choice of x_i is not irrational: it expresses the individual's "true" preference for x_i, v_i over y_i, v_i, the choice he actually faces. Thus, it seems reasonable to say that his real income is enhanced by the ample production of petroleum, but, for his well-being this increase in real income is offset by the increment of pollution v_i–w_i. The difference $\sum p_i x_i - \sum p_i y_i$ is a clue to the money equivalent of that reduction of well-being. (This suggests a willingness-to-pay approach to valuing environmental change.) Further, a Pigovian tax is appropriate to discourage pollution, since v_i and w_i are the same for all individuals in the neighborhood. By contrast an excise tax on barbiturates would reduce the welfare of those who take barbiturates "rationally," that is, temporarily as prescribed. The impact on the well-being of those who might become addicted is unclear. Even for those who do not become addicted because the high price discourages careless use, the reduction of their real income during a period of "rational" use will to some extent offset the benefit from avoiding addiction. In this case regulation seems the unavoidable remedy. The overall point is that externalities are *not* symmetrical with "internalities" but that appropriate corrections for both must be made. This in turn requires attention to "true" preferences, however indirectly it is necessary to infer them.

The growing literature based on surveys and experiments, and our consequent greater learning about the relation of decisions to preferences and of non-market activities to well-being, certainly complicate the job of a welfare economist. But they also enrich it. They are resources for a renewed dialog on the relation of economic activity to human welfare, and if there is little prospect of these controversies being settled in the near future, so much the better – as we have so much more to learn.

Certainly, economic welfare is not the sole criterion for the assessment of public policy. As for example studies by Frey (2010) and his associates have shown, political institutions that encourage citizen participation and work activities that allow a person to act on his own initiative are correlated with higher reported well-being, and this evidence confirms what many earlier writers suggested with less systematic evidence. Like marital happiness, these are instances of what Pigou called non-economic welfare. Nevertheless, economic welfare is an important component of welfare, and so the study of the impacts of public policy decisions on economic welfare is an important tool for the criticism and, we may hope, formation of public policies. To be meaningful, assessments of the impact of public policy must be comparative. Tests such as the Kaldor test provide information for such comparisons. They are, of course, not conclusive, and indeed conclusive arguments in welfare economics are likely to be uncommon. Instead what we may hope for is what Walton called a reasonable dialog and Sen called public reasoning. In that context, something like a Kaldor test places the burden of proof on those who feel that it is misleading, as it indeed may be. Their burden of proof is to show that it is misleading in the particular case. But, as we have seen, this discussion cannot avoid the importance of distribution, nor of the possibility that market choices are biased away from rationality. Both of these issues raise philosophic questions that economists cannot avoid.

In dealing with distribution (once we realize that we cannot avoid dealing with it) there are essentially two possibilities that arise from twentieth-century welfare economics, and it seems unavoidable that the theorist must choose between them. One is, however disguised, cardinal utilitarianism. The other is fairness as it has been understood in the literature on "envy." The "fairness" approaches were originally justified as being more parsimonious with information than utilitarianism, but, in practice, that probably is not true. They require information of a different kind. But they can be supported on other grounds, as the reconsideration of this approach behind a veil of ignorance suggests, and as some other arguments suggest. Taking account of the difficulties of allowing for production, the one concept that seems to survive countercriticisms is income fairness: that is, the distribution is "fair" if the market value of each person's consumption plus the market value of her leisure is the same. (The consumption and leisure valuations require perfectly competitive equilibria.) But this absolute standard may not be much help in making comparisons. (I tried to adapt a version of the theory to making comparisons in McCain 2017, appendix to ch. 10, but I could not claim that my proposal is shovel-ready!) Utilitarianism allows for compromise and comparison is at its heart.

Utilitarianism, however, requires some reasonable approach to the interpersonal comparison of utilities. Here, the survey literature on self-reported well-being comes to our aid. However approximate these reports may be, the emerging consensus is that, after all adjustments are made, self-reported well-being increases with the logarithm of real income. Until we have better information, then, it seems reasonable to proxy individual utility with a logarithmic transformation of (appropriately corrected) individual real income. Moreover, the survey literature provides strong guidance on how to correct for known exceptional cases, such as disability, and some guidance on correction for some aspects of non-economic welfare, such as marriage, and semi-economic welfare, such as unhappiness directly caused by unemployment and inflation. Since the marginal utility of real income would then vary with the inverse of real income, this might (as Harberger speculated in 1978) result in some striking deviations from unweighted efficient allocations. This would be evidence of the relative importance of other matters not directly reflected in the economic evaluation. One remedy for this would be to reorganize our society so that the inequality is much reduced, so that (as again Harberger suggested) efficiency would be the main determinant of policy recommendations. Another and more likely remedy would be to confess that equity is not really very important to public policy in our society (and perhaps efficiency isn't either). If that is so, it is a point that a critic would want to make, and a reconstructed welfare economics could be the tool with which to make it.

If the different approaches to the evaluation of the distribution of economic welfare were in broad disagreement, that would be a problem. But it does not seem likely that they would be. An additive utilitarian, a concave-welfare-function egalitarian, and a fairness theorist would be likely all to agree with Rawls that "both the absolute and the relative differences allowed in a well-ordered society are probably less than those that have often prevailed" (Rawls 1971, p. 536), Suppose, then, a proposal for a policy change were made with an argument that the change would be a potential Pareto improvement. Suppose then the counterargument is made that this would make the poor even more miserable, and thus should not be implemented despite its incremental efficiency. The utilitarian, egalitarian and fairness theorist would agree with Rawls that it is a reasonable counterargument, depending on the reason and evidence supporting the counterargument. They might disagree as to the weight that ought to be placed on the distributive shortcoming against its efficiency gain. Only in cases that are very near the doubtful margin – and clearly known to be so – need we stop to ask whether the utilitarian or one of the more extreme distributive evaluations is the appropriate one.

If welfare economics is to be restored, as Atkinson demanded – and it should be – it could hardly be as one specialization among many. No-one can know everything. If a specialist in the economics of transportation knows nothing of the economics of health care, this is understandable and no disgrace. If either of them knows nothing of welfare economics, given the policy basis of their specializations, this approaches negligence. Economics has an intellectual core. Both of these specialists will have learned the Hicks-Allen comparative static analysis. The Hicks-Allen analysis is very important historically, as a resolution of questions that arose in Walras' model of market equilibrium. Is it more important, for applications to the economics of transportation and health care, than Scitovsky's critique of the Kaldor test? Welfare economics should again become part of the core of economics, so that the term "welfare economics" would be seen as the redundancy it is. Of course, specialized research in theoretical welfare economics may be best done by people with specialized skills. On the other hand, welfare economics without applications is vacuous, so that economists who focus on applications such as transportation and health care may bring to welfare economic theory important innovations arising from their own specializations. If a restored welfare economics is to be a specialized field within economics – and this probably is unavoidable – it must be a more open intellectual community than many of our professional silos must be or are. Surely economists have a stake in this, no less than do the citizens whose lives are affected by our work product.

References

Armstrong, W. E. (1939) The Determinateness of the Utility Function, *Economic Journal* v. 49, no. 195 (Sep) pp. 453–467.

Atkinson, Anthony B. (2011) The Restoration of Welfare Economics, *American Economic Review* v. 101, no. 3 (May) pp. 157–161.

Frey, Bruno S. (2010) *Happiness: A Revolution in Economics* (Cambridge, Mass.: MIT Press).

Harberger, Arnold C. (1978) On the Use of Distributional Weights in Social Cost-Benefit Analysis, *Journal of Political Economy* v. 86, no. 2.2 (Apr) pp. 87–120.

Kahneman, Daniel, Peter P. Wakker and Rakesh Sarin (1997) Back to Bentham? Explorations of Experienced Utility, *Quarterly Journal of Economics* v. 112, no. 2 (May) pp. 375–405.

Kennedy, Charles (1954) Concerning Utility, *Economica, New Series* v. 21, no. 81 (Feb) pp. 7–20.

McCain, Roger A. (2017) *Approaching Equality: What Can Be Done about Wealth Inequality* (Cheltenham: Edward Elgar).

Ng, Yew-Kwang (1980) *Welfare Economics: Introduction and Development of Basic Concepts* (New York: Wiley Halsted Press).

Rawls, John (1971) *A Theory of Justice* (Cambridge, Mass.: Belknap Press).

Walton, Douglas (2011) Defeasible Reasoning and Informal Fallacies, *Synthese* v. 179, no. 3 (Apr) pp. 377–407.

Index